'This overview of women and politics broadens the definition of political action and raises some core arguments and ideas that will stimulate discussion.' – **Sue Johnson**, *University of Worcester*

Krista Cowman's highly approachable account offers the first examination of women's political activity in Britain to span the period from the Glorious Revolution to the election of the first female prime minister. Cowman shows how women had worked in a variety of locations and organisations in the decades before the suffrage campaign, and that women's politics did not begin with the demand for a parliamentary vote. The volume also demonstrates how women's political activity continued after equal suffrage in 1928 in a number of directions within and beyond Parliament.

Key topics include:

–   court politics in the age of Queen Mary and Queen Anne
–   Victorian 'pressure group' politics
–   suffrage campaigns from 1867 to 1928
–   the Women's Liberation Movement.

Clear and wide-ranging, this is an essential book for anyone with an interest in the history of British women's involvement with politics over nearly 300 years.

Krista Cowman is Professor of History at the University of Lincoln. She has published widely on the history of women's suffrage and on women in politics before the First World War.

Gender and History

Series Editors: Amanda Capern and Louella McCarthy

Published

Ann Taylor Allen
WOMEN IN TWENTIETH-CENTURY EUROPE

Trev Lynn Broughton and Helen Rogers (eds)
GENDER AND FATHERHOOD IN THE NINETEENTH CENTURY

Krista Cowman
WOMEN IN BRITISH POLITICS C. 1689–1979

Shani D'Cruze and Louise A. Jackson
WOMEN, CRIME AND JUSTICE IN ENGLAND SINCE 1660

William Henry Foster
GENDER, MASTERY AND SLAVERY: FROM EUROPEAN TO ATLANTIC WORLD
FRONTIERS

Rachel G. Fuchs and Victoria E. Thompson
WOMEN IN NINETEENTH-CENTURY EUROPE

Laurence Lux-Sterritt and Carmen Mangion (eds)
GENDER, CATHOLICISM AND SPIRITUALITY: WOMEN AND THE ROMAN
CATHOLIC CHURCH IN BRITAIN AND EUROPE, 1200–1900

Perry Willson
WOMEN IN TWENTIETH-CENTURY ITALY

Angela Woollacott
GENDER AND EMPIRE

Forthcoming

Paul Bailey
WOMEN AND GENDER IN TWENTIETH-CE NTURY CHINA

Ana Carden–Coyne (ed)
GENDER AND CONFLICT SINCE 1914

Natasha Hodgson
GENDER AND THE CRUSADES

Gender and History Series
Series Standing Order ISBN 978–14039–9374–8 hardback
(*outside North America only*)

You can receive future titles in this series as they are published by placing a standing order. Please contact your bookseller or, in case of difficulty, write to us at the address below with your name and address, the title of the series and the ISBN quoted above.

Customer Services Department, Macmillan Distribution Ltd

Women in British Politics, c. 1689–1979

Krista Cowman

First published 2010 by
PALGRAVE MACMILLAN

Palgrave Macmillan in the UK is an imprint of Macmillan Publishers Limited, registered in England, company number 785998, of Houndmills, Basingstoke, Hampshire RG21 6XS.

Palgrave Macmillan in the US is a division of St Martin's Press LLC, 175 Fifth Avenue, New York, NY 10010.

Palgrave Macmillan is the global academic imprint of the above companies and has companies and representatives throughout the world.

Palgrave® and Macmillan® are registered trademarks in the United States, the United Kingdom, Europe and other countries.

ISBN 978-0-230-54556-4 hardback

ISBN 978-0-230-54557-1   ISBN 978-1-137-26785-6 (eBook)
DOI 10.1007/978-1-137-26785-6

A catalogue record for this book is available from the British Library.

A catalog record for this book is available from the Library of Congress.

10   9   8   7   6   5   4   3   2   1
19   18   17   16   15   14   13   12   11   10

For Guy
A book he might actually read

Contents

List of Abbreviations   viii

Acknowledgements   x

Introduction: Shaping the Narrative: Waves, Peaks and Troughs   1

Part 1   Forging a Political Presence   7
1   From Glorious Revolution to Enlightenment: Women's
     Political Worlds, 1689–1789   9
2   Organised Politics before Suffrage   30

Part 2   The Women's Movement Organises   57
3   The Campaign for Women's Suffrage   59
4   Women and the Liberal Party   77
5   Women and the Conservative Party   89
6   Women and Socialism   101

Part 3   Women's Politics after the Vote   113
7   Women Members of Parliament   115
8   Women in Political Parties, 1918–45   131
9   Beyond Party Politics – the Reconfiguration of Feminist
     Organisations, 1920–79   150
Conclusion   169

Notes   171
Select Bibliography   199
Index   206

List of Abbreviations

ASS	Adult Suffrage Society
BF	British Fascisti
BUF	British Union of Fascists
CDAs	Contagious Diseases Acts
CLWS	Church League for Women's Suffrage
CPGB	Communist Party of Great Britain
CUWFA	Conservative and Unionist Women's Franchise Association
CWSS	Catholic Women's Suffrage Society
EFF	Election Fighting Fund
ELFS	East London Federation of Suffragettes
EOC	Equal Opportunities Commission
EPCC	Equal Pay Campaign Committee
FCLWS	Free Church League for Women's Suffrage
FLWS	Friends' League for Women's Suffrage
ILO	International Labour Organization
ILP	Independent Labour Party
LNA	Ladies' National Association
MP	Member of Parliament
NUSEC	National Union of Societies for Equal Citizenship
NUWM	National Unemployed Workers' Movement
NUWSS	National Union of Women's Suffrage Societies
NWCA	National Women Citizens' Association
ODC	Open Door Council
OMS	Organisation for the Maintenance of Supplies
PSF	People's Suffrage Federation
SDF	Social Democratic Federation
SPEW	Society for Promoting the Employment of Women
SPG	Six Point Group
SJC	Standing Joint Committee
SWHA	Scottish Women's Hospitals Association
US	United Suffragists
VFWF	Votes for Women Fellowship
WAUTRA	Women's Amalgamated Unionist and Tariff Reform Association
WCA	Women Citizens' Association
WCG	Women's Co-op Guild
WFL	Women's Franchise League
WFL	Women's Freedom League
WFW	Women for Westminster
WI	Women's Institute

WIL	Women's International League
WLA	Women's Liberal Association
WLF	Women's Liberal Federation
WLL	Women's Labour League
WLM	Women's Liberation Movement
WLUA	Women's Liberal Unionist Association
WNLF	Women's National Liberal Federation
WPPA	Women's Publicity Planning Association
WPC	Women's Peace Crusade
WSPU	Women's Social and Political Union

Acknowledgements

Single-authored studies are rarely lone endeavours, and a number of debts have been incurred during the writing of this book. Some of these are institutional. At the University of Lincoln the School of Humanities and Performing Arts provided a much-needed research leave to speed the process of writing. Library staff at the University of Lincoln processed voluminous requests for inter-library loans while the university libraries at Leeds and York and the Women's Library in London were extremely helpful during my many visits. I would also like to thank Sonya Barker and the series editors at Palgrave Macmillan for their help and patience as the book progressed.

Other debts are more personal. Readers of historian's biography may recall how the early British women's historian Eileen Power expressed her longing for a historical friend to share the excitement of her research. I am fortunate to have many such friends who have shared aspects of this particular intellectual journey with me. Mark Jenner and Jane Rendall helped me to define the shape and scope of the original proposal. Lynn Abrams, Henrice Altink, James Chapman, Barry Doyle, Jonathan Draper, Mary Eagleton, June Hannam, Kate Hill, Jon Lawrence, Jim McMillan, Ian Packer, Ruth Robbins and Susan Watkins have responded to certain questions or have listened, discussed, prompted and provoked at various stages as the project unfolded. Rosamund Carr, Kathryn Gleadle and Pat Thane all generously shared some of their own relevant work with me prior to its publication. I owe even more thanks to Amanda Capern, Ann Gray, Simon Gunn and Andrew Walker who were kind enough to comment on draft chapters (sometimes more than once), which helped me to clarify the more elusive points. Any errors that remain are mine, but thanks to their patient attention I hope these will be few.

Finally, I am also grateful to a number of friends outside academia. Pippa Carr, Harvey Dowdy, Laura Hapgood Joya, Anita Jamal and Sarah Wilcox have all helped in innumerable practical ways in the final stages of the book's production as have my family, Joan Cowman, Jim Sharpe and Guy and Elfreda Cowman-Sharpe. I thank them, yet again, for their encouragement and support.

Krista Cowman

Introduction:
Shaping the Narrative:
Waves, Peaks and Troughs

Woman have no voice in Parliament. They make no laws, they consent to none, they abrogate none.

(*The Lawes Resolutions of Women's Rights*, c.1632)

[Women are] too liable to be seduced from their attention to the public weal, by the smooth and silken pursuits who constantly invest a court, to rule a state.

(London Debating Society, March 1790)

The fear I have is, lest we should invite her to trespass upon the delicacy, the purity, the refinement, the elevation of her own nature, which are the present sources of its power.

(Rt Hon William Gladstone MP to Samuel Smith, MP, 1892)

I do not think this House is a fit and proper place for any respectable woman to sit in.

(Admiral of the Fleet Sir Hedworth Meux MP, 23 October 1918)

These four quotations from four different centuries are each concerned with the relationship between women and parliament, the epicentre of political power in the British state. All respond to direct or indirect suggestions that women might participate in the political life of the nation by voting for and serving in Parliament by suggesting that such activity is in some way unsuited to them. *The Lawes Resolutions of Women's Rights* was a legal textbook published some time after the reign of Elizabeth I had provoked discussions about how much political power women could exercise. The second quotation emerged from an eighteenth-century public debating society as members considered whether women might vote or sit in a democratised parliament. Gladstone's response to Samuel Smith reflected a growing interest in the question of women's suffrage in the late nineteenth century, and Sir Hedworth Meux was voicing his opposition to the bill that would allow women to become MPs in the early twentieth century. The time that elapsed between each quotation shows that women's place in national politics has been a recurrent theme in British history, both within Parliament and beyond it in the realm of print and debate, where public opinion is formed. Discussions of women's relationship to politics are as old as discussions of politics itself.

Yet, despite ample evidence for earlier precedents, much of the historiography of women in British politics has taken a shorter timeframe. A popular starting point is 1867, when Parliament received its first collective petition for women's suffrage. A few studies go further back to the end of the eighteenth century, with the publication of Mary Wollstonecraft's *Vindication of the Rights of Women*, which is positioned as the precedent for later activities. Most accounts end in 1918, when the Representation of the People Act gave votes to some British women (although some studies continue up to the arrival of equal suffrage in 1928). In other words, for the most part, the story of women and politics in Britain is presented in terms of the history of the nineteenth-century women's movement, and more particularly the history of the campaign for the vote, offering no space for describing women's relationship to politics in an earlier (or indeed a later) period.

This focus on suffrage has encouraged over-reliance on what Amanda Vickery termed 'the heroic voice' within the history of women's politics.[1] The heroic version suggests that there is no history of women and politics before suffrage. It describes a linear progression whereby suffrage agitation grew from small beginnings into a mass political movement, the 'women's movement', which ended in triumph in 1918 (or 1928). Participants in the suffrage campaign had written its history in similarly Whiggish terms even as it was unfolding. Bertha Mason's *Story of the Women's Suffrage Movement* (1912), for example, moved readers through nineteenth-century developments in chapters with titles such as 'Light of Dawn', using the metaphor of a ship to argue that the movement had all it required to 'carry it to victory'.[2] This version is attractive to feminist historians, not least because it describes women's presence in an arena which non-feminist political historians would recognise. Political history, despite the growth of history 'from below', still inclines towards high politics, diplomacy and affairs of state. So although women's history shared social history's concern with telling the hidden stories of the powerless, these were not easily integrated into existing grand narratives of state formation. Studying women in British politics from the beginnings of the suffrage movement up to the point at which there was a woman prime minister was one way of disrupting a male consensus; it positioned the historical subject 'woman' on the winning side and made her more difficult to ignore.

Focusing on successes has inherent problems, however. Verta Taylor and Leila Rupp's research on 1950s American feminism alerted them to the perils of failing to study women's political activity in those periods when the women's movement appeared to be in abeyance. They explained that while 'the metaphor of "waves" of the women's movement ... features the cresting waves but ignores the troughs between', considering the concept of abeyance could show women deploying 'a variety of strategies to nurture and sustain an opposition collective identity'.[3] This echoes the findings of Dale Spender in the early

1980s. Spender interviewed a number of women who had been active in first-wave feminism, intent on discovering what they did politically between the vote and the emergence of second-wave feminism in the 1960s, when there was 'no women's movement in Britain'. The furious response of one interviewee, that 'there's always been a women's movement this century', gave Spender the title for her book but did not alter the fact that the historiography of women's politics still tended to stop in 1928 and recommence in the late 1960s.[4]

Turning our attention to the 'troughs' or abeyances that lie between periods of marked activity has expanded how we view the scope and extent of women's politics. Studies of inter-war feminism by scholars such as Johanna Alberti and Cheryl Law, as well as recent graduate theses by Jessica Thurlow and Samantha Clements, have challenged the suggestion that political activity by women ceased at this time.[5] However, they are not always immune from the tendency to present women's politics in terms of a linear progression. Spender was alert to the danger of minimising women's history through accepting the twentieth century as 'a period of unparalleled progress'; nevertheless her presentation of the lives of an earlier generation of activists fits them into this narrative rather than questioning why women's politics were less visible at a national level at certain times.[6] Such work also accepts the established chronology of women's involvement in politics, with research on inter-war feminism situating it between the nineteenth and twentieth-century 'waves'. Recent recognition of a 'third wave' of British feminism does not change this. Meanwhile, women's politics in the early nineteenth century, the mid-eighteenth century or earlier are set aside from the linear version of women's political history. They are not seen as part of a 'trough' as they stand outside the timeframe bounded by feminism's waves; consequently they are often afforded less consideration.

This book attempts to move the study of women's politics beyond the chronology implied by the wave metaphor by demonstrating that women were active political agents long before the campaign for the vote began. It offers some suggestions as to the processes of change which brought women to the point at which something resembling a 'women's movement' might be possible, and considers how the existence of this movement impacted on women's politics in turn. To do this is to do more than to offer a series of earlier precedents from which women's increased political involvement might be dated. Taking a longer view uncovers a narrative which is much patchier than studies concentrating on later periods might suggest. Women were active throughout the period of this study, but not continuously. The precedent of their political activity in one decade or century did not reduce opposition to it in later years. Periods that saw comparatively high levels of political participation by women were often followed by phases of backlash in which their presence was considered exceptional and rejected. From Leveller petitioners to Chartists, from Anti-Corn Law Leaguers to suffragettes, and from Primrose League Dames to Reclaim the Night marchers, each generation of politically active women has had to justify its presence afresh in what was and arguably still is seen as a male space.

This is not to say that women consistently forget their own histories. There are many examples of women invoking historical precedent as part of their justification for political activity. Suffragettes referred back to the Chartists, and the

Women's Liberation Movement deliberately evoked both militant and constitutional suffrage at different times. What it does do is refute the suggestion that each instance of political activity by women expands their involvement up to the point at which it becomes seen as natural or unproblematic. Placed within a longer timeframe, the heroic narrative of forward progress is thus replaced by a much less confident but more nuanced picture of multiple progressions and successes interspersed with periods of stagnation, defeat and even regression.

Defining the political

Writing about women and politics challenges the way in which politics is conceived. The equation of 'political' with parliamentary-focused activity and activism has been revised by social and cultural historians alongside historians of women and gender whose research has called for a broader definition for political actions. For the early modern period, Hilda Smith has argued that studying women's politics requires a 'broader and more inclusive understanding of politics than we possess today. They considered local office holding, political obligations of families among the governing class, as well as voting and political rights, as constituting politics, while we would be more apt to equate the term only with the latter.'[7] The idea that women of a certain class were expected to participate in the political obligations of their family informed the activities of aristocratic women in seventeenth-century royal courts (as it had done in earlier periods). In the eighteenth century, upper-class women took part in electoral politics on behalf of their husbands, fathers or brothers, and undertook considerable political activity in their own homes through facilitating networking opportunities for ambitious party men. Familial obligations persisted beyond the early modern period. Kim Reynolds' study of the role of aristocratic women in the Victorian age showed how they continued to play an important part in maintaining 'a distinctive cohesive political culture' at local and national level.[8] Even in the twentieth century, familial obligation did not vanish completely; the phenomenon of 'male equivalence' through which some of the first women MPs succeeded to seats vacated by their husbands carried overtones of this.

Smith's further point about the importance of local office holding is equally valid beyond the early modern era. The local has always been an important site for women's politics for a variety of reasons. A strong community dimension has facilitated women's involvement in a number of campaigns over the centuries, including seventeenth and eighteenth-century food riots, Chartism, First World War rent strikes, opposition to the 1930s means test and the Women's Liberation Movement's fight for refuges for victims of domestic violence. Even where there was no obvious community function, women would often be more active in local branches of political organisations than at the national level. Local activity fitted well around the competing demands of home, work and family. It was also easier to get involved; as political organisations expanded, national activity became more bureaucratic and membership of national committees was often drawn from a small pool of previously elected regional delegates. Local organisation was less rigid, with all members eligible for office. Although local political studies have tended to concentrate on the grass-roots activities of radical groups, local politics were not necessarily oppositional. As local government expanded in the nineteenth century, women participated in its growth, often justifying their presence through emphasising its connection with domestic or private life. Local government politicised areas of life previously seen as both nonpolitical and feminine, including educating and feeding children, caring for the sick and the elderly, and improving the environment immediately around the home. And if numbers are any guide, local government remains a more welcoming arena for women's politics up to the present day; in 2008 almost 30 per cent of the United Kingdom's councillors were women as opposed to just over 19 per cent of MPs.[9]

Defining what the political means for women broadens understandings of the term in other ways. It was not until the twentieth century that British women became full members of all political parties. This did not mean that they were not involved in party politics before; by the end of the nineteenth century the Liberal and Conservative Parties each had large female auxiliary organisations, while socialist parties always admitted women to membership on equal terms with men. It did, however, mean that much of women's politics took place outside of the main party structures, sometimes in quite unexpected places such as the sewing meetings in which nineteenth-century socialist women gave their working-class membership space for lively political discussion without drawing them away from their domestic labours more than they would wish. Women could act politically in organisations that were not attached to parties; Catriona Beaumont has pointed to the Women's Institutes and Townswomen's Guilds as places where women's broader political concerns were addressed in the inter-war period.[10] Before the party era, women's politics could be equally diverse; Bernard Capp has shown how women's 'informal networks [and] gossip' were essential in enabling 'the politics of the parish' to function in the early modern period.[11]

We should be careful not to construe every instance of collective public activity by women as political. Although there are ways in which their actions can be read this way, it would be difficult to argue that the large numbers of young women who joined girls' clubs in the late nineteenth and early twentieth century were being political in the same way as their contemporaries who opted for the suffragette movement. Yet it remains important to recognise that including women's politics in political history widens its scope, and involves looking beyond the world of party and Parliament as well as within it.

Finally, some words about the organisation of this book. Its intention is to cover women's participation in politics within the three nations of England, Scotland and Wales in such a way as to produce a collective version of the history of women in British politics. Achieving a reasonable balance between the national historiographical fields as they currently stand is no easy task. It is no longer sufficient, as Kirsti Bohata remarked, 'to insert a Welsh narrative into existing histories of English feminism', a point which also holds true for Scottish examples.[12] National histories require developing in their own specific context. Yet in the case of studies of women's political participation, there has been little attempt to do this. Beyond the important collections edited by Angela John and Jane Aron, and Deidre Beddoe's outline of the twentieth century, little research exists on Welsh women and politics; the early modern period, for example, lacks any comprehensive survey.[13] Scotland has received more attention, although as Lynn Abrams observed, 'despite more than two decades of research into Scottish women's history ... there is still a battle to be fought' in terms of its incorporation.[14]

The approach taken here has been to attempt a balance in terms of examples, and to suggest instances where the Welsh and Scottish experience differed, but the work ultimately reflects the current state of the historiography of women and British politics, which remains predominantly English. The significant body of work that has been produced in the wake of devolution has much more to say about women and politics, although it lies beyond the chronological scope of this work.[15] This has included attempts to place recent developments within a historical context, suggesting avenues for further research which open the possibility that a more inclusive historiography of women and British politics in the late twentieth century will be achievable.

In any textbook a degree of selectivity is required, and a study that attempts to compress 300 years of women's political activity into nine chapters is no exception. The approach is both thematic and chronological, intended to offer sufficient detail on key organisations whilst at the same time avoiding too much repetition of the external events that provoked or impacted on them. The book is divided into three sections which describe women's experiences of politics in three periods, before, during and after the nineteenth-century women's movement. The first two chapters outline women's political activity across a variety of locations and organisations from the Glorious Revolution to the mid-nineteenth century. The second section comprises four chapters which consider a more distinct 'women's movement' in relation to suffrage and to organised political parties. The three chapters in the final section look at the impact of women's political citizenship in Parliament, in established and emerging political parties and in a broader women's movement from 1918 to 1979.

The subject matter of the chapters reflects the current focus of research into women and politics in each of these periods. The chapter on women MPs, for example, is mainly concerned with the period up to 1945. This is not to suggest that there were no women MPs after this time, or that their work was insignificant. However, the limited literature that exists on this topic between 1945 and 1979 repeats many themes covered in studies of earlier periods. Meanwhile the final chapter on women's non-party political organisations after 1928 considers the Equal Pay Act and thus returns to the question of women in Parliament. Selectivity has also required hard choices about the amount of detail to include on individual organisations, and the result is bound to disappoint on some levels as familiar groups are omitted or skirted over. There is, however, much on organisations about which little has been said before, and I hope that this will go some way towards compensating the reader.

Part 1
Forging a Political Presence

1

From Glorious Revolution to Enlightenment: Women's Political Worlds, 1689–1789

Introduction

This chapter examines aspects of women's political activity from the Glorious Revolution to the closing years of the eighteenth century. Until recently this approach would have seemed unusual: early modern political history concerned itself with 'high politics', the narrow world of court and government where men held sway, with occasional attention paid to groups such as the Levellers.[1] Lately this has been challenged by research that has argued the need for a broader definition of the political in an age when few men had access to governmental institutions. Studies such as those by Wrightson have demonstrated alternative sites for political activity in the everyday world of the early modern parish.[2] Women's historians have expanded these approaches to query the gendering of early modern politics. Women, it has been shown, took part in politics at all levels of society.[3] Their participation was not always separate. Lower-class women joined with men to voice concerns over religious, economic and social matters in popular demonstrations and riots throughout the seventeenth and eighteenth centuries. Yet, as Mendelson and Crawford have noted, early modern women developed 'their own objectives in political action,' which were not always identical to those of men.[4] Sometimes these linked directly to their role as wives or mothers. On other occasions religion gave women a public platform. Again this was not unique in a period when state and church were inseparable. Nevertheless, religion 'authorised women in public political action', and they often exceeded men in public expression of dissenting beliefs.[5] This included direct action; a woman was credited with sparking the rioting against the Scottish Prayer Book which opened the Covenanting Revolution of 1637. Recent research suggests that Jenny Geddes, the servant whose attack on the Dean of Edinburgh initiated the protest, is better understood as a composite of several women, confirming female participation.[6] Religious protest was not without risk for women; Covenanting activities led to a number being executed in the 1680s.[7]

Exceptional events in this period disturbed the gendering of politics. The English Civil War saw women of all classes active in support of both sides. Sometimes their involvement was pragmatic; a besieged town demanded the resistance of all its inhabitants. Elsewhere, women acted less spontaneously as couriers, as spies or as nurses to the wounded, as well as raising considerable funds for the Royalist and Parliamentarian causes. The Civil War prompted an upsurge in women's petitioning. Such public activities decreased after the Restoration, as society sought 'a return to normality including the customary gender order'. Dissident voices were repressed but did not vanish; small numbers of women still published political demands throughout the eighteenth century, particularly on religious matters.[8]

Women were not absent from high politics either. The Glorious Revolution of 1688–9 has been seen as 'an event of decisive significance in the internal development of the United Kingdom'.[9] It settled the issue of royal succession, and furthered a shift in the balance of power from monarch to Parliament. The timing and length of parliamentary meetings and elections were regulated, which in turn encouraged the development of party politics. The Toleration Act of 1689 fostered a more open attitude to religious dissent (but not to Catholicism).[10] More recently it has also been read in terms of gender.[11] Lois Schwoerer has described women's participation at several levels as petitioners and publishers, as financial supporters and in the crowds that welcomed William and Mary.[12] Women were also involved in the Jacobite movement, which sought a return to the Stuart (and hence Catholic) monarchy. More obviously the presence of Queen Mary as regnant queen put a woman at the heart of political power as head of state. During Mary's reign and the subsequent regnancy of her sister Anne, British politics were headed (if not dominated) by women. Studying regnant queens has encouraged women's historians to turn their attention to the world of the royal court, where scholars such as Helen Payne found aristocratic women wielding considerable levels of political power which they exercised for their own ends as well as for those of their families.[13]

Aristocratic women's power did not diminish as the importance of the court declined. As Parliament's power rose, so did party political affiliations. These extended beyond the metropolitan world of Parliament into constituencies; by 1700 O'Gorman found evidence of strong and consistent party feeling amongst the electorate.[14] Party loyalty fed into – and was fuelled by – a growing number of contested elections, which in turn assisted the beginnings of party organisation. Women had several roles to play here, as political hostesses, financial supporters and active canvassers. Although she could not stand or vote, the figure of the party woman was as visible as that of the party man at election time.

Alongside considerations of women's relationship to the institutions and mechanisms of state power, women's historians have used the concept of political culture to expand understandings of the political. Particular attention has been paid to women's role in the development of print culture from the mid-seventeenth century onwards.[15] Women were involved in all aspects of the printing industry as well as authoring pamphlets, disseminating their ideas to a broader reading public. Published writings by women covered a number of political themes including religion. A small number used print to challenge sexual inequality in ways Crawford and Gowing feel we 'might label feminist', although they were not acting within a collective political movement at this stage.[16]

Approaches from cultural history have also had important implications for historians concerned with women and the Enlightenment. The practitioners of the Enlightenment are now recognised as more diverse than was previously claimed, comprising not only a small group of Parisian *philosphes* but a host of less familiar figures, 'novelists, poets, medical men, salon hostesses, utopian thinkers and itinerant lecturers'.[17] Collectively they diffused different aspects of Enlightenment through conversation, debate and print, with national and local variations in its emphasis and spread. This wider interpretation has brought greater acknowledgement of women's role in the dissemination of Enlightenment thought. Assessments of their contribution to Enlightenment philosophy has been further aided, in the British context, by studies which have considered its distinctive Protestant/Anglican dimension in comparison with continental anti-clericalism.[18]

At the end of the eighteenth century the French Revolution brought fresh impetus to debates concerning political rights. Adjacent to calls for the recognition of a universalising 'Rights of Man' came the first tentative calls for women's political emancipation, which many scholars have taken as the marking the birth of modern feminism.[19] These were not yet being made collectively, although they appeared more frequently. Nor were they the only response to considerations of where women might fit in an expanding political world. A more restrictive discourse was simultaneously developed, which argued that woman's nature made her unsuited for equal participation in a broadening polity. Some women rejected this; others such as Hannah More argued that subordination benefited women through offering them distinctive spheres of activity which complemented those of men. Whether women were equal to or different from men continued to occupy feminist thinkers in the nineteenth and twentieth centuries.

Seventeenth-century antecedents: popular politics and petitioners

Women involved in political protests in early modern Britain often justified their actions in terms of their role as wives or mothers. This can be seen in their constant presence in disturbances connected to the price or availability of food for almost two centuries.[20] John Walter has described how women assumed the leadership of the notorious grain riots at Maldon, Essex in 1629, boarding a Flemish ship loaded for the export market and forcing its crew to 'fill the[ir] aprons and bonnets' with grain.[21] The women put on trial after the riot drew attention to their poverty in court through words which implied their right to obtain food. One, Ann Spearman, explained how she acted 'because she could not have Corne in the m[ar]kett & [because] certain fflemishe shipps ... [lay] at Burrow Hills ... there to receiue in Corne to carry beyond the sea'.[22]

Women were also to be found in disturbances connected with control over aspects of the local environment which fed into the domestic economy.

Women mobilised to retain rights over common land which they accessed to graze animals or collect firewood. They protested against the enforced drainage of fenland in the Isle of Axholme in the 1620s and the 1690s.[23] Scotswomen resisted the Highland clearances, and were prominent in direct actions against the dykes put up by landowners in Dumfries and Galloway in the 1720s.[24] When military spending sparked inflation and protest at the end of the century, women's participation was so marked that they comprised almost 50 per cent of those accused of felony in London.[25]

Women had other political concerns too, particularly in urban areas where they acted in defence of their wage-earning potential. In Scotland in the early 1700s, Rosalind Carr has argued that financial concerns provoked women's part in anti-Union protests when female 'shopkeepers, traders and consumers' feared that Union would redistribute wealth to London.[26] There were women amongst the crowds of rioting London weavers in 1675, prefiguring their later participation in Luddite protests by calling for the destruction of new engine looms.[27] In 1697 between 4000 and 5000 women descended on Parliament demanding a bill to prohibit the wearing of East India silks, as their popularity was damaging the indigenous trade of silk weaving.[28] These economically motivated examples show that women did not only legitimise their political activity through referring to their role as wives or mothers. Rather, as Bernard Capp has demonstrated, they were willing to voice their opinions on broader political issues, even when this carried extreme personal risk, as in the case of Mary Cleere, executed in 1577 for 'pronouncing Elizabeth [I] a bastard and no rightful queen'.[29] Nicholas Rogers has shown that such attitudes persisted into the eighteenth century, with women figuring prominently in trials for seditious words, frequently 'cursing the King in the street', as in the case of Mary Jones, gaoled for declaring 'the Prince of Wales is a bastard, his mother's a Whore'.[30]

The English Civil War augmented women's political activity in support of both sides. Some of their action was circumstantial; as Capp commented of women's part in the defence of Coventry, 'all hands were needed in a town under siege'.[31] At the same time, a distinctive feminine reaction can be traced in women's opposition to the war. This could be extremely personal; Samuel Priestley's mother walked the first quarter of a mile of his journey towards Fairfax's army with him whilst she 'besought him with tears not to go'.[32] Other women petitioned and demonstrated for peace, approaching Parliament in increasing numbers, culminating in a demonstration of over 5000 in August 1643.[33] Women justified their actions in terms of their identity as wives, mothers and non-combatants. Their opponents dismissed them in equally sexualised terms, calling them 'Oyster wives, and other dirty or tattered sluts', or suggested that they were being manipulated by more experienced political actors to articulate demands they did not understand.[34] Critiques of political women as either naive or sexually deviant would reappear throughout the next four centuries.

Women's petitioning was also a prominent part of the Leveller movement, peaking in 1649. Leveller women too were charged with political ignorance, and advised that as 'the matter ... is of an higher concernement than you understand ... you are desired to goe home, and looke after your owne business'.[35] Despite such gendered dismissals, Ann Hughes' study has concluded that the problem lay with what the women were saying rather than the fact that they, not men, were saying it. Warning us to be wary not to 'take for granted that the Leveller women's petitioning of 1649 was unprecedented and outrageous', Hughes claims that petitioning by early modern women was 'seen as normal in many accounts, irritating or embarrassing, perhaps, but a part of political life'.[36] Patricia Higgins, whose pioneering work on women petitioners took a more literal reading of their claims for exceptionalism, perceived an early feminist consciousness amongst women Levellers in their demands for equality and citizenship.[37] If this is true, it was short-lived; collective activity such as petitioning had declined by the end of the century. It did not vanish completely. Schwoerer has shown that a small number of women continued to produce strong statements of their religious dissent through pamphlets, and occasionally ventured into other modes of public address, up to the period of the Glorious Revolution and beyond.[38] Others such as Margaret Cavendish and Mary Astell began to publish writings that questioned women's status in society.

Queens and elite networks: Mary II, Anne and models of queenship

From 1689 to 1714 two British women wielded power at the highest level. Unlike other European countries, English (then British) queens could reign if there was no male heir. For the first time in over a century, the Glorious Revolution raised the possibility of the (contested) crown passing to a woman, Princess Mary of Orange, wife of the Dutch Prince William, and elder daughter (and eldest surviving child) of King James II by his first wife, Anne Hyde. Unlike her namesake predecessor Mary I, Queen Mary II was able to draw on historical precedents to define her role as regnant queen, as both Mary Tudor and her half-sister Elizabeth had succeeded in overcoming opposition based on their sex to take the crown and thus establish a model for female sovereignty.[39] Their monarchies demonstrated that women could rule, and that they could do so successfully. Furthermore, just as with Mary I and Elizabeth, Mary II and Anne reigned in close proximity, although they developed markedly different concepts of queenship. These showed some of the ways in which individual women could wield significant political power in an age in which this was overwhelmingly gendered as male. Their contrasting styles had wider repercussions for understandings of the relationship between gender and politics in their own time, as within their individual constructions of queenship, very different qualities were equated with femininity. Such different constructions, Rachel Weil has argued, 'must have unsettled any idea that women had natural roles or characteristics'.[40] They also offered markedly different models for how women might negotiate and exercise political power.

Of course, royal women are by their nature exceptional, separated from the majority of society by the privilege of birth which afforded them elite social status with all its attendant benefits. Clarissa Campbell Orr has gone so far as to classify them as 'an extreme case of "relational" women' deriving their status and power from their positions as the wives, mothers or daughters of powerful men.[41] Regnant queens may require different analysis, however, as suggested by Charles Beem. He argued that they are best understood as 'female kings' performing a role which remained gendered as male, in the same way that a hereditary monarchy would occasionally admit 'little boys, senile old men, and lunatics' to the throne.[42] Campbell Orr also sees the immediate post-Restoration period as one in which some masculine characteristics of monarchy were displaced by more feminine concerns, which in turn diminished concerns about the suitability of female rulers.[43]

Mary's conceptualisation of queenship was complex, and attempted to balance her position as heir with her role as wife. Although William of Orange had a claim to the throne (his mother Mary was sister to Charles II and James II), his wife's was stronger. Several contemporary commentators concurred. In the years of political turmoil preceding the Glorious Revolution, many publications outlined women's political capabilities, or celebrated them indirectly through laudatory biographies of Queen Elizabeth I, preparing public opinion for the re-ascendance of a female monarch.[44] This literature contrasts starkly with the anguished discourse that surrounded Mary Tudor's accession.[45] However, when the time came, Mary expressed no desire to reign alone. She took the throne alongside William, ostensibly in a dual monarchy but in reality with little personal power. This was a long-considered decision; unlike her sister Anne, Mary had little political ambition. She was not prepared for the crown. Tudor princesses were educated in a range of subjects; the aristocratic daughters of the post-Restoration era were not.[46] In common with other girls from elite families, Mary and Anne followed a curriculum centred on accomplishments such as dancing and needlework, which did not prepare them to rule.[47] Their only serious study was religious instruction, during which the Bishop of London inculcated a lifelong commitment to the Anglican Church in both sisters.

This is not to say that Mary was unintelligent. As a young bride she endeared herself to her new countrymen and women by mastering the Dutch language; she also developed a good command of French, and attended to some of the gaps in her education through reading religious books.[48] Yet she remained diffident, which was possibly what led her to accept aspects of patriarchal convention which later interpreters saw as weaknesses. These crystallized around her relationship to the husband she married at her parents' insistence at the age of 15, having reputedly wept for more than a day between her first meeting with the older, unattractive Prince and her decision to accept him. Despite this inauspicious beginning, Mary developed a genuine affection for William, which may also explain why she did not assert her claim to the throne over his.

Princess Mary was a popular figure in the Netherlands, but her situation on her return to England was less assured. As the daughter of the deposed monarch she was in a dangerous position: if not open to accusations of parricide, then at least seemingly guilty of flouting patriarchally delineated conventions of father–daughter relationships. Jacobites compared her with Tarquin's wife Tullia, who persuaded her husband to murder her father to gain his crown.[49] Jacobite ballads emphasized her double treachery, regretting 'The day our King's ae daughter came/ To play so foul a play'.[50] Mary learned quickly that she could not take public opinion for granted. Her deportment when she arrive at her new palace at Whitehall, wandering through rooms in her dressing-gown, trying out the beds and rummaging through the closets, attracted strong criticism.[51] Such exuberance, understandable in a young woman, would not be tolerated in a queen. Despite frequent public denials that she held any interest in politics, Mary displayed strong political acumen in curbing her public behaviour from this point. She deferred to her husband, taking care that she was anointed and crowned after rather than with him at their coronation ceremony. Her public persona rested on a carefully constructed identity as a collector and patron of the theatre, music, architecture and garden design.[52]

Mary was also an extremely devout Protestant, which endeared her to all who supported her joint rule against the claim of her Catholic father. Her faith allowed her some significant power within the affairs of state as William, less interested in Anglicanism, often followed her lead. Bishop Burnett claimed that 'the king left the matters of the church wholly in the queen's hands'. This was not strictly so, but she did have a hand in clerical appointments, including that of Tillotson to Canterbury in 1691.[53] Faith emboldened Mary to press for certain changes. On her return to England she confessed herself surprised 'to see so little devotion' in the people, and attempted to alter this. She established 'singing the Prayers in the Chapel' on Sundays, and had Sunday afternoon sermons delivered at Whitehall, but grieved that she 'could not make the people mind the Sunday more', despite trying to tighten up implementation of laws against public drunkenness or debauchery on this day.[54]

Mary's subservient role changed when William determined to secure his throne through pursuing conflict against Jacobite and French forces in Ireland. This raised the question of who would govern in his absence. Public opinion was not universally behind Mary; many doubted her ability to rule. Concerns were also raised that she might side with her father James whilst William was away.[55] Mary was far from enthusiastic about the new prospect, writing that William's decision:

> gave me a very melancholy prospect of things. I saw my self going to be left alone, in my country, it is true; but alas I was a stranger to it, to all persons in it, and most of all to business. I saw myself to be left in many difficulties not knowing whom to trust.[56]

She was not calmed when Lord Shrewsbury, the man her husband 'named as … one who might be [trusted] entirely', resigned his position in the Cabinet Council appointed to advise her during William's absence.[57] Nevertheless, Mary governed successfully during three regencies, steering her way through serious problems including a naval crisis, numerous plots and questions of treason, and the constant threat of invasion. Recent appraisals of her life have concurred that she displayed a 'competent discharge of political and administrative duties' which was rendered unthreatening through her obvious reliance on William and her insistence on consulting him as frequently as communications made possible.[58] Her demure persona, her devoutness and her unfortunate early death from smallpox in 1694 ensured that she was remembered as both an exemplary wife *and* a queen, utilising political power in pursuit of accepted feminine interests.

Queen Anne's reign offers many contrasts with her sister's. The two women had a somewhat stormy relationship when Mary was queen. The settlement that she had approved for herself and William effectively moved Anne out of the succession by ensuring that the crown would remain with William in the event of Mary's death. It did, however, guarantee the precedence of Anne's children over any who may have been born to William and Mary, which may have accounted for the lack of any public protest over her marginalisation on Anne's part. On her accession Anne, recently described as the queen provoking 'the most equivocal press' of all female rulers, developed her own views on how to resolve her position as both queen and wife. She signalled her difference from Mary immediately, intending to rule in her own right, with no role for her husband, Prince George of Denmark, from the coronation ceremony onwards.[59] Anne's decision to affect what Beem described as 'the political emasculation of her husband' prompted comparisons with Elizabeth I, although despite Prince George's marginalisation, Anne was very definitely married.[60] George, who appeared to enjoy an affectionate relationship with his wife, did not object. He was content to adopt the – at the time unique – role of male consort, unlike Prince William (already ruler of the Netherlands in his own right), who had reputedly refused to be his 'wife's gentleman's usher'.[61]

Anne did not set aside all aspects of femininity on her accession. She encouraged the image of herself as the 'nursing mother' of the nation, drawn from verses from Isaiah which inspired her coronation sermon.[62] Although this image (also occasionally applied to Mary) was hardly appropriate to a woman who had undergone 17 miscarriages or stillbirths, its original context suggested equal roles for monarchs of either sex regardless of biology: 'Kings shall be thy nursing fathers, and Queens thy nursing mothers'.[63] Like Mary, Anne was a committed Anglican. She took her role as Defender of the Faith to heart, reintroducing the displaced ceremony of monarchical 'touching' to cure scrofula (the king's evil) and supporting charitable schemes such as Queen Anne's Bounty, a fund established in 1704 to benefit poor clergy. Such actions were applauded in Mary as feminine virtues; conversely in Anne, very much a sole queen, they were condemned as instances where she showed 'Tenderness to a Fault'.[64] Anne had to adopt more masculine roles than her sister, as her single rule put her at the head of the army and navy. Her biographer, Edward Gregg, has suggested that Anne's 'sex was an obvious disadvantage in a reign dominated by a great war'.[65] Yet there appears to have been little contemporary comment on this during the War of the Spanish Succession beyond the acceptance that, as 'Her Majesty was no Amazon, it was not expected that she should ride her self in the Head of her Troops' as William had done.[66] Furthermore, although she was initially portrayed as a rather ineffectual bystander, demanding rather than commanding military victories, Anne's femininity proved useful when she moved away from the Whigs' pursuit of the war to the Tories' opposition, as her diminishing enthusiasm could be presented as evidence of her nurturing concern for her subjects rather than an example of political inconsistency.[67]

Other dimensions of Anne's femininity were rendered more problematic. She surrounded herself with women, a point which will be returned to below. Mary had also done this; propriety at the very least dictated that the queen's closest servants who performed intimate duties for her must be of the same sex. However, as Mary did not rule alone, her circle of women attendants attracted no criticism. Anne, without a king, found that suspicion lighted on her relationships with her intimate servants and confidantes. They were suspected of having too much power over her, the suggestion being that, as an apparently (for political purposes at least) unhusbanded woman, she must be being manipulated by somebody (and in all probability by a pushy woman) rather than acting on her own. Natalie Davis has noted how Anne's dependence on 'womanly connections and female friendships invited a perception of her as "weak" and dominated by favourites', a perception which was augmented when, following a very public break, her former confidante Sarah Churchill published her damning memoirs.[68] As Gregg has noted, although Anne's reign was favourably received in some quarters at the time, the tenacity of Churchill's memoirs coloured later assessments of her work. It is only recently that her diligence in attending to affairs of state has been positively appraised.[69]

Mary II and Anne presented two different models of female political power. Both were married women, but they handled the complex relationship between themselves, the state and their husbands in opposite ways. Mary's construction of herself as dutiful and subservient wife met with approbation at the time, although how much of this was to do with her unexpected early death, which gave rise to extreme levels of public grief, it is difficult to assess. Certainly her periods as effective sole ruler during William's repeated military absences do not appear to have drawn significant amounts of adverse criticism. Anne, by contrast, attracted more hostile comment in her own day, notably from those fearing the influence of the female friends and servants with whom she was surrounded. This fuelled depictions of her as weak and stupid, unaware of the affairs of state, which sit at odds with more recent biographical reassessments of her very diligent work in this sphere. As regnant queens, both women conformed to certain gendered expectations of behaviour, but challenged others, attempting to define their roles in their own terms.

Aristocratic women and the royal court

Queen regnant was the most powerful political position available to women in post-Restoration Britain, but it was beyond the reach of most women. Other positions were more attainable. The furore surrounding Queen Anne's relationships with her attendants leads us into an arena where women exercised considerable political power. From Elias onwards, historians have been attentive to the royal court as the centre of power in early modern Europe.[70] Court influence was arguably declining in the post-Reformation era, its position as employer being replaced, as Robert Bucholz has described, by 'a burgeoning governmental bureaucracy and the rising professions', yet it still proved an irresistible magnet to many of the elite.[71] For young women in particular, the court offered unequalled opportunity to achieve an advantageous marriage. Such marriages could take women to the heart of state power, as in the case of Anne Hyde, mother to Queen Mary and Queen Anne. Hyde, daughter of the first Duke of Clarendon, was serving as maid of honour to the Princess of Orange at Breda when she met James, Duke of York. They embarked on a relationship, and James married her in secret when she became pregnant, confessing the marriage later, to the fury of his mother. Reliance on sexual attraction and the decision to embark on a sexual relationship outside of wedlock were risky strategies. Girls less lucky than Anne Hyde were sent back home in public disgrace if their pregnancies did not prompt an offer of marriage.[72] Women who became the mistresses of kings could translate their sexuality into power and wealth, but in a more dependent manner that those who became wives. Elizabeth Villiers, the former childhood friend and maid of honour to Mary II, had a longstanding relationship with King William, but found herself rapidly put aside in his guilt after Mary's early death.[73] Royal mistresses were subject to gossip and suspected of having undue influence, and a deposed mistress enjoyed no rights to retain the privileges extended to her during her relationship with the king.

A safer role for women was that of the courtier, a defined job with a salary. The latter could be substantial; Sarah Churchill derived an annual income of around £6000 from her various official positions as mistress of the robes, groom of the stole, keeper of the Privy Purse and ranger of Windsor Park.[74] These positions were not necessarily the preserve of aristocratic women. Bucholz's prosoprographical analysis of 1424 courtiers at the court of Queen Anne concluded that the 'strenuous and manual work' required to keep the Queen and her wardrobe in order appealed to women of slightly lower origins, making such appointments 'a potential ladder upon which an ambitious young woman could rise in status' or advance her family.[75] Women courtiers' status grew during Anne's reign as they enjoyed access to the monarch rather than to his consort. The perceived power of women such as Sarah Churchill, Abigail Masham (who replaced Sarah as Queen Anne's favourite) and Elizabeth Seymour can be inferred from the levels of popular concern that they aroused. Although Geoffrey Holmes suggested that regnant queens were 'peculiarly susceptible' to the ways of 'bedchamber politics', it is probable that it was not her sex, but Anne's frequent bouts of ill-health that fuelled concern, as they confined her to her bedchamber or quieter rooms away from the open court.[76] Being accepted at court did not guarantee proximity to the queen. To achieve this, it was necessary to be admitted into her private apartments, easier for Anne's courtiers as she spent more time there. This, coupled with her penchant for controlling the balance of political power between Whigs and Tories in her parliaments by meeting individual ministers in private, meant that the women who controlled access to her bedchamber appeared to control what was effectively the only private space in the Augustan court, and along with this, access to the monarch herself.[77]

Close contact with the queen did not automatically advantage bedchamber women. Many intimate duties lacked prestige. Abigail Masham's work included 'sleeping on the floor of the royal bedroom at night, and emptying the royal slops in the morning', which initially dissuaded Anne from ennobling Abigail's husband, as she feared that it would be inappropriate for a titled lady to undertake these tasks.[78] Conversely, there were occasions when the lines between the political and personal worlds of the court became blurred, placing bedchamber women in a privileged position. The critical status of legitimacy to a hereditary monarchy empowered women who had expertise around maternity. There was significant female participation in the 'warming-pan scandal' of 1688. Supporters of the Orange claim to the throne suggested that the Jacobite heir, born to James II and his catholic wife Mary of Modena, was an impostor, smuggled into the royal bedchamber in a warming-pan after Mary had faked a pregnancy. Published propaganda tracts invoked the words – and authority – of Mary's bedchamber women both in her defence and against her, presenting them as trustworthy, loyal witnesses or 'scheming women who conspired with priests and midwives', depending on the perspective of the writer.[79] The fear of 'scheming' or manipulative and pernicious collective female influence was exacerbated when it surrounded the monarch rather than his consort. and could be used to question a regnant queen's capacity for independent judgement, as in some assessments of Queen Anne's reign.[80]

Jacobite women

Not all instances of political involvement by elite women were associated with crown or parliament. Many Scots women supported Jacobite attempts to restore the (Catholic) Stuart monarchy. Family loyalty often prompted their action. Karl von den Steinen's investigation into the political activism of the daughters of Anne, Duchess of Hamilton, concluded that 'the perceived political victimisation of their husbands' motivated Katherine, Duchess of Atholl, and her younger sister Margaret to embark on a series of political activities culminating in Katharine's intelligence gathering during the Queensbury Plot of 1703.[81] Other wives risked more direct actions when faced with more desperate circumstances. When Lady Nithsdale failed in her attempt to petition King George to spare the life of her husband, one of a number awaiting execution after the '15, she and other women took matters into their own hands. With two women friends she visited her husband in the Tower of London, dressed him in women's clothes and helped him escape.[82]

Family loyalty was important in determining attachment to the Jacobite cause, but not all Jacobite women acted as dutiful wives. As a rebel movement which set itself against the prevalent political consensus, Jacobitism was perhaps less concerned with observing appropriate gendered behaviours, and would 'accept all volunteers, regardless of sex'.[83] This allowed for more direct involvement, perhaps most notoriously in the shape of a woman such as Jenny Cameron, separated from (so arguably uninfluenced by) her husband, who led a detachment of 300 men to join Bonnie Prince Charlie's army in 1745, or Lady Anne Mackintosh who donned riding habit, blue bonnet and pistols to raise a similar number of troops, earning the name of 'Colonel Anne'.[84] In 1715 and 1745 women raised money for the Jacobite cause and offered shelter to combatants seeking to escape at the end of the uprisings. Paul Monad has gone so far as to suggest that 'it is not anachronistic to [describe as] feminists' many early female writers who also had a demonstrable attachment to the Jacobite cause in the eighteenth century.[85] Yet although their participation was welcomed within the movement, it attracted predictable external criticism. 'Female Rebels', one pamphleteer argued, 'seldom observe[d] any Medium in their passions' but were prone to excessive extremes of behaviour.[86] Recent appraisals of women

Jacobites have suggested that it is this belief in their transgressiveness that has led to the elevation of Flora Macdonald, arguably not in complete sympathy with the Jacobite cause, to the status of heroine. Flora's motivation for aiding the Prince in his escape was pity rather than political conviction, which she underlined when she later explained to the Prince of Wales 'that she would have done the same thing for him had she found him in distress'.[87]

Women and the beginnings of party politics

Post-Restoration Britain witnessed a gradual shift in the locus of political power. Successive legislation from the Bill of Rights of 1689 to the Act of Settlement of 1701 (only really enacted after Anne's death) shaped the circumstances through which power shifted away from the person of the individual monarch and royal prerogative to Parliament. This was a period in which parliamentary power was in the ascendency, the monarch held in check by members of the House of Commons elected by votes which could not be taken entirely for granted. Politics became participatory, up to a point, although there was no linear progression in this. The early eighteenth century brought a flurry of activity in England and Wales, with 16 general elections between 1679 and 1716 and a contest in almost every constituency.[88] The Triennial Act of 1694 required elections every three years, but this was replaced by a Septennial Act in 1716, after which the number of elections decreased. There was also a steady decline in the number of individual contests up to 1747, when fewer than 10 per cent of constituencies polled, then another rise in the second half of the century, during which around a third of elections involved contests.[89] One of the reasons for this patchy pattern is the cost of elections; the Tories spent an estimated £20,000 on a contest at Oxfordshire in 1754. Contested elections also required a willing body of workers, plus careful nurturing between contests to ensure loyalty.

Women's initial relationship to this remains unclear. Compared with the surrounding centuries, the eighteenth century has enjoyed less attention from women's historians until recently. In the field of women's involvement in politics the absence of research is even more marked, and has moved little since Karl von den Steinen noted how studies of the period forced readers to 'chose between politics without women or women without politics'.[90] More recently, James Daybell has suggested that the centralisation of government and the growth of Parliament 'may have reduced the role of great noble households as political institutions', thus reducing the political roles of aristocratic women by the end of the seventeenth century.[91] On the other hand, work by Ingrid Tague and Elaine Chalus has suggested that elite women simply moved their sphere of activity in response to the rise of party and electoral politics.[92] There were political institutions beyond the court that were open to women. There was no law that formally debarred women from voting before 1832. Property ownership governed who voted in most boroughs and all counties, and on certain occasions, women did vote if they were unmarried and independently qualified to do so, or if they were widows. Some women even stood as candidates for local office. Patricia Crawford uncovered an instance of a woman voting in a parliamentary election in 1654, and suggested that the practice may have extended beyond this date.[93] In another notable election in Richmond, North Yorkshire, in 1678, women who demanded to exercise what they saw as their right to vote were permitted to assign their votes to men to cast on their behalf.[94] Yet such instances were rare, and established custom generally debarred even qualified women from exercising their franchise.

After 1689 Schwoerer has suggested that 'barriers against [women's] voting were hardened'.[95] Their presence hereafter tends to be noted on occasions when they were prevented from engaging in the ballot. Sarah Bly's election as sexton for a London parish in 1738 provoked her defeated opponent to challenge the case, with the result that her victory was upheld, but only because the office 'did not concern the public or the care and inspection of the morals of the parishioners'.[96] This judgement effectively curtailed women's opportunity to exercise a parliamentary vote, throwing them back onto their more familiar role of attempting to influence rather than to participate directly. Nevertheless, the small but continuing number of satirical publications that ridiculed women's political ambitions suggested that this was at least a question being aired in some quarters.[97] Furthermore, as Susan Staves has demonstrated, women continued to vote for local office holders and participate in elections linked to companies and private trusts, which could be very politicised affairs.[98]

Voting was only one way of participating in electoral politics. Elaine Chalus has recently suggested that assessments that view the ten parliamentary elections between 1695 and 1715 as a 'watershed' in British politics need to be extended to consider their impact on women.[99] Early eighteenth-century politics was not restricted to Parliament or official institutions, but extended into a variety of cultural milieux. Party allegiance determined attendance at race or hunt meetings, or at social venues such as assembly rooms, which shaped the rhythms of polite society into the eighteenth century.[100] This shifting of political activity to the locale offered ample opportunities for elite women to undertake political work. Chalus has identified four roles which they were able to undertake: confidante, adviser, partner and agent.[101] These reflected the extent to which party politics was becoming a family affair, in which women's participation was both expected and, on occasions, demanded. Women were not passive in these roles. Lavinia, Lady Spencer urgently wrote to her husband for accounts of debates in the House, while Lady Charlotte Wentworth helped her brother, Lord Rockingham, prepare his Parliamentary speeches.[102]

When numbers of contested elections were high, electioneering became important to both parties. The image of deferential voters controlled by the interests of their landlords or employers has been challenged by Frank O'Gorman and John Phillips, who have pointed to the diversity of the electorate to query the extent to which control might be effectively exercised. The electorate varied in size between counties; Yorkshire had around 20,000 voters whilst Rutland had only 800. In Scotland the electorate was much smaller, barely reaching 2000. O'Gorman and Phillips each found high turnouts in contested elections, suggesting that electoral politics was becoming a participatory activity in the eighteenth century.[103] Elite women participated in electioneering, taking up activities such as canvassing with enthusiasm. Prior to the nineteenth century Reform Acts, canvassing was seen as more than a means of predicting – or attempting to influence – the outcome at the polls. Eighteenth-century elections were frequently preceded by vigorous bouts of canvassing, intended to ascertain whether it was worth a particular party putting up a candidate at all. Canvassing could be public: Catherine Talbot encouraged bell ringing and the wearing of green cockades in an election in 1758 without attracting criticism.[104] Others were less sure of themselves, but played an equally important role canvassing and shaping political support in the newer social spaces of assembly rooms and public balls, as well as around their own dinner tables.

Women's canvassing was expected to stay within certain boundaries. Obvious transgressors attracted attention at the time, so they have arguably become overrepresented in historiography by those who have presented women's involvement as rather risqué, involving 'a kiss, a smile, a wave, and a dress of flamboyant party colours' to seduce (figuratively if not literally) the undecided voter.[105] Such characteristics underpin interpretations of the better researched examples of politicking women in post-Reformation elections, although less subtle methods could also be employed. Mrs Webb, who intervened in a contest in Chippenham in 1702, offered Margaret Burges 'a good waistcoat for her husband and a dressing for herself, and promised her a bushel of wheat and a pair of breeches for her husband to vote for Sir Basil Firebrace'.[106]

Sarah Churchill, one of the most frequently cited female canvassers, embraced the more robust sides of electioneering when she headed for St Albans in 1705 to thwart the ambitions of the Tory John Gape. On this occasion she did little more than use her close friendship with Queen Anne to attempt to persuade the voters that Gape, as a 'Tacker' (in support of the attempts to tack the Occasional Conformity Bill onto the end of the Land Tax Bill of November 1704) was pro-French and the sort of candidate the Queen did not wish to see succeed, being 'against the Queen's interests and the good of the nation'.[107] Sarah's intervention, which included publicly debating with clergy, shopkeepers and other interested locals, drew charges of 'unwarrantable interference' in the proceedings from Tory voices, even though Gape won. The complaints went as far as the Parliamentary Committee of Elections and Privileges, where witnesses repeatedly described how she had 'sent for them and desired their votes', being prepared to enter into debate 'as to several points of state' with opponents.[108] Sarah's behaviour was thus publicly condemned despite her insistence that as a substantial landowner in the constituency, her involvement was not unusual or improper.[109]

Towards the end of the century, Georgiana, Duchess of Devonshire was similarly censured for moving too frequently and freely amongst the lower-class voters on behalf of the Whig campaign in 1784, leading to accusations of a 'kisses for votes' scandal.[110] 'We hear the D–s of D– grants favours to those who promise their votes and interest to Mr Fox', was how the *Morning Post* reported her campaign.[111] Sarah and Georgiana were condemned for their behaviour rather than their presence. Other women participated in elections without criticism when they kept within expected norms.

The politics of print culture

The *Morning Post*'s role in spreading awareness of the Duchess of Devonshire's scandalous behaviour reminds us that the sites of political activity were broadening.

The eighteenth-century growth in newspaper and periodical titles and circulation was prefigured by a vibrant print culture in the seventeenth century. The Civil War removed press controls, and their brief reassertion during the Restoration lapsed in 1695.[112] This, along with raised literacy rates and different modes of literary production, brought an expansion in the range of titles, with 700 new ones published between 1620 and 1700.[113] Women took their part in this work, as 'distributors ... publishers, printers, bookbinders and booksellers'.[114] Furthermore, they 'were not merely the producers and distributors of other people's political ideas', but used print to address a variety of political subjects themselves.[115]

Women's seventeenth-century publications often had religious content, although they could simultaneously address broader social concerns; Hester Biddle's *Warning from the Lord God of Life and Power Unto Thee O City Of London* predicted dire consequences for wealthy metropolitan residents who ignored the plight of the city's poor.[116] By the end of the century, elite women such as Mary Astell were publishing works that spoke to women's circumstances directly. Astell's *A Serious Proposal to the Ladies* (1694) covered the poor state of girls' education, an issue that would preoccupy feminist campaigners for the next two centuries, and bring her subsequent recognition as one of England's earliest feminists.[117] Less developed but equally important was the discussion in an emerging periodical press which deliberately sought to attract – and inform – a female readership. E. J. Clery's analysis of one title, the *Athenian Mercury*, argues that its interactive format (readers' letters determined its subject matter) offered women an unparalleled 'open platform for voicing their views and experiences'.[118] The spread of political writings by and for women in the seventeenth and eighteenth centuries helped pave the way for a more coherent women's movement in the nineteenth century. By the end of the eighteenth century, networks of women writers were connecting 'English rational dissent and Scottish Whiggism across Edinburgh, Glasgow and Northern England as well as London and Bath', disseminating political ideas far beyond the metropolis.[119]

The spread of print culture had other implications for women's politics. It reflected a growing level of women's literacy. This was strongest in urban areas, although for rural Scotland Smout has estimated that reading literacy rates were much higher than for writing, suggesting that dissemination of ideas in print might be wider than hitherto considered.[120] Knowledge gained through reading had broader political implications; Elaine Chalus has recently outlined how the 'Rag Plot' concerning (unfounded) fears of a hive of Jacobites in mid-eighteenth century Oxford could not have functioned without high levels of literacy of all involved.[121] More immediately, print culture aided the evolution of certain spaces where pamphlets, newspapers and periodicals could be read and their ideas discussed. Central to this was the spread in popularity of the coffee house, the first of which opened in Oxford in 1650, spawning numerous metropolitan and provincial copies.[122] Coffee houses were not just places for socialising; as Melton noted, they were 'politicized spaces of public discussion'.[123] The inflammatory potential of coffee-house politics prompted calls for their suppression in the 1670s, and they remained an important location for the formation of political ideologies into the next century, alongside other forums such as salons and public debating clubs.[124] By the late eighteenth and early nineteenth century some coffee houses – such as the Drum in Liverpool – were hosting meetings of radical groups. The political clubs that underpinned the associational culture of party in the nineteenth century arguably owe their origins to such institutions.

How far women were able to access coffee houses remains a matter of debate, although practice clearly varied across Britain. Carr has argued that in Scotland 'women were generally excluded from those spaces in which extra-parliamentary citizenship could be practised' such as the coffee house.[125] In a study of English coffee houses Steven Pincus has refuted claims of women's exclusion, although as Markman Eliss noted, his conclusion that their presence was welcomed rested on a small sample of evidence.[126] Women were far more likely to be found in coffee houses as workers, running establishments in their own right or serving in them. Their presence was often criticised by male patrons, and according to Cowan, 'cannot be taken as clear-cut evidence of their equal participation' in the milieu of coffeehouse culture.[127] Nevertheless, the fact that women were there physically, and in the print culture which underpinned the political dimensions of the coffee house, makes it impossible to interpret such politics as exclusively masculine.

Women, politics and the Enlightenment

Some historians have argued for an emerging sense of feminist consciousness during the Enlightenment. For Margaret Jacob, the period 'put women's rights ... on the agenda as never before'.[128] This connection is not always obvious, however; many discussions of women's roles in the period did not demand increased social or political rights, but emphasised a distinct female 'nature' and sexual difference. Identification of specific, biologically determined female roles (which tended to be subordinate or auxiliary to those of men) had been prefigured in earlier centuries, but the Enlightenment preoccupation with science encouraged their presentation as rational scientific discourses. Nevertheless, the intellectual atmosphere of the time provided spaces for women to argue against such claims or to develop their own ideas. In London women took part in public debating societies, a key site for the formation and spread of Enlightenment thought. Debating societies were considered more democratic than salons as they required no invitation, but welcomed anyone who could pay the attendance fee. They became popular from the 1750s, first as male-only groups, then (after some discussion) opening to women observers and members. In 1780 La Belle Assemblée, the first female debating society, was launched, followed by a small number of imitators.[129] In Scotland too, women attended and voted at debating societies, although there is no evidence that they spoke in debates.[130]

Debating society discussions often took a political turn; in 1780 alone there were at least 11 debates focusing on women's role in education and politics.[131] Some of these questioned whether women too might be entitled to demand political rights, as part of wider discussions about the form that a more democratic or participatory government might take. Others went further, to consider whether women might have the right to vote or even to sit in Parliament. Debating societies provided women with a public space where they could articulate their own analysis of varying aspects of their subordination. Despite their popularity amongst a small group of women, the all-female debating societies found it difficult to sustain themselves financially and were short-lived. Some of their participants who had developed a taste for public debates through attending them continued to join in mixed groups, but these were closed by the government in 1798 as part of a broader clamp-down on seditious activity in the wake of the French Revolution. Nevertheless, while they existed, women's debating societies allowed women to consider their relationship to politics, constituting an important location where women could begin to develop a sense of themselves as political actors. Their repeated attention to themes such as education and voting rights combined with the opportunity they provided for women to speak to a mixed audience has led Anna Clark to consider them 'extremely significant for women's role in the political public'.[132]

The French Revolution and women's political role

The French Revolution did not start a debate about women's participation in the political life of the nation. This had been the subject of lively, if intermittent, discussion in previous centuries, and was expanding into newer spaces, debating clubs and a variety of print media. Nevertheless, the seismic upheaval across the Channel provoked renewed interest in the question, and the first direct calls for women's political emancipation. Much of this was connected to broader discussions of the nature and extent of participatory government and citizenship. How citizenship ought to be defined, and who should possess it, were critical in deciding how a post-revolutionary state might be arranged. Women's extremely visible part in events in France, most noticeably in the march on Versailles in October 1789 but also in revolutionary clubs and salons, put them at the heart of these discussions. As Joan Scott noted, 'the gendering of citizenship was a persistent theme in French political discourse' at this time.[133]

In the event women were excluded from full political citizenship in the French Republic (and remained so until after the Second World War). Not all French women accepted this, however. Vociferous counter-arguments for the extension of men's post-Revolutionary rights to women were raised by Olympe de Gouges, Etta Palm d'Aelders and others. Their work inspired and fed into demands in other countries, gathering momentum; a recent study of European women's political writings found women in Belgium, the Netherlands, Italy and Germany were agitating for greater rights in the wake of the French Revolution.[134] In Britain too, increasing numbers of women – and men – took up the subject.

The best known example remains Mary Wollstonecraft, whose name 'was inextricably linked in the public mind with the French Revolution'.[135] Wollstonecraft's *Vindication of the Rights of Women* (1792) is seen by many as the founding text of British feminism. The extent to which the *Vindication* merits its foundational status is questionable. Many of its eighteenth-century ideas are, unsurprisingly, out of step with later feminist consensus. The *Vindication* was critical of the effect of contemporary education, yet as Jane Rendall has noted, 'there is no doubt' that its author 'saw the domestic sphere as that in which women would most likely excel, and that for which they should be trained'.[136] Wollstonecraft's text said little about the extension of specific civil or political rights to women – at one point she suggests that they ought not to complain when the majority of working men 'whose very sweat supports the splendid stud of an heir-apparent' were equally disenfranchised.[137] Yet in its own time, it represented one of the earliest attempts to critique the gendered nature of Enlightenment thought which universalised virtue on the one hand while questioning women's embodiment of this on the other hand.[138] The sense of possibility contained in the *Vindication* helped it to achieve 'symbolic stature ... transformed by its times into a revolutionary manifesto'.[139] Recent interpretations have taken a broader view of its content, reassessing Wollstonecraft's religiosity to place her within a longer tradition of dissenting thought.[140]

Unlike earlier proto-feminist writers, Wollstonecraft was not operating entirely alone; other women were expressing similar views. Catherine Macaulay, often cited as a 'feminist historian', prefigured some of Wollstonecraft's ideas, influencing her in her denial of sexual difference and her indignation at women's exclusion 'from every political right'.[141] Women such as Mary Hays turned to the imaginative form of the novel to critique women's 'sensibility' and issue tentative calls for their right to experience sexual passion.[142] While there was not yet anything that could be described as a women's movement, a greater number of voices now raised similar arguments to Wollstonecraft and called for an enhanced status for women. By the end of the century there was even a name – the Wollstonecraft School – denoting those who supported a range of progressive ideas about women.[143] Such labelling suggests that a greater degree of coherence was surrounding women's political activity than in its earlier, more episodic phases.

The calls for an extension of women's political rights were not welcomed in all circles. Linda Colley noted how the sexualised demonisation and execution of Marie Antoinette, coupled with equally vituperative attacks on other aristocratic French women during the Revolution, provoked discussion in which the prominence afforded to women by the *ancien régime* became a key area for criticism amongst British commentators perturbed by the consequences of an inappropriately feminised state.[144] In the wake of the Revolution, sections of British society that were frightened rather than inspired by events in France delivered a powerful conservative backlash against the Wollstonecraft School and against those ideas which we might describe as 'feminist'. Wollstonecraft's own unconventional private life was invoked as a means of discrediting her thought and that of her supporters. The dangers of 'unsexed' women interfering in the affairs of state came to symbolise the inevitable societal breakdown which would follow any British revolution. So in many ways the legacy of the French Revolution for the women's movement was paradoxical. On the one hand, it extended discussions of political rights which enabled some women to raise claims on behalf of their sex. On the other hand, the potential of such discussions to subvert existing gender roles became a powerful weapon in the hands of those who wished to preserve current social orders and prevent revolutionary upheaval.

Separate spheres

Many readers will be familiar with the retrospective model of 'separate spheres' to explain divisions between the public and private worlds of men and women.

While this is most frequently applied to the nineteenth century, some historians have sought its origins in the eighteenth century, arguing that women found it more difficult to take part in public life from this point.[145] Much of the evidence for this difficulty is drawn from a growing body of prescriptive literature published in the late eighteenth and early nineteenth centuries. This argued that women were unsuited for the public world of commerce and politics and should remain in private, domestic life.

Attempts to define the scope of women's private role coincided with an expansion in what might be considered public. New locations for social and cultural activities developed, such as the debating society, the assembly room, the subscription library and the coffee house. Historical investigation of these sites has drawn heavily on the work of Jürgen Habermas, who argued that they represented the emergence of a new, bourgeois public sphere in eighteenth-century Europe.[146] For Habermas, these physical locations, combined with developing print culture, journals and pamphlet literature, moulded the new phenomenon of 'public opinion' which acted as a powerful counterweight to absolutist systems. Public opinion was much more than a set of common ideas; it could shape a variety of social and political practices. Hence the public sphere played a critical role in shaping and upholding emerging political systems.

Women's relationship to this has been controversial. Habermas' descriptions of the public and private sphere ascribed no gendered qualities to either. Nevertheless, his thesis informed the views of a number of scholars who have demonstrated that as 'public' embodied a number of masculine characteristics ('rationality', 'virtue'), 'private' or domestic life became feminised. A number of exclusionary practices supported this, marginalising women from the growing associational culture surrounding the public sphere as its institutions became more formalised. Histories of nineteenth-century women often started with descriptions of 'middle-class wives who remained in their homes while their husbands sallied forth into the world of business, politics, bureaucracy and the professions'.[147] This view of restriction and closure for women characterised Davidoff and Hall's study of how gender helped to shape nineteenth-century middle-class identity.[148] Davidoff and Hall's thesis did not go unchallenged, particularly by Amanda Vickery who argued rigorously against its implication that there had been a 'golden age' for women which preceded the more restrictive epoch of separate spheres. Vickery cautioned against a too literal reading of the prescriptive literature of the early nineteenth century, noting that 'women like men were evidently quite capable of professing one thing and performing another' in the period, while Linda Colley went further to suggest that the rise in such literature might be better understood as a backlash against an increasing public role for women rather than a successful attempt to deny them one.[149] Historians of women's politics have been at the forefront of establishing a complex picture of coexisting 'counter publics' which engaged in vigorous and sometimes successful competition with the dominant model.

Numerous political and philanthropic societies welcomed women's involvement in the nineteenth century, as the next chapter will show. As Simon Morgan's recent study of women's civic activities in Leeds suggests, 'rather than beating on the doors of an ancient fortress, women were very much part of' the process of constructing a public sphere in the city.[150] Such arguments have done much to widen the debate around public and private to the point at which Kathryn Gleadle has advised the adoption of a plural interpretation of 'separate spheres' as a more accurate reflection of when and how women positioned themselves within politics.[151]

Some historians of feminism have noted how 'separate spheres' rhetoric was not exclusively deployed by men. Many women took up their pens to embrace its tenets, and took on active public roles in the process. One example is Hannah More, who founded a number of schools and Sunday schools in Somerset as well as the Religious Tract Society. Some of More's arguments echoed those of Mary Wollstonecraft. She was critical of contemporary girls' education, particularly its emphasis on the acquisition of 'accomplishments'. Her *Strictures on Female Education* (1799) argued the need for curricular reform in terms which, Jane Rendall has suggested, placed it firmly 'as a text of the Enlightenment'.[152] She wished society to place greater value on women's domestic, familial role. Yet More loathed Wollstonecraft and refused to read the *Vindication* on the grounds that its title was 'fantastic and absurd'.[153] Most of More's writing was deeply conservative; she rejected the notion of a political role for women, approved of existing gender hierarchies and believed that women's education ought to prepare them for a life of discreet subordination. Nevertheless, as Anne Stott's biography noted, More's writings could persuade her readers to 'dip their toes into public life' in pursuit of a number of causes.[154]

There were paradoxes, too, in More's own beliefs and actions. She took on a more public role in support of William Wilberforce's parliamentary campaigns. She argued that marriage and motherhood were the roles that suited women's nature, yet she remained unmarried and childless. She spoke out against the inappropriateness of female polemicists while publishing her own *Cheap Repository Tracts* to convert the poor. The contradictions More embodied demonstrate some of the difficulties in defining early feminism; many of its opponents also questioned women's role in society and participated in activities that paved the way for greater female involvement in politics. More rejected women's rights as 'impious' and would have been horrified to find herself associated with feminism. Yet by the early twentieth century, Ray Strachey was claiming that her educational work, although limited, 'was marking out a new sphere for the young women of the middle classes, and their revolt against their own narrow and futile lives followed as a matter of course'.[155] Placing More into a feminist trajectory complicates assessments of feminism, as Harriet Guest has suggested, by recognising that not all articulations of women's interests emanated from a radical or even a liberal base.[156]

Conclusion

From the Glorious Revolution to the Enlightenment, women played an active part in British politics at a variety of levels. Several factors determined the direction and level of their participation. For much of the period, women from the lower orders were more likely to be involved in manifestations of popular politics such as demonstrations and riots. Their elite counterparts could enjoy more formal involvement in the world of the court through powerful kinship networks, so were more likely to practise their politics in this area. Yet there were occasions when the lines were drawn less firmly. External circumstances shaped women's participation in politics. They were extremely active in a number of political activities around the Civil War. During the Glorious Revolution, when James' flight and William and Mary's arrival heightened the political temperature, women across all classes found a part to play. And, as politics moved into different locations, women too took part in these moves, involving themselves in political debates and electioneering, and committing their ideas to paper for wider dissemination.

It would be a mistake, however, to present the seventeenth and eighteenth centuries as a period of women's steady advancement into political life. In some cases, particularly among the lower levels of society, women's activities were sporadic or short-lived. With the exception of queens, women never achieved equal access to the key sites of political power in this period, and at times their presence was less welcome in public life, or more contested. Women's participation in the Civil War was disparaged during the Restoration as representative of the ills of social upheaval. Jacobite women were dismissed as 'damn rebel bitches'.[157] Similarly, at the end of the eighteenth century, a rise in women's involvement in political debates provoked a hostile backlash which questioned their role in public life. Women's participation in the French Revolution was presented as unnatural and exemplifying all that was wrong with a republic. Such reactions suggest that women's presence in politics remained precarious.

It also needs to be remembered that, despite the collective terms attached to women's political activity in this period, there was no attempt to connect it at the time. Women involved in popular protest did not link their actions into a broader critique of their social position as women. Elite women's politics remained separate from the popular politics of riot, concerned with familial rather than sexual advancement. Some individual women started to tentatively explore their circumstances as women, and consider whether their social position might be open to change, but they did this as individuals and did not view themselves as part of a movement. The 'Wollstonecraft School' suggested a collective identity but it did not engender a formal political grouping with organisational structures or quantifiable membership, nor did it seek to do so. It would not be until the next century that women's politics would develop such structures and hence transform into a recognisable movement.

2
Organised Politics before Suffrage

Introduction

According to Ray Strachey, 'The true history of the Women's Movement is the whole history of the nineteenth century'.[1] Many historians suggest that an identifiable 'women's movement' did not appear until the mid-nineteenth century, when the suffrage campaign gathered momentum (although its concerns were far greater than the simple aim of the parliamentary vote). Yet this movement did not come from nowhere. From the early nineteenth century, women combined independently or alongside men to make political demands. This chapter outlines some of the main areas of women's collective activity prior to the point when a distinct women's movement emerged. It shows how their experience brought them invaluable political skills as well as helping them to develop analyses of a range of social questions relating to sexual inequality. These skills and analyses facilitated the coalescence of what we might consider feminist demands into a women's movement which lasted beyond the First World War.

The characteristics of women's nineteenth-century political activism differed from previous centuries. This can partly be explained through simultaneous changes to the British polity. The increased powers of municipal government, a rising number of parliamentary voters following Reform Acts of 1832, 1867 (1868 in Scotland) and 1884, a rise in contested elections and reforms such as the Corrupt Practices Act of 1883 opened up different routes to political participation, which will be discussed in later chapters. The consequence of such reforms for political behaviour is a matter of some debate. Some historians see this as part of a broadening of democracy which brought increased political participation. Others such as James Vernon believe that the nineteenth century brought a marked 'decline in the power of the people to create their own politics' as new developments were controlled by a political centre.[2] Women remained outside of the national political framework but with more opportunity to engage in collective political action. They could now involve themselves in numerous tiers of elected local governance, which could make national p tics appear less remote.

The late eighteenth and early nineteenth century saw a rise in the numbe of political pressure groups. These were often dominated by middle-class men, disenfranchised but able to exercise considerable political power beyond Westminster through collectively organising for the abolition of the slave trade or increased religious toleration.[3] Politics was now something that people did, and not just at election times. Miles Taylor has argued that an increase in pressure group politics in the wake of the 1832 Reform Act showed 'the new popularity' of reformed government and political activity.[4] Women joined pressure groups with men or in all-female auxiliaries where they articulated sexually specific responses. Although their broader demands matched those of the men they worked with, women often justified their participation on the grounds of distinctive feminine qualities or experiences, including motherhood. They also joined voluntary associations with more philanthropic aims. By the mid-point of the century a few groups were starting to employ paid organisers, offering some women the opportunity to turn political activity into a paying career. The importance of print culture to collective politics continued. Books and pamphlets were joined by a radical press and a small number of specific titles such as the *Englishwoman's Review*. The *Review* reported on the work of a number of single-issue campaigns aimed at improving girls' education or reforming various laws relating to women, but saw itself as a site where campaigns would be initiated as well as developed and discussed.

The single-issue campaigns that preceded the women's movement were dominated by middle-class women. Local groups were important but were part of organisations which developed national structures, committees and conferences. Few working-class women had the time and money required for political work, which could be all-consuming and poorly remunerated. Also, in many mixed campaigns, politics began as a familial affair, with women joining as wives, sisters or daughters. As Philippa Levine has noted, this familial dimension facilitated the development of strong friendship networks between political women, which themselves underpinned later campaigns but simultaneously helped replicate the class composition of their leadership.[5] Yet this is not to say that working-class women were completely absent from political organisation in the nineteenth century. The example of the Chartist movement which will be discussed here inspired working-class women in the suffrage movement in later decades.

Women also developed political skills through philanthropic work. This was easily presented as 'feminine', which facilitated women's involvement, but once in place many women developed professional attitudes to the work, and used it as a basis to argue for a greater public role. Philanthropy drew some women into local government, which forms the final section of this chapter. Their participation in numerous new, elected roles peaked after the beginnings of the suffrage campaign, after the other organisations described in this chapter. Elected women ascribed different meanings to their work. Some expressed ambivalent feelings about having a parliamentary vote themselves, and were content with the powers invested in them under local franchises. Many, including Mrs Pankhurst, found that the experience of local government work convinced them of the need for broader political rights for all women. Others did not move into suffrage but found themselves drawn into the mechanisms of political parties at local and national level. Local government thus bridges single-issue reform campaigns and women's later involvement in suffrage and party politics, which forms the next section of this book.

Owenism

Despite a retreat from the radical demands of the late eighteenth century, some historians have suggested continuity in aspects of women's politics that emerged in the early 1800s. Barbara Taylor situated women's participation in radical Utopian movements such as Owenism in the popular democratic tradition of the late eighteenth century associated with figures such as Wollstonecraft.[6] Owenism, founded by Robert Owen, a wealthy industrialist, sparked a number of local associations and experimental communities which encouraged women's participation. Owen sought to create a 'new moral world' based on cooperation and mutuality rather than the competitive ways of capitalism. His philosophy of the 'doctrine of circumstances' explained the role of environment in shaping the life and outlook of an individual, and thus provided for a reconsideration of women's role in society by challenging the idea that existing gender hierarchies were 'natural'. The movement was firmly committed to equality and opposed to distinctions of class, religion and sex.

Taylor's study showed that some of the women who came to prominence as Owenite writers and lecturers raised the subject of women's oppression. On the other hand, few women had leading positions in local Owenite associations, and the most famous Owenite discourses on women were by men like William Thompson. Taylor also found discrepancies between the Utopian ideals of Owenism and the way that these worked in practice. Owenite communities were intended to be based on equality, but women complained that they still did most of the domestic work, and Jane Rendall's analysis concluded that women's responsibility for this was never questioned.[7] In one Scots community in Orbiston, disagreements over how to implement communal housekeeping came close to prompting the entire female membership to leave. Owenism's support for 'moral marriages' which might be ended by mutual consent was also contentious, given that many of those who set up Owenite communities were married couples. When the leader of the community at Manea Fen attempted to initiate freer sexual practices the community collapsed. The scandal that radical thinking on sexuality provoked outside the movement deterred many working-class women from further involvement, as they felt less able to brave the subsequent public hostility.[8]

Although Owenism was relatively small and short-lived, it has an important place in the history of the women's movement and of women in British politics. In some ways it can be seen to connect aspects of Enlightenment thought to the women's movement which emerged in the mid-nineteenth century. Although some women moved out of public life, disillusioned by the collapse of Owenite communities, others continued to press for a greater public role. Catherine Barmby wrote articles arguing for a greater social and political role for women in the Owenite journal the *New Moral World*; she later suggested the need for a woman's journal to Barbara Bodichon and Bessie Rayner Parkes, who went on to found the English Woman's Journal (later the Englishwoman's Review).[9] Owenism's commitment to communal living was instrumental in founding the cooperative movement, in which women were to play an increasingly key role in the nineteenth and twentieth centuries.

Anti-slavery

Women's participation in the anti-slavery movement also bridged two centuries, although the movement gained national cohesion after 1800. Eighteenth-century women showed their support in a number of ways. They donated substantially; around a quarter of the published income of the Manchester abolition society came from female subscribers in 1788.[10] They made public display of their opposition, wearing Wedgwood cameos featuring a kneeling slave above the words 'am I not a man and a brother' as brooches, hairpins and bracelets that made fashion into a political statement. They were enthusiastic supporters of William Fox's abstention campaign, which urged the public to employ their economic power to undermine enterprises which relied on slavery. As Vron Ware has noted, women, who 'fully recognized their power within the domestic economy', played a vital role in abstention's success, while it simultaneously injected a political dimension into their domestic role.[11] Abstention anticipated the exclusive dealing of Chartist women by some 40 years, and has been associated with a broader, more radical challenge to anti-slavery's London leadership through its connection to the demand for immediate emancipation regardless of parliamentary schedules.[12]

When the slave trade was abolished in 1807 the campaign's emphasis shifted to slavery more broadly. A national Anti-Slavery Society was formed in 1823. Then in 1825 Lucy Townsend, a West Bromwich clergyman's wife, set up the first women's abolition group, the Ladies' Society for the Relief of Negro Slaves (later called the Female Society for Birmingham). The Birmingham society 'acted as a national rather than a local organization' and encouraged the formation of similar women's groups throughout Britain.[13] Between 1825 and 1833 73 ladies' associations formed across England, Scotland and Wales. Not all men in the movement welcomed this move; William Wilberforce believed that women's activity was unbiblical. Nevertheless, the popularity of women's groups convinced the National Society to endorse the effort. Their importance was summarised by the anti-slavery activist George Thompson, who wrote to the Quaker campaigner Anne Knight: 'Where they existed they did everything ... they formed the cement of the whole anti-slavery building – without their aid we never should have been united'.[14]

Most women who campaigned against slavery did so in own neighbourhood. Ladies' associations organised several large petitions. They developed new ways of propagandising to extend their appeal, calling door-to-door to speak to women who were not sufficiently interested in the issue to attend a public meeting. Their propaganda addressed women either directly, through media such as Elizabeth Heyrick's pamphlet *Appeal to the Hearts and Consciousness of British Women*, or by emphasising the brutal treatment of slave women and children. Ladies' societies extended the abstention campaign cautioning all 'Christian females' to guard against being 'bribed by the greater cheapness of this or the other article of daily consumption'.[15] Yet there were limits to their activity; women remained apart from the national leadership and were not called upon to speak on public platforms. Women sometimes criticised the movement's male leaders; in the late 1830s Mary Anne Rawson from Sheffield led an open revolt against the local men's society over their compromising attitude to calling for immediate emancipation for West Indian apprentices.[16] However, as Alison Twells has shown, this was atypical of Rawson's involvement and was motivated by a disapproval of certain actions rather than a broader concern to advance women's position within the movement.[17] Rawson and other leading women campaigners usually contented themselves with working within the parameters available to them.

The anti-slavery movement provides a good example of early gender-based politics, but it did not always overcome differences between women. Divisions emerged around class. Middle-class leaders sometimes attempted to enlist working-class women to sign petitions or support abstention campaigns. A few societies made special provision for working-class members, such as in Glasgow where the Female Anti-Slavery Society's decision to set no minimum subscription drew a number of poorer subscribers.[18] Overall, though, the more usual pattern for women's anti-slavery activism was one of middle-class membership and working-class support. Support could not always be relied upon; some poorer women were quick to point out the unfairness of wealthier activists urging them to buy dearer, 'free-grown' sugar without realising the economic implications this had for poorer households. The middle-class leadership too differed amongst itself as to the basis of women's opposition to slavery. Some women such as Elizabeth Heyrick argued from an egalitarian perspective, which encouraged her to demand a more active and equal role in the campaign. Others such as Hannah More believed in spiritual equality regardless of gender or race, but retained a commitment to a hierarchical social order and did not wish their campaign to lead to women being given a broader political role.

Research into women in the anti-slavery movement has fed into broader investigations of the relationship between women and Empire in the nineteenth and twentieth centuries. The scope of women's involvement in empire has been suggested through popular studies of their role as the wives of an expanding colonial bureaucracy as well as their independent work as missionaries, nurses or even explorers. This recovery work has been developed by scholars who have demonstrated the extent to which many women were active imperialists. Julia Bush has described the detailed networks through which upper and middle-class women developed their own imperial projects through organisations such as the Girls' Friendly Society and the Victoria League. Their imperialism developed a distinctive 'vision of a nurturing, feminized empire' in which women could play a particular role.[19]

For the mid-nineteenth century Antoinette Burton has drawn attention to the extent to which liberal feminists involved in numerous welfare or equality campaigns 'conceived of the empire as a legitimate place for exhibiting their fitness for participation in the imperial state'. Bush similarly showed how female emigration societies opened up employment opportunities for women while simultaneously upholding colonial rule.[20] From a different perspective a number of scholars have considered how colonialism affected indigenous women, and looked more critically at how alliances based on gender were complicated by relationships between the coloniser and the colonised.[21] Another important strand of research has focused on the impact of imperialism in Britain, showing how women came to play a key role in domestic missionary work in Victorian urban centres as well as in supporting missions overseas.[22] Considerations of the relationship between feminism and empire have complicated presentations of an inclusive, progressive history of western feminism, demonstrating how on occasions the empowerment of one group of women was indivisible from the disempowerment of another.[23]

Women in the Chartist movement

The 1832 Reform Act, commonly called the Great Reform Act, redrew political boundaries and created new constituencies which reflected the population shifts of an industrialising, urbanising Britain. It also defined voters as 'male' for the first time. Belief in its pivotal nature is central to many later analyses of women's engagement in politics in the mid-nineteenth century, which see it, in the words of James Vernon, as an event whose 'significance … can not be over played'.[24] For nineteenth-century suffragists, 1832 was the turning point which 'absolutely excluded women from the parliamentary franchise'.[25] More recently Kathryn Gleadle has argued that depictions of the Reform Act as a moment of 'political closure' for women underplay the complexity of its impact on their political behaviours. Noting that the Scottish legislation did not exclude women explicitly, Gleadle suggested that their presence in the English version reflects awareness of 'a theoretical possibility' of the female vote arising from their recurrent presence in a variety of political settings including the reform movement.[26]

The Reform Act provoked no immediate organised opposition to women's political exclusion, although there was a reaction from some working-class women. The Chartist movement, which followed in its wake, is seen by many historians as the point at which working-class radicalism came of age to create a national movement. Chartism drew working-class women into collective political action on a larger scale than ever before. Chartists based their campaign around the People's Charter, published in May 1838, which demanded a wide-ranging overhaul of the electoral system. The Charter's six points (universal suffrage for adult men, annual parliaments, payment for MPs, removal of the property qualification for MPs, equally sized constituencies and voting by ballot) revealed some of the limitations of the 1832 Reform Act. Chartism also showed the disappointment of a large section of the population who hoped that much higher levels of political inclusion might follow the Act, and who now regarded it as a betrayal. The Chartists' campaign peaked over the next decade but lasted until 1858. Large petitions to Parliament were organised and presented in 1839, 1842 and 1848. Regular national conventions took place. Local associations were established throughout Britain which held their own rallies and meetings. News of all of these events and organisations circulated through the vibrant Chartist press, which capitalised on new print technologies and improved transport links to support over 120 publications during the movement's lifetime.[27]

At first Chartism did not replicate the gendered language of the Reform Act. One early draft of the People's Charter included universal suffrage with no mention of the sex of the voter, but women's suffrage was omitted from the final version, for fear that 'its adoption ... might retard the male suffrage' according to the Chartist leader William Lovett.[28] This was not an impossible fear; female political activists were demonised in the wake of the French Revolution as we have seen, and Anna Clark's research found that opponents of Chartism would raise 'the spectre of a female franchise ... to ridicule the philosophy of universal suffrage'.[29] Although it offered them no promise of political rights, Chartism recruited a significant female following. In its first two national petitions women comprised around a third of the total signatories.

Some Chartists attempted to reinstate the demand for female suffrage. Reginald J. Richardson, a Salford Chartist imprisoned for his political activities, wrote a pamphlet, *The Rights of Women*, which stated that women had a 'natural' 'civil' and 'political' right 'to interfere in the political affairs of the country' including voting.[30] The question was occasionally raised via interruptions at Chartist meetings, and the women of Ashton wrote wryly of wishing to see 'intelligence as a necessary qualification for voting' so that they could 'enjoy the elective franchise as well as our kinsmen'.[31] A few, such as the 'working woman of Glasgow' who wrote to the Northern Star in 1838, observed the irony of a male franchise persisting in the Victorian era 'now that we have got a woman at the head of our Government'.[32] Chartist women who remained uncritical of the demand for male suffrage only did not merely seek to uphold the claims of their male friends and relations. As Malcolm Chase has recently observed, Chartism grew to encompass a wide range of demands that went way beyond its original aim of political reform, making women's involvement quite compatible despite its restrictive concept of suffrage.[33]

Chartism's organisation surpassed anything previously available to working-class women in its size and scope. Around 150 women-only societies developed, with names such as female reform associations, female political unions and women's charter associations. Some of these emerged from a small number of existing groups which had been campaigning against the New Poor Law. Others were new ventures, inspired by Chartist leader Thomas Salt, who established the Birmingham Female Political Union in 1838. The success of the Birmingham initiative which recruited over 1000 members encouraged Chartist men – and some women – to emulate his actions. Women's societies developed throughout Britain, although they were more numerous in textile districts. They proved extremely popular; 2000 Leicester women attended inaugural meeting of the local women's society. They also endured beyond the initial excitement engendered by their establishment. Some time after their formation the Halifax and Rochdale female societies were attracting between 30 and 40 women at their meetings each week.[34]

The provision of separate organisations for Chartist women partly derived from men's expectations that they would be supporters rather than activists. The *True Scotsman* appealed to women to join the movement in terms that identified their secondary role, reminding them that 'we need your aid to assist us'.[35] Women used similar language to justify their own involvement: Stockport women regretted being 'driven by dire necessity to depart from the limits usually prescribed for female duties'.[36] Others explained that they had a moral duty to defend the interests of their families. Yet, although women were frequently urged to 'help', 'aid' or 'assist' Chartist men, some forged a more proactive role for themselves. Jutta Schwarzkopf's detailed study of female Chartist associations describes how they developed their own momentum, allowing women scope to build up a range of political skills.[37] Mrs Lapworth, chairwoman of the Birmingham Women's Political Union, explained how although at first 'the women knew little of politics ... they were daily becoming better acquainted with them and ought to feel thankful to those gentlemen who took the trouble to instruct them'.[38] Members of women's associations paid a weekly subscription and elected a committee of a treasurer, secretary and chairwoman, who arranged the programme of activities. The focal point was the regular weekly meeting where new members were enrolled, national and local developments in the movement discussed and resolutions passed. There might also be a guest speaker, a man or a member of a different female association. By training and hosting speakers, female associations allowed women to engage with the wider movement. A number of women became lecturers and addressed meetings throughout Britain. Published reports of their women's speeches show them gaining in confidence and experience. Anna Clark found that Chartist women in Glasgow first addressed a wider public with hesitant speeches, but soon presented a more militant profile, 'defining themselves as heroines and not just as victims', and explaining that they had 'improved their habits of thought' through mutual study.[39]

Chartist women were prepared to take an equal share in all aspects of the movement, including instances of physical force. Some used menacing language in their speeches. Mrs Collie told a crowd in Dunfermline that Chartist women were willing to 'die to have our liberty', while a Stockport delegate informed a national meeting in 1848 that northern women were 'ready to take the place of the men who [were] cut down should it come to that'.[40] Women did engage in direct forms of action. In Lancashire, they bought pikes for their men to take on demonstrations. In Mansfield when 50 Chartists were arrested after a demonstration, the only one found to be armed was a 43-year-old framework knitter, Elizabeth Cresswell, who was carrying a loaded revolver.[41] Jutta Schwarzkopf noted how 'whenever Chartists rioted, women were also involved', and that their 'presence in Chartist riots was often conspicuous'.[42] It is, of course, possible that press reports exaggerated women's involvement as a means of discrediting protests, as had happened in other forms of violent demonstration. Yet even if this were the case, the persistent references to women in reports of Chartist violence makes their participation certain. Schwarzkopf also found areas of militancy which seemed eminently suited to women, such as the popular form of community punishment, 'riding the stang' (being flung into the local beck) meted out to those who had provided witness statements against Chartists in Bradford.[43]

Not all activity by Chartist women was controversial. They proved themselves to be successful petitioners and enthusiastic fundraisers. They used traditional feminine skills in support of their broader political aims, making scarves or caps of liberty which were presented to the male leaders of the movement at large public meetings. Women designed and stitched the intricate banners carried at most large Chartist demonstrations. In Nottingham, the Female Political Union mobilised women's domestic role in charge of the household economy to embark on a campaign of exclusive dealing after anti-slavery's abstention campaign, urging its members to use those shops whose owners supported the charter. Supporters were reminded that they had a 'public duty' to recognise 'the necessity of expending their money only with people or shopkeepers friendly to the cause of freedom, justice, universal suffrage etc', and the women circulated lists of businesses that could safely be patronised.[44] Because these activities drew on women's traditional roles, they have been interpreted as confining. Conversely, they allowed Chartist women to devise their own fields of work which could be taken up by the whole movement, as in the case of exclusive dealing.

Involvement in Chartism offered women avenues of political work beyond the more obvious forums of the meeting room or public platform. Many Chartists believed that education was the best way to precipitate reform, as a better educated population would not be content to remain disenfranchised. Chartists in Elland, near Halifax, were 'determined not to wait … for national education', and set out to educate themselves.[45] Other associations followed this lead and established a variety of initiatives, including discussion classes and adult schools. These were open to both sexes, but Thomis and Grimmett found that they placed greater emphasis on provision for women who had responsibility for educating young children.[46] Women did not have to pay for the classes offered at Elland, while in Gorbals the local women's organisation made provision for members to read 'instructive essays or extracts from popular works' so that they might be better placed to impart such knowledge.[47] Chartists valued women's education as it had the potential to transform the views of a coming generation; Chartist leader Henry Vincent described how the movement had transformed 'every kitchen' into 'a political meeting house' with 'the good mother … the political teacher'.[48] Similarly, the Birmingham Chartist writer 'Sophia' appealed to 'Chartist women and mothers [to] instruct and encourage each other that our children shall be better informed of their rights as citizens'.[49] Some women ran successful Chartist Sunday schools, which educated adults and children together, while others opened their own schools for children, moving their educational involvement beyond the immediate domestic arena.

Just how far Chartist women were able to challenge existing gendered structures through their involvement remains a key question. For Jutta Schwarzkopf the movement's emphasis on female domesticity ultimately 'did much to deprive women of any effective means to exert an influence on the forces shaping their own lives'.[50] Schwarzkopf recognised the pragmatic factors which encouraged some Chartist women to define their political work in unthreatening terms as supportive wives and mothers, but concluded that the movement's failure 'left women doubly disempowered' and made it more difficult for working-class women to involve themselves in politics in the future.[51] Thomis and Grimmett admitted that the movement brought some 'temporary gains' for women in terms of their 'new awareness and self-confidence', but believed that these were lost by the middle of the nineteenth century as women reverted to a more domestic role.[52] Conversely Michelle de Larrabeiti's analysis of the domestic rhetoric employed by Chartist women suggests that their construction of themselves as 'militant mothers' offered them a greater degree of agency.[53] What is certain is that Chartism did set a precedent for large-scale organisation amongst working-class women. Less is known about the involvement of working-class women in mid-Victorian politics, but the precedent was not lost on later generations; militant suffragettes would sometimes invoke Chartist women when seeking to locate their own political activity in a longer radical tradition.

Women in the Anti-Corn Law League

Chartism was not the only political movement that attracted women in the early nineteenth century. Similar opportunities for large-scale organisation grew out of the campaign to repeal the Corn Laws. These laws, which were introduced in 1815, outlawed the import of grain into Britain until the domestic price had reached 80 shillings a quarter. Amendments in 1822, 1828 and 1842 refined this via a complicated sliding scale. The Corn Laws represented a victory for landed interests in Parliament along with a broader wish to expand agricultural production and safeguard self-sufficiency in the wake of the Napoleonic wars. Many manufacturers opposed the measures, which they saw as favouring agriculture over industry. Sporadic protests took place throughout Britain, and repeal societies formed in cities such as Sheffield and Dundee. Their effect was limited when corn prices were low, but a combination of economic depression and a number of bad harvests prompted the setting up of the Manchester Anti-Corn Law Association in September 1838. When a parliamentary motion calling for the laws' repeal failed in 1839, the Manchester Association organised a meeting in London which inaugurated a national Anti-Corn Law League. The League retained Manchester as its base but developed into a British movement with strongholds in Wales, across Northern manufacturing districts and in Scotland. Predictably it enjoyed less success in rural districts, although it did achieve some significant recruits such as the East Lothian border farmer George Hope, who spoke authoritatively about the effects of the laws on farm workers.

The Anti-Corn Law League was led by men, but its membership was open to women. This allowed middle-class women to involve themselves directly in politics at both a local and a national level; tens of thousands signed the League's petitions, while smaller but still significant numbers took advantage of the opportunity for involvement in activities such as canvassing or fundraising, or attending the League's main events. The importance of League participation to their politicisation was often cited by later generations of women. Helen Blackburn described it as 'the nursery in which many a girl of that generation learned to know how closely public questions concerned her', while Sylvia Pankhurst used her grandparent's membership of the League as a means of establishing her own radical credentials.[54]

The League's significance for women was not immediately apparent. Women attended some lectures but took little part in its organisation, possibly because of the League's early reputation for supporting violence and class antagonism.[55] One early historian of the League saw women's more active involvement in its affairs as originating at an Anti-Corn Law League tea party in Manchester in October 1840. The success of having women presiding at the tables led to attempts to recruit more women into membership and to make more direct use of their abilities.[56] Women thereafter contributed to the League in a number of ways. They proved themselves successful petitioners; Manchester women members gathered a petition of 50,000 signatures in December 1841.[57] They established themselves as effective fundraisers using subscription cards and door-to-door canvassing to raise money; £47 6s was raised in this way in Halifax.[58] Jane Rendall observed how they raised the popular fundraising technique of holding a bazaar to 'a new degree of effectiveness', angering contemporary observers such as J. Cocker, who wrote to the *Quarterly Review* to complain that the Manchester bazaar in 1842 'did not even pretend to be for any *charitable* object but entirely for the purposes of *political agitation*'.[59]

In 1845 the League held its Great Bazaar in Covent Garden, a political fundraising event that was the largest ever seen. Simon Morgan's research into the Great Bazaar showed how women were involved in its organisation at a number of levels. Each branch of the League involved with the Bazaar had responsibility for staffing and stocking its own stalls, and local ladies' committees sprang up to oversee the efforts in their own towns. Over 1000 women from all over Britain busied themselves making items to sell at the event. Morgan argues that through such activities the Great Bazaar offered women 'a way of breaking out of their local circles [to] appear on a national stage' in an era when women's politics tended to be practised closer to home.[60] The committees set up to prepare for the Bazaar came to function as women's branches of the League. They created a space where women could discuss their own concerns, such as in 1842 when the Manchester Ladies' Committee produced its own take on exclusive dealing by refusing to buy goods that carried government duties as a form of political protest.[61]

Alex Tyrrell's analysis of the League suggested that it combated criticism of women's involvement in its work by emphasizing its compatibility with 'Woman's Mission'.[62] This emphasis presented women's involvement in the League as an expansion of their supposedly natural nurturing role. While not disagreeing with this, Simon Morgan's study found a wider variety of discourses in operation. In particular, Morgan found that the League deployed rhetoric that acknowledged women's position in the domestic economy but sought to develop this into something more public. An editorial comment in the *Anti-Corn Law Circular* connected the worlds of home and politics, and urged women to remember that participation in the League was 'merely performing, on a larger scale, the duty which they everyday perform as good housekeepers, in obtaining at the cheapest possible rate, their domestic supply of provisions'. Through such arguments the League was beginning to develop a political concept of women's domestic role rather than simply using their daily experience as a means of justifying their temporary excursions into public politics.[63]

The Langham Place Circle and the Kensington Society

Jane Rendall's exploration of the origins of modern feminism identified the mid-nineteenth century as a critical moment for the emergence of an organized women's movement.[64] The precedents of middle-class women's involvement in anti-slavery and anti-Corn Law campaigns, along with women's involvement in Chartism, increased calls for their greater social and political involvement. Yet, although there were exceptions, the overall focus of these campaigns was not for improvements specifically aimed at women. This altered in the mid-nineteenth century when a number of women began to agitate for greater rights for their own sex. At this point they were not united behind a single demand, but were starting to articulate a number of concerns which we may now think of as 'feminist'.

The most influential grouping was an informal network of women named for 19 Langham Place, the office of the early feminist paper, the *English Woman's Journal*. The *Journal* was founded by Barbara (Leigh Smith) Bodichon and her friend Bessie Rayner Parkes in 1858 to offer a wider platform for discussion of women's work and concerns. Bodichon and Parkes shared family backgrounds in a number of radical political causes and a frustration at the limits that social conventions attempted to place on their own public activity. They wanted the *Journal* to be a campaigning tool as well as a periodical. Parkes wanted to set up a bookshop and club around it, but had to content herself at first with a small reading room in its offices at Cavendish Place. A network of women active in various campaigns developed around this, including Emily Davies, Adelaide Procter, Matilda Hays and Emily Faithfull. In December 1859, Matilda Hays' wealthy friend Theodosia Monson rented more spacious premises for the *Journal* at Langham Place. These included a coffee shop and a reading room which offered a base for broader activities. New readers began to visit Langham Place to meet like-minded women. Jessie Boucherett, the daughter of the high sheriff of Lincolnshire and a well-known philanthropist in her own county, caught sight of the *Journal* on a railway bookstall and, delighted to find 'her own unspoken aspirations' underpinning its articles, headed to London to meet with the editors.[65]

Other women arrived at Langham Place for less altruistic reasons. The *Journal* reported women's employment opportunities and had started a small register of women seeking work for circulation amongst its subscribers, whereupon Langham Place became deluged with women looking for jobs. Jessie Boucherett took charge of the register and established the Society for Promoting the Employment of Women (SPEW). In a paper read at the 1859 meeting of the Social Science Association, Boucherett reported that SPEW had placed 75 women into permanent jobs in its first year, and found temporary positions for a further 100.[66] This success encouraged the formation of some local branches throughout Britain, including one in Gateshead established by Emily Davies. Boucherett identified lack of training as one of the main obstacles to women's employment, so SPEW attempted to compensate for this. It started classes in bookkeeping and literacy, and liaised with potential employers to place its students. Other initiatives aimed at combating lingering prejudices over hiring women. Emily Faithfull set up a printing firm, the Victoria Printing Press, which trained and employed a small number of women compositors. The press gained a royal warrant and printed the *English Woman's Journal* as well as Faithfull's own later venture, the *Victoria Magazine*. Maria Rye, who had helped with the Press, opened an office in Lincoln's Inn where she employed a team of women at the specialist job of copying legal documents. The *Journal* carried a range of articles discussing the sort of labour women might be able to undertake, as well as arguing for better educational provision to enhance women's employability.

Langham Place women campaigned for better educational provision for girls. In 1864 campaigners were cheered when the Taunton Commission, a far-ranging enquiry into secondary education, included girls' education in its final report (thanks largely to the persistent efforts of Emily Davies). This meant that the Commission heard evidence of investigations into the relative mental capacities of girls and boys which found no significant difference, offering a powerful argument that women could use in support of their attempts to improve girls' education. A small number of institutions were opened, including the North London Collegiate School (1850) and Cheltenham Ladies' College (1854). The success of such establishments led to the foundation of the Girls Public Day School Company in 1871, which offered a broad, liberal curriculum in the 30 schools it was running by 1900. Similar initiatives were undertaken in Wales by the Association for Promoting the Education of Girls in Wales which began in 1886, although W. G. Evans' study of its work suggests that it was as motivated by a desire to provide an equivalent standard of education in Wales to that available in England for all Welsh adolescents as with the wish to raise girls' education to the level of boys'.[67] Langham Place women were involved in attempts to expand higher education for women, most notably through Emily Davies who set up a college at Girton, outside Cambridge, with financial support from Barbara Bodichon. As women's educational opportunities expanded, they supported calls for greater access to the professions, backing Elizabeth Garrett as she struggled to qualify as a doctor.

The *English Woman's Journal* was never a financial success and it was wound up in 1864. At Langham Place there were disagreements about the focus and direction of the women's movement. Parkes became increasingly cautious, criticising married women's work outside the home and wanting to avoid contentious issues such as women's suffrage or sexuality. Others adopted a different perspective. From 1865 a new group met at the home of Charlotte Manning in Kensington. This was the Kensington Debating Society, and its object, according to Emily Davies, was to 'serve as a sort of link between persons, above the average of thoughtfulness and intelligence who are interested in common subjects, but who have not many opportunities of mutual intercourse'.[68]

Its debates were extremely well organised; members submitted questions to a small committee which invited written papers on the three themes considered to be the most interesting. The Society tackled controversial issues such as women's suffrage. Its membership was not restricted to London but included a number of 'corresponding' members such as Elizabeth Wolstenholme Elmy, who helped spread its thinking into the provinces.

Neither the Langham Place Group nor the Kensington Society can be described as large organisations, but they represented a significant development in the way that women organised themselves. Women had previously come together around particular political issues, often working with men in groups which disbanded when their aims were achieved or when campaigns floundered. In the meetings at Langham Place and Kensington something different was taking place. Women were now beginning to tackle issues that related directly to their own social and legal status. They were also starting to connect campaigns and articulate broader critiques of their social position. Thus, as Jane Rendall has noted, 'through identifying their own needs they also began to define a cautious liberal feminist politics' which set the tone for an emerging women's movement.[69] Its participants did not always share the same ideals. Some, like Emily Davies, were committed to equality and sought to remove the hurdles that obstructed women's opportunities. Others like Josephine Butler, were strong believers in female superiority. They argued that the entire nation would benefit from greater female participation, but came very close to replicating the language and logic of separate spheres. Some women felt that retaining respectability was crucial if the women's movement was to advance; others like Elizabeth Wolstenholme Elmy were more willing to experiment with new forms of relationships and were less concerned about the consequences. Yet despite very real differences, the common desire to overcome women's oppression was sufficient to bind the women's movement together as it grew throughout the nineteenth century. This unity of purpose was at its most apparent in the campaign that grew up around votes for women, as we shall see.

The campaign for Married Women's Property Acts

Other single issues drew women into formal organisations. Many of these focused on achieving specific legal reforms. A lengthy and well-documented campaign to give married women greater control over their own property began in 1855. Nineteenth-century common law offered some protection for married women to retain their rights over 'real' property (generally land), but their personal property became the legal responsibility of their husbands on their marriage. The result of this is illustrated in a story told by Millicent Garret Fawcett, who was the victim of a street robbery and went to court to face her attacker, only to hear him charged with stealing 'from the person of Millicent Fawcett a purse ... the property of Henry Fawcett'. Fawcett described how the understanding of her legal powerlessness which stemmed from this played a vital part in defining her later feminism.[70]

The inequity of the law around married women's property was an obvious target for women like Barbara Bodichon. In 1854 she published a pamphlet,

Summary of the Laws in England Concerning Women, Together with a
servations Thereon. Bodichon argued that the laws concerning married
1's property would offer 'a simple, tangible and not offensive point of
attack', and set about preparing one. She gathered a small committee consisting
of herself, Bessie Rayner Parkes, and some friends acquired through previous
radical causes. This held meetings and collected examples of women who were
unjustly treated under the Acts. It also organised a petition which attracted
26,000 signatures, including the poet Elizabeth Barrett Browning and the
writers George Eliot and Mrs Gaskell. The petition failed but some of its
demands were incorporated into the 1857 Divorce Act, linking the two areas
for reform and encouraging broader feminist critiques of the legal foundations
of marriage.

In 1867 a larger and more nationally representative Married Women's
Property Committee (MWPC) was formed by Elizabeth Wolstenholme
Elmy and Jessie Boucherett, with Lydia Becker as secretary. The presence of
Wolstenholme Elmy, Becker and Josephine Butler reflected the North West's
growing status as an important locus for the women's movement; many MWPC
members were simultaneously involved in the Manchester Women's Suffrage
Society. The MWPC secured some success when a bill was passed in Parliament
in 1870, but this had very limited results. It allowed women to retain control
of their earnings after marriage, something that had little effect for most
middle-class women, while doing nothing to enable them to retain control
of property they brought into a marriage. Becker and Wolstenholme Elmy
wrote to *The Times* declaring that the committee would continue its campaign.
Ursula Bright's appointment as treasurer connected the MWPC with many
leading Liberal politicians, and expanded its support. The Liberal government
elected in 1880 agreed to further legal amendments, and the Married Women's
Property Acts of 1881 (Scotland) and 1882 (England) increased women's independence. Although the English Act did not end coverture (the legal premise
that a wife was subordinate to her husband) it weakened it significantly by
allowing married women to act as independent legal entities. Lee Holcombe
has interpreted it as 'the most important of all the legal reforms won by feminists in the nineteenth century'.[71] However, economic historians have argued
that the Acts represented a reaction to changing economic conditions rather
than a feminist victory.[72] They did not immediately provoke wider reforms, and
campaigners still had many issues to occupy their energies.

The repeal of the Contagious Diseases Acts

The campaign that grew up around the Contagious Diseases Acts (CDAs) also
targeted legislation that impacted disproportionately on women. These Acts
were a series of measures passed in 1864, 1866 and 1869 which applied in
districts with a high military presence such as ports and garrison towns. They
empowered police to compel any woman suspected of prostitution to undergo
a medical examination, with the aim of controlling the spread of venereal
disease in the armed forces. Infected women would be hospitalised either in
specific venereal hospitals (also known as 'lock hospitals') or in hospitals with

'lock' (venereal) wards where they could be detained for up to nine months. Uninfected women who were identified as prostitutes through the process were forced to sign a police register and attend for further medical examinations every fortnight. When the Acts' implications became clear a repeal campaign gathered speed, rooted in the 'social purity' movement. Social purity concerned itself with a number of moral questions including prostitution, eugenics and sexuality. Despite its focus on policing or regulation, many scholars have suggested that it was not incompatible with feminism, as the campaign against the CDAs demonstrates.[73]

The most significant of these organisations for women's politics was the Ladies' National Association (LNA). A National Association for the Repeal of the CDAs had formed in 1869. This excluded women, so Elizabeth Wolstenholme set up a separate auxiliary Ladies' National Association (LNA) in December. Josephine Butler, whom Wolstenholme knew through the North England Council for Promoting the Education of Women, assumed its leadership. Butler was also known for her philanthropic work with Liverpool prostitutes. Like many LNA activists, Butler was motivated by religious convictions. She did not hide her opinion of unchaste behaviour as sinful, but her campaigning consistently aimed to make men take responsibility for their actions rather than blaming women. LNA women were usually older, single and well off, which Walkowitz felt offered them 'an unusual freedom to engage in public activities and move about the country', although the subject matter of their campaign made their work controversial.[74]

Under Butler's leadership the LNA surpassed its parent body in numbers and activity. Its structure became the model for non-party political organisations of women. By 1871 it had a national network of 57 branches and over 800 members, and a newspaper, *The Shield*, which juxtaposed political reports with lurid stories of the Acts' worst results. It helped some women to make politics into a paying career by employing a small number of staff, such as Miss Duffett, a former seamstress whom the Bristol branch funded to work up support for the repeal campaign in Plymouth in 1870.[75] LNA campaigns connected into the broader rhythms of Parliament through supporting repeal candidates at by-elections. The provincial strength of the LNA prevented it from becoming dominated by London women, while reports in *The Shield* and the movement of speakers and organisers between branches cemented links between groups of women activists in different locations.

The LNA deployed a number of arguments. Repeal was presented as part of a broader struggle of the liberal middle class against an older, corrupt regime which deployed excessive state power against the interests of its citizens. Aristocratic corruption underpinned accounts of young servants forced into prostitution following their seduction by their employers. Butler made frequent references to Wat Tyler, the fifteenth-century rebel leader who had been a favourite figure amongst Chartist speakers.[76] Magistrates, politicians and doctors were criticised for their growing power which enabled them to oppress women, epitomised by the act of 'instrumental' or 'specular rape' that comprised the enforced medical examination. Mixed-sex audiences were shocked at the sight of women speakers displaying the speculum for public view.

Other arguments centred on the CDAs' representation of the so-called 'sexual double standard', which criminalised and punished woman's sexual behaviour while attaching no penalty to men's. To illustrate this point, Butler quoted the testimony of one prostitute imprisoned under the acts by a magistrate who 'had paid [her] several shillings a day or two before, in the street, to go with [her]'.[77] LNA members challenged the Act's assumption that the state had a duty to ensure a supply of healthy prostitutes for men, arguing that man's desires could be controlled. They recognised that a variety of different circumstances pushed women into prostitution, and acknowledged that it was frequently undertaken as a temporary recourse, countering the simplistic notion that all women were either 'virtuous' or 'fallen'. They attacked the Act's potential to increase prostitution through forcing women to register, explaining that registration gave them a label that could prove hard to escape, but did not go so far as to defend the practice as a valid economic choice. Walkowitz noted that LNA members could become 'morally indignant when confronted with a registered woman who did not desire to be rescued and reformed'.[78]

The LNA exceeded the aims of previous single-issue movements by attempting to create a gender-based campaign of opposition and to unite all women through appeals to common female experiences. Butler believed that prostitution would not stop 'til it is attacked by women', and personalised her response to the enforced medical examination, publicly declaring that she would 'much rather die than endure it'.[79] Another League member, Mary Hume-Rothery, wrote a letter to the prime minister in 1870 in which she acknowledged that she and others of her class 'might have slipped' into prostitution 'had she been born in the same unprotected, unfenced position, in the very jaws of poverty'.[80] As discussion became more open by the standards of the day, some LNA activists demanded women-only meetings, concurring with Priscilla Bright McLaren that these alone would provide space for women to 'speak freely of the false idea of morality in which our *gentlemen!* are educated'.[81]

The LNA's woman-centred approach involved making strong efforts to work with prostitutes. Some branches challenged the inadequacies of local state medical provision for prostitutes by opening their own venereal hospitals in cities such as Winchester, where Butler reported that patients were cured without internal examinations.[82] They offered legal advice to prostitutes and paid for defence lawyers. This frustrated the authorities; one police inspector in Plymouth wrote that the LNA had familiarised prostitutes with 'all possible methods by which they could evade the provisions of the acts'.[83] Women were encouraged to refuse voluntary examinations. LNA members attended court to support women charged under the Acts, and defied magistrates' attempts at excluding them arguing that this was a woman's issue and that their presence saved the accused from being forced to face an entirely male court alone.

The LNA also criticised the class bias inherent within the CDAs, and emphasised the link between poverty and prostitution. Barbara Caine's claim that Butler 'did not attempt to bring working-class women … into the campaign' overlooks the LNA's efforts in arranging meetings aimed specifically at working women in a variety of locations, including those such as Nottingham which were not themselves subjected to the CDAs.[84] It is true, though, that the initiatives *The Shield* reported as successes did not translate into sustained working-class involvement. Judith Walkowitz has suggested that this may be due to reluctance on the part of working-class women to mix with prostitutes.[85] The division between the middle-class repealer and the prostitute was clear, but working-class women, who resembled their prostitute neighbours in speech and appearance, may have feared that LNA activity could cast doubt on their own moral status. Despite the practical level of its aid, the LNA never recruited any prostitutes to its ranks but remained an organisation that spoke on their behalf, often portraying them as helpless victims. It could also be insensitive. Criticism of the authorities' failure to distinguish between prostitutes and 'innocent' women was intended to show respectable men that this threatened their wives and daughters, but it simultaneously enforced the divide between different categories of women, undermining the LNA's emphasis on shared female experience. With working-class men, the LNA had a little more success. A number of groups of male supporters were set up, mainly in industrial centres where they recruited a working-class membership especially amongst those recently enfranchised by the 1867 Reform Act. The LNA in Edinburgh was one branch that reported good results in attracting working men to meetings.[86]

The LNA saw the repeal of the CDAs in 1886 as a victory. Many historical evaluations concur, presenting the movement as an example of a successful political campaign by women. This is a tempting conclusion to draw, but other factors require consideration. One is the unpopularity of the repeal campaign even amongst women who opposed the Acts. Sandra Holton's important contextualisation of the early suffrage movement pointed out that the formation of the LNA caused a rift amongst suffragists. A significant faction agreed with John Stuart Mill that suffrage would suffer from close association with the LNA's public discussions of sexuality, vice and venereal disease.[87] This opens up another issue less linked to questions of success or failure: the extent to which the campaign enabled women to participate in discussions previously considered taboo despite the fact that their outcomes shaped women's everyday lives. Themes raised through discussions of the CDAs radiated out into other campaigns. Elizabeth Wolstenholme Elmy articulated a powerful critique of the CDA's implications that men could not control their sexual urges, which she extended to men's behaviour towards their wives, arguing that rather than submit to unwilling sexual attention, 'the functions of wifehood and motherhood must remain solely and entirely within the wife's own option'.[88] Elmy's critique led her to campaign for the criminalisation of rape within marriage, although the state did not concede this until the end of the twentieth century. Other LNA activists drew different conclusions from their work. Several went on to other social purity bodies such as the National Vigilance Association, where they behaved as 'feminist vigilantes', endorsing repressive behaviours aimed at reducing prostitution such as closing music halls and clamping down on streetwalkers.[89]

Each of these organisations brought women considerable experience in the organisation and administration of politics. Through the district branches of Chartist groups, the Anti-Corn Law League, the Anti-Slavery Society and the Ladies National Association women learned the mechanisms of campaigning.

They raised funds, organised petitions, built branches, and recruited friends and strangers into membership. A smaller number gained further experience as public speakers, and some even managed to make a national name this way. Although there was no automatic progression from one organisation to another, there were some examples of women moving from the Anti-Corn Law League into the Ladies National Association. Members of the Ladies National Association were aware that the subject of their campaign required careful handling, but this was eased by the precedents of earlier organisations. By the 1870s political organisations of women looked less unusual.

A broader public role: women, philanthropy and local government

As well as organising around specific issues, nineteenth-century women undertook a variety of charitable or philanthropic work which proved useful in later political activity. Women's philanthropic involvement was less controversial, easily justified through its caring and nurturing dimensions which translated seamlessly into an extension of 'natural' feminine qualities. The nineteenth-century notion of 'woman's mission' developed such understandings to suggest that women (or more accurately middle-class women) had a duty to deploy these qualities beyond their own homes, imparting middle-class values to their 'less fortunate sisters', as the objects of their charitable endeavours were described. Sarah Lewis, author of *Woman's Mission*, believed this involved the extension of maternal love to the wider community, irrespective of whether the women concerned were mothers themselves. This feminine conceptualisation was valuable, according to Patricia Hollis, as it 'encouraged women to come forward with the confidence that their domestic and family background was as useful and relevant to public service as men's commercial and business expertise'.[90] They also had time to perform such tasks. This did not mean that philanthropy was viewed as a hobby. Middle and upper-class women devoted considerable time to philanthropic vocations which they conceptualised as work, and through which they developed acknowledged expertise. Philanthropy developed a strong political dimension as local government began to take over much of the work of voluntary societies, as will be shown.

Women in philanthropic organisations

Philanthropic activity often began at parish level, when churchwomen entered the homes of the local poor with food, warm clothing, biblical tracts or good advice. As the scope of charitable work expanded, women began to visit institutions that brought them into direct contact with aspects of the Victorian state. Women visitors were not always welcomed by the authorities. As Prochaska commented, 'no one asked the poor for their permission to be visited. Public and charitable institutions were different'.[91] Women sometimes had to resort to covert means to gain access. Catharine Cappe in York campaigned for many years to persuade the County Hospital to open its doors without success. When the hospital ran short of funds in 1813 she recognised the opportunity.

Cappe convinced several wealthy women friends to promise an annual subscription if the hospital agreed to appoint women visitors, which it duly did. Once admitted, however, many women found men were happy to let them get on with the work of attending to the needs of women and children.

Many of the mixed-sex philanthropic organisations engaged in visiting now sought to recruit women volunteers. Most societies were still run by men, placing women's involvement mainly on the ground, although some larger societies established ladies' auxiliaries. Auxiliaries were supposed to concentrate on fundraising but often exceeded their remit to advise male directors on policy. At the same time women developed separate societies whose work depended on their size and scope. Some were restricted to a small area (sometimes a single parish) or to alleviating distress amongst a particular group such as needlewomen, the widowed or the blind. Smaller institutions were not necessarily less formal or successful. Mary Claire Martin's study of women's philanthropic activity in Walthamstow and Leyton found that the four institutions initiated and managed by local women matched or outstripped those of men in size and financial viability.[92]

The growth of philanthropic and charitable organisations in the nineteenth century encouraged their professionalisation. Many new societies were supported by voluntary subscriptions so they had to be accountable to their subscribers. In all-female societies the requirement to keep accurate accounts and records fell entirely on women. Volunteers who did not hold committee office were also affected by the drive towards a more effective, streamlined model of organisation. The Charity Organisation Society was formed in London in 1869 to rationalise the many overlapping charitable bodies, and established a number of provincial branches. It was a controversial organisation (sometimes called 'Cringe Or Starve') which feared that giving relief without questioning the character of its recipients encouraged a state of feckless dependence amongst the poor. Nevertheless it took its work seriously and provided training for its volunteer visitors, many of whom were women. Volunteers were encouraged to behave more like paid case workers and to produce detailed files on their visits. In some districts women visitors were encouraged to wear a uniform to identify them as they went about their work.

The growing rationalisation of philanthropy brought some women national recognition. Kathryn Gleadle has described how a small number of 'female experts' were able to make significant contributions to national debates surrounding the levels and nature of state intervention in welfare issues. Louisa Twining, who began workhouse visiting in the 1850s, drew on this experience to present a range of papers and publish articles in the national press. She later gave evidence to the Royal Commission on Education about workhouse schools.[93] Women like Twining could not just narrate their own experience; they had to remain conversant with a range of policies across numerous government departments if they were to present a case effectively to parliamentary committees. Women's expertise could prompt legislative change; a boarding-out scheme which Hannah Archer devised for the workhouse children of Wiltshire informed the Pauper Education Act of 1862. A downside to this, noted by Gleadle, was that women often lost authority over their own schemes when these passed into state control.[94] Yet their acceptance as experts in certain areas provided a valuable argument when some women sought to press claims to greater political involvement later in the century.

There is no straightforward trajectory from women's philanthropic activity in the early and mid-nineteenth century to their increased political involvement in its latter decades. For some women, philanthropy provided an important step that offered a taste of life beyond the domestic arena and set them on the way to a range of other campaigns. Gleadle found examples of women fusing politics and philanthropy in their communities. In Kirkstall, Mrs Scatcherd (later an active suffragist) took a group of young men in a regular political discussion class on Sunday afternoons, while Elizabeth Pease, who visited unemployed handloom weavers in Darlington, used their example in letters she wrote to the local press describing the distress caused by the Corn Laws.[95] Despite its equation with 'natural' feminine characteristics, women's philanthropic involvement was not without its critics. Simon Morgan has noted that it was often seen as radical, and contested by men 'concerned about the 'public' nature of much philanthropic work' as well as by those who simply resented women's interference.[96] Yet, as June Hannam has pointed out, much philanthropic work had the potential for a deeply conservative streak.[97] It could promote women's supposedly natural roles and privilege the opinion of articulate, middle-class women over its working-class recipients.

A different interpretation has been suggested by cultural historians who have shifted their analyses beyond the implications of philanthropic involvement for particular political organisations by pointing to its potential to empower individual women. Mica Nava described how philanthropy established women's

> right to look. It authorised the observation and classification of the homes, lives and even marital relationships of the poor. Middle-class women involved in the philanthropic enterprise were not obliged to conduct their affairs with a lowered gaze. They could indulge the pleasures of urban spectatorship – of the voyeur – with a sense of entitlement.[98]

Nava's compelling picture does not reflect the experience of philanthropy for all women. Mrs Wightman, wife of the rector of a Shrewsbury parish, agreed to start visiting the poor of Butcher Row, a poor part of the parish. On her first visit she set out fortified by communal prayer with her husband, but returned within minutes in tears, overpowered by her fear of being alone on the streets at night, while a visitor friend of hers confessed she was 'afraid of working men; if one happens to enter a cottage … I walk out at once'.[99] Wightman became more resigned but was never comfortable with the public nature of her work. Ann Taylor Gilbert, involved in philanthropic work in Nottingham, wrote of the difficulties she found in 'drawing the line correctly between in door and out of doors business'.[100] Many women clearly viewed philanthropic work as a duty to be endured rather than as something that transformed them into empowered *flâneuses*.

Women and local government

Many historians see women's philanthropic work as a step towards their increased participation in local government in the final decades of the nineteenth century. A combination of population growth and increasing urbanization prompted a series of reforms in this area. The various forms of local government that shaped and regulated new urban centres expanded, extending opportunities for political participation. Across England and Wales, Poor Law Amendment Acts in 1834 and 1844 established Boards of Guardians elected annually to administer the New Poor Law. The Municipal Corporations Act of 1835 reformed the government of around 200 towns and cities, replacing municipal corporations with elected councils. Multiple representation of council wards provided for annual elections, with a third of councillors being replaced each year, and required registers of local electors. A further Local Government Act in 1888 reformed rural government, providing for county councils. The 1870 Education Act set up 2000 elected school boards in England and Wales (extended to Scotland from 1872) to provide elementary education for working-class children. Although there were independent candidates for councils and boards, these formed important sites for party-political contests, increasing contacts between party and population, fuelling the development of local party machines and allowing those who were not candidates to develop political activism.

Nineteenth-century local government became an important site for women's political activity. This was an unintended consequence of local government expansion. The Municipal Corporations Act agreed with the 1832 Reform Act that 'male persons' only comprised the electorate. Then in 1869, Jacob Bright moved an amendment to the Municipal Corporations (Franchise) Act arguing that the 1835 reform had removed the local franchise from suitably qualified women. His argument, that he was merely seeking to restore a previously held and exercised right, was accepted by both the Commons and the Lords, giving the municipal vote to thousands of women (although a High Court ruling in 1872 subsequently reduced their number by excluding married women). The Education Acts allowed women to vote for school boards, and exceeded contemporary practice in accepting them as candidates whether they were married or not. Women's eligibility to stand as Poor Law Guardians had been assumed in the 1834 Act, and was successfully tested in 1875. Women ratepayers in England and Wales gained further rights to vote for county councils from 1888, as well as to stand themselves. In Scotland, legislation opening up local government to women came later but followed a similar timetable. The Scottish Education Act of 1872 made women eligible to vote and stand in school board elections (voting but not standing required a property qualification). Women ratepayers could vote in burgh elections from 1881, 13 years after similar rights were awarded in England and Wales, and for country (1889) and parish (1894) councils, although they could only stand for the latter. Town councils accepted women candidates from 1907, as in England and Wales.

School boards

Eleven women were elected at the first school board contests in 1870. Numbers grew steadily; by 1902 when school boards were abolished in England and Wales there were around 370 women members. Seventeen women were elected at the first Scottish school board elections in 1873, with 'every woman on the poll' turning out to vote in one town.[101] Seventy-six women had been elected on to Scottish boards by 1906, proportionately higher than the figure for the rest of Britain.[102] Scottish school boards remained in place for longer, so were an important site for women's political engagement into the twentieth century. Reaction to the first women candidates was mixed. Some observers worried about women standing for election or working in mixed elected bodies; others argued that as children's education was a 'natural' focus for women's interests, 'feminine influence' on school boards was desirable. The remit of school boards encouraged women to emphasise the gender-specific qualities they could bring to the work. It was easy to argue that elementary education was a 'suitable' field for women who cared for infants themselves. Many successful candidates had considerable educational experience outside of their families. They had taught in Sunday schools or run girls' clubs or private schools. Board members also had to manage teachers as employers, but women argued that they were suited for this role too, as most board school teachers were women.

There were other reasons for women's success on the boards. As new public bodies they were not seen as exclusively male, and as the qualifications for standing were less complicated than those required for voting, women candidates were not disadvantaged by income or marital status. Some candidates saw board work as an important stage towards women's political equality. In London the first two women elected, Elizabeth Garrett and Emily Davies, were associated with the Kensington Society and known as female pioneers, Davies in the field of higher education for girls and Garrett in medicine. Rose Crawshay, the first woman school board member in Wales, was vice president of the Bristol and West of England National Society for Women's Suffrage, while Flora Stevenson, elected to the Edinburgh School Board in 1873, was an active local suffragist. The women's movement used such successes as an example of what women could achieve in arguing for greater involvement in a variety of fields.

Women guardians and women councillors

Women were more numerous on the Boards of Guardians that administered the Poor Law. Susie Steinbach ascribed this to the lower status of these boards, which may be correct, although this initially complicated women's presence.[103] Guardians dealt with the mentally unstable, the morally suspect and the workhouse, with its filthy VD wards. Male guardians had shaped the boards as they wanted them for almost 40 years, treating them as an extension to gentlemen's clubs, playing practical jokes and passing lewd remarks about women applying for Poor Law relief. It was not until 1875 that the first woman, Martha Merrington, was elected at Kensington. In Scotland, where the Poor Law was administered through parochial boards, Margaret Foulton was elected at Inverkeithing the following year.

The numbers of women guardians remained small for many years, something Patricia Hollis attributed to a combination of the complex qualification requirements and the hostility their presence attracted. One Birmingham guardian felt that the board 'should be an Eden which no Eve should enter', while Walsall's mayor worried about the subjects they would hear discussed.[104] Women countered that they were better suited to the work than many men, as managing a workhouse and its inmates was household management on a larger scale. Women subverted the masculine humour of the boards, reacting with amused incredulity to male guardians who were at a loss to decide on the size of pie dish for a workhouse kitchen or whether pauper girls' dresses required buttons or hooks.[105] On sexual matters they argued that 'some of the women who are brought before the Guardians require the care and consideration of their own sex'.[106] Precedent went some way to undermining the concerns of prejudice, and the numbers of women guardians grew slowly, then increased after the property qualification was abolished in 1894, rising from 136 to around 900 by 1895.[107]

Women in local government carved out distinct roles that drew on their 'motherly influence ... [and] womanly experience and sympathy'.[108] School board women were noticeably child-centred, advocating Frobel methods of learning through play and campaigning for school meals and school medical officers.[109] Many pushed for continuing education and better pay for women teachers. On the Boards of Guardians women attempted to soften institutional life through what Hollis described as 'a culture of domesticity and emotional warmth'.[110] This ranged from lobbying for major building changes to bringing books, pictures and tobacco to cheer 'their' poor. Through these approaches women's presence came to be seen as a measure of a board's progressiveness, and boards without a female member often tried to co-opt one. School board seats passed 'down the female line' in Sheffield, Bradford, Bristol and elsewhere.[111] When there were two women on a board they would often work together. One exception was the London School Board, whose size allowed for greater numbers of women than its provincial counterparts. Jane Martin's detailed study of the work of its 29 women members has concluded that they 'did not argue from a shared feminist perspective above that of party but often divided on issues such as corporal punishment or subsidised school meals'.[112] Politics also divided women on Boards of Guardians, especially when greater numbers of socialist women were elected and used their platform to attack the broader causes of poverty.

Women in local government were sustained by the broader women's movement. A Society for Promoting the Return of Women as Poor Law Guardians supported their candidacy. In 1888 a separate committee was formed in London by Annie Leigh Browne to secure the return of women to the London County Council. This became the Women's Local Government Society, which offered practical help and advice to women candidates. Links between elected women and the women's movement became less harmonious when suffragette militancy advanced. Margaret Ashton, a constitutional suffragist who was elected as a councillor in Manchester on her second attempt, felt that some of the hostility she had encountered in her campaign could be directly attributed to suffragettes, and publicly repudiated their actions.[113]

Before the First World War local government offered women unprecedented opportunities to participate in the political life of the nation. Much of what they did in this arena has been overshadowed by the more flamboyant history of the Edwardian suffrage campaign. Yet local government work preceded this by several decades, allowing women to seek election at a time when no other European country offered them a similar role.[114] The gap between local and national politics has encouraged historical interpretations which separate women's participation in local government from the campaign for the parliamentary vote. Although Patricia Hollis' thorough and insightful study of women's participation in local government in England concluded that the achievement of parliamentary suffrage 'owed little or nothing to women's local government work', she emphasised that many women hoped it would break down further barriers.[115] Others disagree. Martin Pugh cautioned against affording 'marginal significance' to developments in local government, suggesting that they represented 'one of those small keys that help to unlock large doors'.[116] For Philippa Levine, although the work of local government women and the campaign for parliamentary suffrage 'operated independently of one another for the pragmatic purposes of achievement, their aims and aspirations clearly converged'. She suggests that the links between the two were so self-evident that there was little need to articulate them at the time.[117] Leading anti-suffragists like Mrs Humphrey Ward may have argued that giving women the local vote was quite sufficient and removed the need for them to have the national one, but many politicians now used the opposite argument in debates on suffrage bills, suggesting that the precedent of the local government franchise demonstrated that women were not incapable of voting sensibly, or liable to be physically exhausted by the process.

Conclusion

The years between the publication of *A Vindication of the Rights of Women* and the first school board elections saw women involving themselves in a variety of political movements. Unlike earlier centuries, the first part of the nineteenth century did not exhibit marked peaks and troughs in political activity by women. There were lulls at certain points, but unlike the Restoration or the period after the French Revolution there was no backlash against the presence of women in a movement such as Chartism when the movement itself diminished. Women's organisations remained relatively small and separate at this stage, with distinct aims, although similarities were beginning to emerge in their focus and activities. All placed great importance on education, for example, and developed ways to prepare women activists for canvassing or speaking through offering them training and support. Many devised quite complex regional and national structures, with committees and elections which drew women into contact with campaigners in other areas and familiarised them with the mechanisms of political work.

The connections between single-issue campaigns did not only come from the friendship networks between participants (although these played an important part in developing and sustaining a number of campaigns). They also represented the transition from women in politics to a political women's movement. By the mid-nineteenth century, women were beginning to develop a broader analysis of their situation which recognised connections between a variety of social, political and economic inequalities. They continued to differ over tactics and priorities, but readers of the *Englishwoman's Review* would hold similar views on a number of issues, including the need for better educational and employment opportunities for women, as well as for greater economic and political independence. A growing number of women's organisations offered a shape to women's collective political work, meaning that they did not always have to fit their activities within existing men's groups.

At the same time, the political landscape was changing. Although historians differ over the point at which the process began, there is consensus that by the mid-nineteenth century something resembling the modern party system was emerging. At this stage, no political party recognised women as members (this would not change until the birth of the Independent Labour Party in 1892). Nevertheless, the Liberals and the Conservatives had numbers of women supporters who were to prove themselves of great value in the new organisational structures of both parties. Political women now had the opportunity to work within parties as well as in a women's movement.

Part 2
The Women's Movement Organises

3

The Campaign for Women's Suffrage

Introduction

In Ray Strachey's account of the origins of the British women's suffrage movement, a young Emily Davies visited her friends Elizabeth and Millicent Garrett. Sitting in front of a bedroom fire, they discussed the problems and inequities they faced as women. Emily suggested a three-point strategy to overcome these:

> 'Well, Elizabeth', she said, 'It's quite clear what has to be done. I must devote myself to securing higher education, while you open the medical profession to women. After these things are done,' she added, 'we must see about getting the vote .... You are younger than we are, Millie, so you must attend to that.'[1]

Strachey admitted that the story may be apocryphal; nevertheless it illustrates the perspective of mid-nineteenth-century feminist campaigners. Successive reforms had improved women's social position and expanded their opportunities for public participation. Changes in local government opened up elected offices and drew women into party politics. The irony of women ably determining and enacting local legislation while remaining external to the process at a national level was not lost on many campaigners, who also recognised that Divorce Law Reform, the Married Women's Property Acts and the repeal of the Contagious Diseases Acts had needed sympathetic male MPs to make them law. A consensus began to emerge amongst feminists that the parliamentary vote was essential to further reform. Only this, it was felt, would give women power over their own lives.

From the 1860s to the First World War the British women's movement became indivisible from the campaign for women's suffrage. Occasional calls for the parliamentary vote to be extended to women had been made in earlier centuries by women acting alone. Now a series of nineteenth-century Reform Acts provoked broader debates about who might be included in a growing electorate. These encouraged women to demand the vote collectively, so that by

1914 there were over 50 suffrage societies active in Britain. The suffrage movement surpassed all previous examples of women's political activity in its size and
spread. It was also broader in scope than might be suspected. This chapter charts
the growth of the suffrage movement, and examines its scope and diversity, as
well as its different methodologies up to the point at which some women gained
the parliamentary vote in 1918.

Petitions, legal challenges and early campaigns

Individual women had tried to raise interest in the suffrage question before. Mary
Smith from York petitioned Parliament in August 1832, arguing that as she paid
taxes she should be entitled to a vote, but her claims were ignored. A Quaker
woman, Anne Knight, wasted no opportunity to raise the question of suffrage in
her copious correspondences with leading political figures, and advocated votes
for women in a public meeting at Sheffield in 1851. Then, in 1865, John Stuart
Mill was elected to Parliament. Mill, who had published an article calling for
women's suffrage, made this part of his election address. Bessie Rayner Parkes,
Barbara Bodichon and other Langham Place women campaigned for him. The
following November the Kensington Society held a meeting on the topic, with
papers from Bodichon, Helen Taylor (Mill's stepdaughter), Katherine Hare
and Charlotte Manning, the president. Almost all of the 50 attending voted
in support of women's suffrage. Emily Davies (who was concerned about the
issue's potential to attract those with extremist views) felt this amounted to
'a subdued kind of agitation for the franchise'.[2] She cautioned against a specific
suffrage organisation but events overtook her. In 1866 Parliament began to
discuss the possibility of further franchise reform. Enthused by the chance of a
public hearing, Bodichon and others approached Mill to see if he would raise
women's suffrage in Parliament. He agreed, providing they produced a petition of at least 100 signatures to demonstrate some interest in the question.
A Women's Suffrage Committee was quickly formed which collected almost
1500 names. Mill presented the petition on 7 June, following up with a question, ten days later, about the number of women who would qualify as voters
under property restrictions were they not debarred on grounds of sex.

Suffrage historians concur that the next 12 months 'saw the emergence of an
organized women's suffrage movement in Britain'.[3] Sandra Holton's work has
done much to establish the key role that women's friendship networks – often
established through contacts made in other political campaigns – played in its
early development and spread.[4] They extended it beyond London. Elizabeth
Wolstenholme (later Wolstenholme Elmy) a well-known figure in Manchester's
Radical Liberal circles who had joined the Kensington Society as a corresponding member, set up a suffrage society in Manchester, which collected around 300
signatures in support of the petition. Other events nurtured the northern movement. In the summer of 1866, Barbara Bodichon visited Manchester to deliver a
paper on women's suffrage to a meeting of the Social Science Association. In the
audience was Lydia Becker, president of the Manchester Ladies' Literary Society,
who succeeded Wolstenholme Elmy as secretary of the Manchester group in
February 1867. Jacob Bright, the Manchester MP who took over as women's

suffrage champion in Parliament after Mill's 1868 electoral defeat, was another whose family networks enhanced the national spread of the movement. One of his sisters, Priscilla Bright McLaren, helped to found the Edinburgh society; other relatives were involved in groups in Bristol and Bath. Wider friendship networks spread into other regions; Clementia Taylor, wife of Leicester MP and suffrage supporter P. A. Taylor, helped establish a suffrage society in Birmingham in 1868 with friends such as Priscilla Bright McLaren.

Members of these various provincial committees worked hard to win over public opinion through meetings and petitions as the Reform Bill moved through Parliament. Mill's women's suffrage amendment was defeated, as was a Women's Disabilities Bill, drafted with the help of Manchester lawyer Richard Pankhurst, which Jacob Bright introduced in May 1870. Neither the Liberal nor the Conservative Party would commit to votes for women as a party issue, but private members' suffrage bills were introduced in most subsequent Parliaments up to 1900. Although some passed their first reading, none succeeded, as they were 'talked out' or afforded insufficient debating time. Nevertheless, their regular occurrence encouraged a pattern of parliamentary-focused campaigning for suffragists, who accompanied Westminster discussions with vigorous provincial agitation. Bertha Mason, an early suffrage historian, described the excitement of this early period:

> Lectures were given, great meetings were held, petitions were circulated and literature was distributed .... By these methods public opinion was steadily educated and thousands of adherents were gained for the cause. So energetic was the campaign that there was hardly a town of any importance from John o'Groats to Land's End where the principle of Women's Suffrage was not discussed and explained.[5]

This national scope was enhanced by structural developments. A Central Committee of the National Society for Women's Suffrage drew local groups together from 1868, while Lydia Becker's *Women's Suffrage Journal* kept supporters in touch with suffrage work throughout Britain from 1870.

Provincial societies challenged the legal anomalies surrounding exclusion of suitably qualified women from local electoral registers. They capitalised on the case of Lily Maxwell, 'an intelligent person of respectable appearance', who found herself on the Manchester electoral register and cast her vote for Jacob Bright in November 1867.[6] Maxwell's inclusion was accidental – Lydia Becker felt that 'the overseer must have thought [Lily] was a masculine name' – but her vote was recorded.[7] Campaigners rushed to collect other suitable names throughout England and Scotland. The Manchester Suffrage Society took four cases to appeal, one of which (Chorlton *v.* Lings) was heard in November 1869. Laura Nym Mayhall saw this case as 'a pivotal point' in the suffrage campaign, as it confirmed readings of the wording of nineteenth-century Reform Acts as explicitly gendered.[8] An Act introduced by Lord Brougham in 1859 (frequently cited by suffrage supporters) stated that 'in all Acts of Parliament, unless the contrary is expressly stated, words importing the masculine gender shall apply to women as well as men', but the judgement in Chorlton *v.* Lings held that that 'in modern and more civilized times' women would be 'excluded from taking any part in popular assemblies, or in the election of Members of Parliament'. A similar ruling in Brown *v.* Ingram in Scotland showed that the parliamentary vote would not going be easily achieved.[9] Jane Rendall noted that Maxwell's vote had another legacy. Her presentation as a 'single and industrious householder indebted to no man' translated into that of an 'acceptable woman voter' to many observers. This had serious consequences for the unity of the movement when others argued that married women also deserved a vote.[10]

1870–1904, diversification and unification

The close personal networks which underpinned suffrage branches could encourage factions to develop. Holton situated the origins of the movement's divisions in discussions around the scope of the first suffrage petition. Emily Davies wished to restrict its demand to votes only for single women and widows. Other radical campaigners sought to challenge the premise of sex-based inequality by including married women.[11] The final petition represented a compromise, neither explicitly including nor excluding married women, but the issue remained contentious amongst suffrage leaders, and Davies gradually withdrew her energies to concentrate on educational reform. Other debates proved equally divisive. In Northern England, Josephine Butler recruited radical members of the suffrage movement into her contentious efforts to repeal the Contagious Diseases Acts. This facilitated some contact between radical middle-class women and working-class activists, but disquieted more cautious suffrage campaigners.

There were other factions shaping the suffrage campaign. Women were more formally involved in party politics in the late nineteenth century, as the next chapter will show. Some members of the Women's Liberal Federation attempted to affiliate to the National Society for Women's Suffrage. Resistance to this from Conservative and Liberal Unionist suffragists provoked the withdrawal of a number of suffragists from the Liberal Unionist camp. They formed the Central Committee of the National Society for Women's Suffrage in 1888. This met in Great College Street, so was often referred to as the Great College Street Society. The remaining members of the Central Committee now went under the name of the Central National Society for Women's Suffrage (otherwise known as the 'Parliament Street' society). These divisions were stronger centrally than in the provinces, where research suggests that many women retained affiliations with both groups.[12] Disagreement around a married women's franchise gained sufficient strength of feeling to prompt the founding of another organisation, the Women's Franchise League (WFL), in 1889. The League, led by Elizabeth Wolstenholme Elmy, Harriet McIlquham and Leeds feminist Alice Scatcherd, maintained a radical voice on suffrage and broader feminist issues, and attempted to forge links with the emerging labour movement as well as with working-class women's groups. This, and the presence of such figures as Emmeline Pankhurst in its membership, has led some historians to see the WFL as a precursor to the suffrage movement's later militant wing although during its lifetime it differed from other societies in its aims rather than its tactics.[13]

Few historians would now agree with Antonia Raeburn's observation that suffrage was a dead issue by the beginning of the twentieth century.[14] Sophia Van Wingerden's reassessment of the period between 1885 and 1904 has noted that it brought increased levels of national organisation, making it 'easier for women to affiliate to a suffrage society' wherever they lived.[15] Significant developments in the 1890s paved the way for the movement's Edwardian peak. Suffrage campaigners were enthused by a series of parliamentary successes. The Local Government Act (1894) extended the voting rights of single women and widows to married women, increasing their legal independence. A women's suffrage bill was narrowly defeated in Parliament but attracted the support of the majority of Conservative MPs. When it was reintroduced in 1897 it passed its second reading. Leading members of the existing suffrage societies recognised that a coordinating body would enhance their impact in Parliament and elsewhere. In 1897 the National Union of Women's Suffrage Societies (NUWSS) was set up under the leadership of Millicent Garrett Fawcett, with the object of campaigning to secure votes for women on the same terms that they were offered to men. Most regional and national societies joined. The NUWSS was determinedly non-party, but many of its members held strong party affiliations. Harold Smith noted the conservative leanings of many of the London Society for Women's Suffrage, which played a leading role in establishing the National Union, while Jo Vellacott tempered this with her assessment that its Liberal membership was substantial 'in the country at large'.[16] Other studies by Jill Liddington and Jill Norris have emphasized the NUWSS's connection with Labour and socialist groups in the North.[17]

At the same time a younger generation of campaigners were entering the movement. The *fin de siècle* figure of the 'New Woman' may have been a journalistic construction, but contemporary commentators immediately recognised her in the women graduates from the new redbrick universities and women's colleges. An article in the student magazine of Owens College, Manchester (where women were admitted from 1888) described her:

> She smokes. She rides a bicycle – not in skirts. She demands a vote. She belongs to a club. She would like a latch key – if she has not already got one. She holds drawing room meetings and crowds to public halls to discuss her place in the world.[18]

Progressive, emancipated, and increasingly economically independent, young 'new' women looked beyond the old-fashioned established methods of suffrage campaigning. They were also aware of broader constituencies. In 1900 Esther Roper, secretary of the Manchester National Society for Women's Suffrage, joined Eva Gore Booth to launch a suffrage petition amongst women workers in the Lancashire textile industry which attracted almost 30,000 signatures. Roper, Gore Booth and other socialist and trade union women worked for the Independent Labour Party (ILP) candidate David Shackleton at Clitheroe, where he pledged to push for votes for women if he was elected. When he failed to deliver, Roper and Gore Booth joined trade unionists Sarah Reddish and Selina Cooper to form the Lancashire and Cheshire Women Textile and other Workers' Representation Committee. This supported a small number of independent parliamentary candidates who were prepared to stand on a suffrage platform, raising the suggestion of the radical potential of an alliance between working-class socialist activists and the women's suffrage movement.

Another new suffrage society was formed in Manchester in October 1903. This was the Women's Social and Political Union (WSPU), inaugurated by Emmeline Pankhurst, widow of the lawyer who had helped draft Jacob Bright's bill in 1867. The Pankhursts were early members of the ILP in Manchester, and Emmeline was the first woman elected to its national Executive Committee. She was also a committed suffragist, impatient with what she felt was the ILP's procrastination on the issue exemplified by MPs like Shackleton, who wavered in their support once elected. Mrs Pankhurst saw her new union functioning as a ginger group within the socialist movement to allow women to push the issue forward themselves. It recruited younger women with different political traditions from their Victorian predecessors, who brought fresh attitudes to suffrage work. Women like textile worker Annie Kenney and ILP organiser Teresa Billington Grieg were happy to face hostile crowds at impromptu street meetings, a tactic they had learned in the socialist movement. From quite an early stage such behaviour was described as militancy because of its public nature; its adherents were nicknamed suffragettes, a label coined by the *Daily Mail* as a term of derision, but embraced by Christabel Pankhurst who claimed that its hard 'g' underlined her society's determination to 'get' the vote. Such remarks coupled with the flamboyance of the Union's campaign have encouraged its presentation as the most radical suffrage society, although as Harold Smith has noted, this ignores the fact its demand for votes for women on the same terms as they may be given to men was identical to that of the NUWSS.[19] Yet by adopting militancy the Union offered women a different political experience, which proved extremely attractive to many disillusioned with constitutional approaches.

The National Union of Women's Suffrage Societies, 1907–14

Meanwhile the NUWSS had expanded its national network of branches. The Union still relied on the petitions and public meetings although it took on different characteristics in some districts. In Lancashire, for example, it continued the work initiated by Esther Roper amongst textile workers, and gained significant support amongst working-class women and socialists, whom Jill Liddington and Jill Norris termed the 'radical suffragists'. In 1907 the NUWSS altered its constitution to give more power to its executive committee. The committee was now elected by a council of delegates from local societies who met quarterly. Millicent Garrett Fawcett retained the presidency despite competition from the Conservative suffragist Lady Frances Balfour; nevertheless, according to Harold Smith, one result of the reorganisation was that the growingly radical provincial societies lost ground in the Union to the more conservative policies of its leaders, many of whom came from the London Women's Suffrage Society.[20] The reorganised NUWSS resembled a large political party rather than a women's pressure group. It had central offices in London and a number of full-time staff including a team of ten organisers who worked in the provinces. A newspaper, *Common Cause*, kept members in touch with the Union's work.

These developments fuelled further expansion and diversification. In February 1907 the NUWSS organised the first large-scale suffrage procession in London, which was dubbed the 'Mud March' because of the inclement weather. Millicent Fawcett was initially conciliatory towards the WSPU and praised the way that militant tactics had raised the profile of suffrage. The Mud March shows that the NUWSS changed its methods to adopt more public forms of activity in response to the suffragettes. It arranged similar events up to the outbreak of the First World War, including a national suffrage pilgrimage which converged in London from all over Britain in 1913. However, relations between constitutional and militant societies cooled as militancy advanced, and the NUWSS formally condemned militancy in 1908.

The NUWSS numbered many Liberal supporters amongst its leadership. This had some impact on its policy, particularly in the way in which it arranged its election work. From 1903 the Union had worked to secure the adoption of pro-suffrage candidates. It also questioned candidates during elections, and encouraged its members to work for those who were the strongest friends of the cause, a policy Holton feels 'more generally favoured the return of the Liberal government's candidates'.[21] When no pro-suffrage candidate stood, the NUWSS took no part in an election. This strategy saved Liberal suffragists the embarrassment of attacking their own government, but made the NUWSS look politically confused. In Liverpool during the first general election of 1910 the same NUWSS members worked for candidates from opposing political parties in neighbouring constituencies; the local WSPU coordinated a much simpler campaign which aimed to 'keep the Liberal out'.

By 1910 the NUWSS had over 200 provincial branches across England, Scotland and Wales, necessitating further reorganisation. A federated structure was devised which gave more power to regional groups and provided for provisional councils. This democratic structure contrasted with the autocratic format of the WSPU. At the same time, as Sandra Holton has noted, it was not without its own problems, with 'recurrent tension between London headquarters and local societies' around issues of policy and the internal structure of the NUWSS.[22] The NUWSS could now display greater national and regional variation. The Scottish Federation had 63 societies by 1914 and its own treasurer, and was vociferous in resisting attempts to portray the movement as 'English'. Organising under the slogan 'ye mauna tramp on the Scottish thistle', it made strong protests when a national suffrage procession of 1911 was described by the Union as a march of England's women. Another result of regional autonomy was that some branches began to develop closer links with their local labour movements. seeing labour candidates as the 'best friends' to women's suffrage. Branches in the North of England began to push for closer ties with Labour as the best means of advancing suffrage.

In 1912 the NUWSS forged an electoral alliance with the Labour Party. This was not uncontroversial; many members including Millicent Fawcett opposed this step, but a combination of factors, including the Labour Party's inclusion of women's suffrage in its official programme and the Liberal government's dismissive attitude towards the Conciliation Bill, eased the change. The main result was the Election Fighting Fund (EFF) dedicated to giving practical support to Labour candidates. The NUWSS hoped that a Liberal government with a reduced majority would be dependent on the pro-suffrage Labour Party, but also lobbied hard to persuade the Conservatives to commit to votes for women. The EFF was credited with achieving some Liberal defeats, although these usually involved a split vote and resulted in the election of a Conservative candidate rather than a Labour victory. Not all of the NUWSS leaders supported the scheme. Eleanor Rathbone spearheaded opposition on the Executive Committee, and suggested that she might be prepared to support a breakaway group of local societies who were unhappy with the policy which threatened to break up the Union. Other Liberal women were concerned, but Rathbone only gathered a handful of supporters on the committee and finally resigned over the issue in 1914. The EFF proved popular in Northern England but was more controversial in other areas. In Wales, for example, Ursula Masson has described how a combination of strong local Liberalism amongst suffragists coupled with a lack of organisation amongst working-class women made the task of the local EFF organiser almost impossible.[23]

The Women's Social and Political Union

The WSPU moved to London in 1906, where Christabel Pankhurst felt it could pressure the government more effectively. At the same time it developed a network of branches throughout Britain, with a larger number of paid organisers than other suffrage societies. Organisers' regular reports of branch activities in the Union's paper *Votes for Women* have underpinned a number of recent regional and national studies which give us a far fuller picture of the diversity of the WSPU.[24] Although branch members had to work with organisers they had little say over their appointment, which could cause friction, especially in different national contexts. Sylvia Pankhurst and Ada Flatman both had a difficult time in Aberdeen, and while Leah Leneman's extensive study of Scottish suffrage concluded that 'for the most part Scottish WSPU branches did not object' to the presence of English organisers on principle, Englishness was the reason the Edinburgh branch gave for wanting to remove their organiser, Mary Allen, in 1914.[25] In Wales, where language was an issue, the WSPU took more care, and deployed the Welsh-speaking Rachel Barrett to oversee work in the principality, although Kay Cook and Neil Evans' research found that militancy was strongest in English-speaking towns in the south.[26] Organisers had a degree of freedom to shape local campaigns, but were also responsible to the WSPU headquarters in London. Some branches devised their own forms of militant protest but many were more occupied with recruitment and fundraising.

The militancy that distinguished suffragettes from suffragists is not easily defined. The work of the Suffragette Fellowship in the 1950s pushed a connection between militancy and prison, with an annual 'prisoner's day' celebration in October marking the arrests of Christabel Pankhurst and Annie Kenney at Manchester's Free Trade Hall in 1905. Yet many suffragettes who did not go to prison described themselves as militant. Alice Kedge, a 14-year-old servant from Camden Town, bought a 'votes for women' badge which her mother insisted she threw away. Her compromise, to wear it 'under the lapel of my coat because

I didn't want to upset my mother and I couldn't afford to lose my job', showed the pressures on many working-class girls who sympathised with suffrage.[27] Fear of family disapproval cut across class lines. Margaret Haig Thomas, daughter of a Liberal MP, remembered that although it was 'almost the done thing' to go to prison in her own family, her husband's relations took a different view, so she would hide in side streets if she saw her mother-in-law during suffragette paper sales.[28] As the WSPU extended the scope of its militancy, other women felt able to go further. From 1907 the Union held regular militant demonstrations in London called 'Women's Parliaments', which usually ended in large numbers of arrests. The Union's regional organisation enabled women of different ages and backgrounds from all over Britain to attend. Branches often clubbed together to pay delegates' fares, or offered practical help such as childcare or cooking while women were in prison.

Most accounts divide suffragette militancy into three phases. The first, described above, focused on politicians and Parliament, and involved heckling and low-level civil disobedience. Militancy developed a second phase from 1908. Liz Stanley and Ann Morley's reading of suffrage violence presents it as reactive, where 'each shift in militant tactics was a reasoned response to a yet more repressive treatment of feminist women'.[29] The rhetoric through which suffragettes justified their move to window-smashing supports this interpretation, as the first window-smashers, Mary Leigh and Edith New, linked their actions to the violence used against women on WSPU deputations. Militancy was suspended for much of 1910 while a cross-party Conciliation Committee drafted a suffrage bill. When this was shelved after its second reading, the WSPU responded with a large demonstration which prompted a brutal police response, with many witnesses reporting an overtly sexual component. The violence of this 'Black Friday' was regularly invoked when suffragettes turned to more direct actions, coordinating window smashing on a large scale as part of their London protests.

From 1912, militancy embraced more violent forms of protest, including arson, bombing, and criminal damage to a range of targets such as golf courses, letter boxes and works of art. The WSPU hoped this would create 'an intolerable situation', whereby public opinion would persuade the government to give in to their demands.[30] There was a reactive element in these actions. Suffragette offenders were now receiving more severe prison sentences regardless of their crime; supporters were particularly aggrieved at the 12-month sentence passed on Harriet Kerr, the WSPU's office manager, for conspiracy in April 1913, as she had made non-participation in violence a condition of her employment. Some suffragettes felt justified in augmenting their actions given that a long sentence was likely whatever their crime. Violent militancy brought a shift in the WSPU's policy towards prison, as its members were now expected to evade arrest. This enabled larger numbers of supporters to play a direct role in supporting violence through maintaining a network of safe houses facilitating the work of itinerant arsonists. At least four households in York, Birmingham and London sheltered Harry Johnson when he was on the run after an arson attack in Doncaster in 1913.[31]

Most historians divide militancy into distinct 'early' and 'later' types. This chronological distinction is misleading as it implies that one form of militancy replaced another, which was never the case. The WSPU's leaders were clear that a degree of choice about the level of militancy had to remain, and members could move in and out of different types of militancy throughout the entire campaign. In 1912, Emmeline Pankhurst famously urged her followers to 'be militant in your own way', offering them a variety of options which ranged from the violent destruction of property to silent passive protests in the House of Commons.[32] In the period when violent protests were increasing, a number of new initiatives began, continuing the earlier tactic of civil disobedience. There were many interruptions at cinemas and theatres. In London, suffragettes stood on chairs in Lyons Corner House to deliver impromptu speeches. The 'prayers for prisoners' initiative saw women interrupting church services to pray for suffragette prisoners; women were ejected from York Minster and attempts were made to ban all women from congregations at Liverpool's Anglican Cathedral as a result.

Interpretations of suffragette militancy are mixed. The civil disobedience tactics are not without supporters. Andrew Rosen acknowledged their 'effectiveness', and even anti-militant suffragists such as Ray Strachey admitted that the 'extraordinary behaviour' of militant suffragettes 'came as a new gospel' which inspired a fresh generation of recruits to join the ranks of suffragists and suffragettes.[33] Militancy's more violent forms, by contrast, have been condemned by authors such as Pugh, who believe these achieved little beyond 'trap[ing]' the Union in a 'spiral of decline', and Brian Harrison, who attacked its 'destructiveness' and 'ruthlessness'.[34] Critical interpretations of militancy concurred that it alienated public opinion. The erroneous insistence on viewing the incorporation of different militant tactics as a linear progression rather than an expansion has hampered a broader consideration of the composition of militancy. Martin Pugh's 'revisionist' approach to women's suffrage claimed to find militancy 'a more varied and ... subtle movement than is usually thought', yet his analysis proceeded to focus almost entirely on arson, stonethrowing and the response to these. This misses much of militancy's diversity, and led him to suggest that 'only a minority of WSPU members were personally involved' in militant behaviours.[35]

Feminist historians have challenged this, to offer sympathetic interpretations of all forms of militancy. Elizabeth Sarah's analysis of Christabel Pankhurst's political philosophy considered how militancy affected its practitioners, noting its potential to free women from 'the stronghold' of gendered behaviour in order that they might 'realise ... their power' as political actors.[36] Cultural historians have followed Sarah's attempt to return agency to women involved in suffrage politics through reclaiming broader definitions of militancy. Barbara Green's investigation of the 'performative activism' of suffrage considered, amongst other things, how suffragettes' presence challenged the gendering of Edwardian urban space.[37] Wendy Parkes built on this in work which described suffragettes' use of fashion as 'an integral part of [their] identification and performance as a suffragette', which echoes the experience of Alice Kedge, described above.[38] It is important not to underestimate the political significance of such activities in the context of their time; many men found the public nature of the suffragettes' activities extremely challenging and responded disproportionately.

Suffragettes undertaking theatre protests met with violent ejections, while Mary Richardson was one of many paper sellers to recall having to deal with unpleasant sexual innuendo from the men who passed her in the street.[39]

Other suffrage organisations

The NUWSS and the WSPU were not the only groups campaigning for votes for women. *Votes for Women* listed over 50 separate suffrage societies by 1914. These can be broadly divided into four types: oppositional, religious, professional and political. Three oppositional groups emerged from splits within the WSPU. In 1907, Teresa Billington Grieg and Charlotte Despard left the Union to form the Women's Freedom League (WFL). Their main disagreement was with the WSPU's autocracy; Freedom League members wished for more accountability and democracy, a conference to set policy, and regular elections to the National Committee. This was a similar structure to the NUWSS, but the WFL also practised militancy. It set up a national network of branches, although it was stronger in districts with no WSPU branch or where the majority of WSPU members joined the WFL, as in Wolverhampton. The WFL employed a small number of organisers, and its members undertook a number of militant protests. Some of these focused on broader social inequalities. It was particularly active around the issue of tax resistance, encouraging its members to withhold their taxes until they had votes as a means of emphasizing women's powerlessness within the state. It also initiated protests in police courts. These were not restricted to suffragette trials. A number of simultaneous interruptions took place in Glasgow, London and the Southwest region against the 'application of man-made laws' to voteless women.[40] Elsewhere, Muriel Matters and Helen Fox achieved a degree of notoriety when they chained themselves to the grille that separated the Ladies' Chamber (where women were allowed as spectators) from the House of Commons (the grille was subsequently removed). Many Freedom League members went to prison as a result of militant actions, but the League rejected the more violent forms of militancy practised by the WSPU. The WFL outlived the WSPU by several decades, and remained active up to the 1960s.

There was a further split in the WSPU in 1912 when the Union's treasurer, Emmeline Pethick Lawrence, and her husband Frederick were expelled. The expulsions (which were never satisfactorily explained) were precipitated when the government issued warrants for their arrests, along with Christabel and Emmeline Pankhurst and Mabel Tuke, following the large window-smashing raid in West London in March. Christabel Pankhurst fled to Paris, where she remained until the First World War broke out, organising the Union from a distance. There is some suggestion that she feared that the Pethick Lawrences were taking too much power in her absence, although the couple also disagreed with Christabel and Emmeline over the form and direction of further militancy. The Pethick Lawrences retained control of *Votes for Women* and the WSPU started a new paper, *The Suffragette*. *Votes for Women* had a wide readership but the Pethick Lawrences remained broadly loyal to the WSPU and a united militant campaign, and although Emmeline recalled how several people appealed to her to begin a new organisation, she and her husband determined to put the movement first. They formed a loose affiliation, the Votes for Women Fellowship (VFWF), to unite members of other societies across what they saw as the divisive labels of 'militant' or 'non-militant'.

Fellowship branches formed in many parts of the country, and held regular meetings aimed more at education than recruitment. The Fellowship experience convinced some activists that there was room for a group to unite the militant and constitutional wings of the movement more formally. The United Suffragists (US) was consequently launched in 1914. This was intended as 'an intermediate party ... with a stable organisation that remains above ground and intact for constitutional agitation'.[41] It was open to men and women, to militants and non-militants, and accepted joint membership with other societies. The US recruited several quite well-known public figures who had not previously been associated with suffrage groups, largely because of its separation from the complex controversies that surrounded many other suffrage societies by this date. Its potential was interrupted by the outbreak of war; although it continued low-key suffrage campaigning, this was less necessary as the militant campaign collapsed.

A third, smaller oppositional group was the East London Federation of Suffragettes (ELFS), begun by Sylvia Pankhurst in 1913. This originated in a WSPU campaign in the district the previous year. When George Lansbury was defeated in a by-election at Bow which he fought on a suffrage platform (having resigned as an MP to do this), the WSPU leadership seemed set on withdrawing from the area, prompting Sylvia to respond with a more independent campaign. The ELFS organized on more democratic lines than the WSPU, and recruited a less eclectic, more working-class membership. Its support for broader socialist causes concerned Christabel Pankhurst in particular. When Sylvia spoke at the Albert Hall in support of Jim Larkin, socialist leader of the Dublin lock-out, Christabel publicly distanced herself from the East End campaign, at which point it became autonomous. The ELFS continued to agitate for suffrage during the First World War, and changed its name to the Workers' Suffrage Federation in 1916, then the Workers' Socialist Federation in 1918.[42] Sylvia's work in the East End has been described in detail by historians adopting a socialist-feminist approach to the question of votes for women.[43] While the organisation was significant in terms of its distinctive scope and analysis, however, it must be remembered that it remained rooted in the East End and did not precipitate a national campaign on similar lines.

Religious suffrage societies

Not all suffrage organisations formed from splits within larger groups. Religion, which had long been an important facet of many women's political involvement, underpinned the motivation of several suffrage campaigners. There were a number of religious suffrage societies which recruited men and women as members. In the Anglican Church, a Church League for Women's Suffrage (CLWS) was founded in 1909 by the Reverend Claude Hinscliff, its secretary for many years. In his study of the CLWS, Brian Heeney noted that while its primary aim was the vote, it also wished to emphasise 'the deep religious significance of the women's movement' and to promote suffrage within the Anglican Church.[44] The CLWS held monthly communion services, and was involved in some broader movements for equality within the church, for example in helping to draft recommendations for a new version of the marriage service. It never attempted to develop a mass membership and did not employ organisers, but had over 100 branches and 5000 members by 1913. It was not particularly radical, and steered its members away from contentious issues such as the ordination of women, but was not afraid to take a strong stand on other matters. It refused to expel or condemn members who participated in militancy, despite losing some prominent members including the Bishop of Worcester in protest. The CLWS continued a low level of suffrage campaigning during the First World War, then became the League of the Church Militant, devoted to broader campaigning for equality within the church.

Catholic women were represented by the Catholic Women's Suffrage Society (CWSS), which was formed by two WSPU members who met each other at mass in 1912.[45] This was less supportive of militancy than the CLWS, but otherwise served a similar function in promoting the suffrage cause amongst Catholic congregations and organisations. The CWSS was smaller than the CLWS but very active in Liverpool and in southeast England. In Liverpool it involved itself in broader welfare work, reflecting the working-class nature of many Catholic parishes, which it continued during the First World War. At the end of the war, the CWSS reformed as the St Joan's Social and Political Alliance.

There were suffrage societies for other faiths. Nonconformists set up a Free Church League for Women's Suffrage (FCLWS) in 1910 and a Friends' League for Women's Suffrage (FLWS), whose records appear to have been accidently destroyed in the 1920s.[46] The FCLWS has not as yet been the subject of sustained historical enquiry, so little is known about its activities beyond the more prominent of its members, which included the Pethick Lawrences. In common with other religious societies it published its own newspaper, the *Free Church Suffrage Times*, which reported on its provincial work and continued as *The Coming Day* until 1920.

Jewish suffragists formed the Jewish League for Women's Suffrage, partly, according to the *Suffrage Annual and Women's Who's Who*, as it was thought that it would be more attractive to Jews than a nondenominational organisation.[47] The Jewish society was more directly involved in militancy than other religious societies, with some of its members interrupting synagogue services on Yom Kippur in 1913. Each of these societies complemented the work of the main militant and constitutional groups. While they each recruited women who were not members of other societies, they also enjoyed considerable overlap with the NUWSS, the WSPU and the WFL, offering religious suffragists and suffragettes space to press their claims in different arenas, and to assert spiritual claims which were as important to them as political ones.

'Professional' suffrage groups

As well as groups that sought alternative methods of organising and campaigning from the two main suffrage organisations, and those catering for suffragists of a particular religious denomination or political persuasion, a number of suffrage societies served a narrower membership. Many only recruited members from particular careers, and some were able to direct members' professional skills for the benefit of the broader suffrage movement. Suffrage attracted large numbers of the more bohemian sections of Edwardian society, so several small organisations were linked to the arts. This association was mutually beneficial. All suffrage societies had their own colours (purple, white and green for the WSPU, and red, white and green for the NUWSS), and made great use of visual display at their meetings and in public demonstrations. The Artists' Suffrage League (1907) worked with the NUWSS, and showed its support for constitutional methods in its slogan 'Alliance not defiance'. Its members, who included many professional artists and illustrators, donated their services free of charge. They produced fundraising postcards and advertising posters, and created around 80 colourful and elaborate banners for the large NUWSS demonstration in London in June 1913. Militant suffragettes were helped by the Suffrage Atelier (1909), which described itself as an 'Arts and Crafts Society Working for the Enfranchisement of Women'. Atelier members were supposed to promote suffrage through their work, but were expected to offer such work to the Atelier in the first instance, receiving a percentage of any profit it raised, with the remainder going to the movement. The Atelier made posters and postcards which were used for fundraising purposes, along with banners for WSPU demonstrations. It also worked with the Women's Freedom League, and helped decorate halls for WFL fundraising events.[48]

The larger suffrage societies benefited from the work of the Actresses' Franchise League (AFL), which was formed in 1908. The AFL produced entertainments (singers or recitations) for suffrage meetings free or at a greatly reduced rate. Some of its better-known members, including the actresses Cicely Hamilton and Edith Craig, were also involved in the production of plays and performances intended to raise income for the cause. The best known of these was Cicely Hamilton's *Pageant of Great Women*, first produced by Edith Craig in 1909. The pageant, which involved the allegorical character 'Woman' presenting a number of well-known historical women as a means of legitimising women's current claims, was performed at WSPU and WFL branches throughout Britain. The AFL also produced more broadly feminist plays which dealt with wider issues of gender inequality, such as the sexual double standard and the problems facing working women. In 1913, partly due to the popularity of the League's work, a 'Woman's Theatre' was set up, but only managed one season before the outbreak of war. Unlike the ASL and the Suffrage Atelier, the AFL carried on work during the war. One of its members, Lena Ashwell, initiated the 'Women's Theatre Camps Entertainments' which travelled behind the lines on the Western Front providing entertainment for wounded or resting troops.[49]

There were also a number of political societies, whose work is outlined in subsequent chapters, and groups with a particular national or regional focus such as the Forward Cymric Suffrage Union which was active in Wales. The number of organisations working for the vote demonstrates the size of the suffrage campaign while their different priorities show the diversity of concerns that fed into suffrage. Rather than comprising a narrow movement divided into militant and constitutional wings, the suffrage campaign attracted actresses, teachers,

Catholics, Anglicans, party-political women and countless others. Although some members joined only to get the vote, the majority saw suffrage as part of a much broader fight for a more equal society.

The First World War and women's suffrage

The suffrage campaign united the women's movement behind a common aim, although divisions remained over tactics. The outbreak of the First World War in August 1914 ended the high-profile suffrage campaign and fractured the women's movement. No clear consensus emerged as to how best to respond to the wartime situation. Organisations took a variety of approaches, which can broadly be arranged in four categories: supportive or jingoistic responses, continuity, suspension or redirection of activity, and pacifism.

The best known jingoistic response came from the WSPU, which suspended militancy almost immediately. In return the government released suffrage prisoners, and Christabel Pankhurst returned from Paris. Her first speech signalled the Union's new priorities. When Victor Duval, founder of the Men's Political Union for Enfranchisement, cheered 'votes for women!' Pankhurst snapped 'We can't discuss that now'.[50] The WSPU's national organisation was wound up. Christabel and Emmeline Pankhurst developed a gendered interpretation of the war which denounced the violation of France, described as a female nation, by the masculine German state. They toured the country before conscription was introduced, persuading men to enlist, and headed a government-backed campaign to recruit women into the munitions industry. *The Suffragette* became *Britannia*, filled with bellicose articles condemning pacifists and strikers. This was a decisive shift from the WSPU's socialist origins, which had remained in evidence at the grass roots long after its split with the ILP. However, as Angela Smith has pointed out, there was overlap between the content of *Britannia* and *The Suffragette*, and the Pankhursts continued to press for women's rights in the new wartime context, arguing that patriotic feminists should be rewarded with the vote.[51]

The WSPU leaders were not alone in responding to the war by arguing for a more overtly patriotic role for women. Organisations such as the Home Service Corps and the Women's Volunteer Reserve recruited women in support of the war effort, and adopted military trappings such as drill and informal uniforms. From 1917 women could join the Women's Auxiliary Army Corps or the Women's Royal Naval Service. Between 80,000 and 90,000 women had joined up by November 1918. Recent work by Krisztina Roberts and Janet Watson has shown that uniformed organisations had to negotiate complicated responses, and struggled to maintain clear demarcations between male and female roles.[52] On the one hand, women's support was essential to the war, and women were demanding a more active part, but on the other hand many feared the subversion of gender roles which was suggested by the appearance of large numbers of women wearing khaki. When a WAAC base in Abbeville, France, was bombed, the death of eight young women shifted public attitudes towards their work, and some war memorials later included the names of members of women's auxiliary forces.

Not all in the pre-war women's movement wished to suspend the campaign for the vote. A small number of WSPU activists challenged Emmeline and Christabel Pankhurst's use of the Union's name. Two organisations emerged; the Suffragettes of the WSPU, which formed in 1915 and the Independent Suffragettes, set up the following year. Both attempted to continue some suffrage campaigning but were hampered by lack of funds. Their newspapers (the *Suffragette News Sheet* and the *Independent Suffragette*) were short and sporadic because of wartime paper shortages. The United Suffragists achieved a better level of organisation as it was able to build on pre-war links. Similarly, in the East End of London, Sylvia Pankhurst's ELFS continued to organise working-class women. Franchise reform came back onto the national agenda in 1916 when the coalition government began to discuss how to make sure that men in the armed forces could vote in a post-war election. Suffrage societies were quick to lobby the government, and warn that their current truce would end if women were ignored. Millicent Fawcett used uncharacteristically militant language, warning the prime minister that while the NUWSS 'had buried the hatchet … they had marked the place where it was buried and were prepared if the occasion arose to dig it up.'[53]

Other suffrage groups kept working during the war but shifted the focus of their campaigns. Jo Vellacott has argued that the NUWSS's response showed both 'the extent and efficiency of its network' and the depth of broader concerns beyond the immediate vote within the movement.[54] The NUWSS did not take an overtly jingoistic stance but focused its energies on welfare campaigns that alleviated the distress caused through war, while at the same time supporting the broader war effort. NUWSS work was channelled through a variety of bodies: it officially cooperated with the government's Central Committee for Women's Employment (CCWE), while branches throughout Britain organised women's service bureaux which coordinated a range of local work. Some drew up employment registers and placed women into what had been considered men's jobs, such as lift operators, to free up men for the forces. Others ran training classes in first aid and nursing, or in signalling and welding, preparing women for auxiliary or munitions work. Many branches arranged regular social events for soldiers' and sailors' wives, and collected luxury items such as tobacco and soap to send to servicemen. In some areas this expanded into setting up infant and maternity centres. Suffragists were also involved with wartime schemes for women police, sometimes setting up their own uniformed patrols around military camps to look after the welfare of young girls attracted by the soldiers.[55]

The NUWSS supported initiatives beyond Britain, most notably the Scottish Women's Hospitals Association (SWHA). This grew from the Scottish Federation but was supported by funds raised in NWUSS branches throughout Britain. The SWHA staffed hospitals in France and mobile units on the Eastern Front. Some of the staff were NUWSS members, such as Dr Frances Ivens, who sent regular reports of her work at Royaumont back to her Liverpool NUWSS branch. The SWHA required considerable fundraising; the NUWSS Annual Report suggested figures of around £7000 a month. Sandra Holton has argued for the efficacy of the NUWSS's policy, pointing out that its membership held for much of the war and expanded in some areas such as Glasgow, although it did fall off in other districts.[56] It is, however, difficult to assess how much of this came from the lack of a credible alternative, as in many areas the NUWSS was effectively the coordinating body for a number of broader relief efforts, many of which did not attempt to present themselves as part of a wider suffrage struggle.

The NUWSS also lost members to the women's peace movement. Some suffragists felt that winning the vote through demonstrating patriotic support for the war was too much of a compromise. Socialist parties throughout Europe had opposed the First World War, and some attempted to continue opposition once war was declared. Clara Zetkin called a meeting of the Women's Bureau of the Second International in March 1915, which was the first time any members of the International had met formally since the beginning of the war. Four British women attended. A broader, more politically mixed gathering was held in The Hague the next month with the help of the International Women's Suffrage Alliance. This time the government used new passport legislation to prevent British attendance, but a small number of women managed to join the meeting. The Hague conference established the Women's International League (later the Women's International League for Peace and Freedom). Its British branch demonstrated the complexity of feminist responses to the war, with leading members from across the militant/constitutional divide: Helena Swanwick, Catherine Marshall and Maude Royden from the NUWSS; Emmeline Pethick Lawrence and Barbara Ayrton Gould from the WSPU/US; Charlotte Despard from the WFL. The WIL stood for arbitration as well as votes for women, combining pacifism and suffrage in a direct challenge to the attitude of other suffrage groups, which continued to undertake work that was broadly supportive of the war effort as a means of proving women's fitness for citizenship.

Conclusion

In 1918, the Representation of the People Act gave votes to a number of British women over the age of 30. The timing of this Act, at the end of a war in which women's contribution had been critical, suggests a connection between the two which has made the link between the suffrage movement and the vote a difficult one to quantify. Some historians have followed the lead of Arthur Marwick, who suggested that the pre-war movement was less relevant than women's war work, and that the Representation of the People Act in 1918 was the reward a grateful government offered its patriotic female citizens.[57] Certainly some politicians who changed their minds about suffrage found that the overt patriotism of sections of the women's movement offered them a useful reason for doing so. Yet, as Nicoletta Gullace has observed, the Act did not start from this premise, but was more to do with enfranchising soldiers. Many soldiers had no vote, and those who did were now largely disqualified under the residency requirements of the 1884 Reform Act.[58] Conversely many young women who had been most active, including members of the auxiliary forces and the majority of working-class munitions workers, remained voteless in 1918. A further restriction limited the vote to those women over 30 who had a local

government vote (or with husbands who did), which Duncan Tanner calcu-
lated left 22 per cent of older women disenfranchised.[59] These restrictions
suggest that the link between women's suffrage and their war work is less clear.
Furthermore, some leading suffragists had opposed the war throughout, and
combined their demand for the vote with peace campaigns.

The contribution of women's wartime work towards the vote needs to be
placed in the longer context of a suffrage campaign which ran from 1866 to
1928. At its Edwardian peak the suffrage movement drew unprecedented
numbers of women into political activity in Britain. Although the movement
divided over its tactics and scope, all suffragists adhered to the basic principle of votes for women, and combined behind this demand. Together they
made the issue so ubiquitous that to discuss further franchise reform without
including women in 1918 would have been extremely difficult for any political
party. Suffrage campaigners presented the 1918 Act as a victory, even though
it fell short of giving votes to women on the same terms as they were given
to men. A large celebration was held in London, and many societies including the Conservative and Unionist Women's Franchise Association and the
United Suffragists wound themselves up, suggesting that their work was over.
Not all suffrage campaigners felt this. Others believed that the 1918 Act was
a step on the way to the fuller political equality they wanted. Groups such as
the Women's Freedom League and the National Union of Women's Suffrage
Societies continued to press for further reform, aware that the war had brought
neither the vote on the terms which they had wanted, nor an end to the suffrage
movement.

4
Women and the Liberal Party

Introduction

The nineteenth century brought changes in British politics which altered the practices associated with political involvement and activity. Successive Reform Acts in 1832, 1867, 1868 (Scotland) and 1884 expanded the electorate. Although the parliamentary franchise remained exclusively male and was based on a property or residency qualification, around 60 per cent of adult men could vote for Parliament by the end of the century. The political map altered, mirroring Britain's pattern of industrialisation, with more constituencies, reflecting population shifts towards larger urban centres. The two-party system which had been a feature of British politics since the end of the seventeenth century also began to change. Liberals and Conservatives dominated elected offices before the First World War but were challenged by the success of a small number of socialist candidates, particularly at local level. This suggested that party affiliation could no longer be assumed, particularly in urban districts where many working men voted after 1884. Urbanisation also meant that levels of support could not easily be predicted from old allegiances based on familial networks rooted in generations of residency. New electors required courting and canvassing. Votes were now considered as something that had to be won.

The transition to a larger, more active model of party membership was boosted by the 1883 Corrupt and Illegal Practices Act. The Act responded to an enlarged electorate by tightening up the rules surrounding electoral behaviour. Corruption and bribery became punishable by imprisonment, and election expenses were capped at around £1,000 for every 5,000 voters. At the same time the number of contested elections, which had tailed off in the mid-eighteenth century, rose throughout Britain, particularly after the later Reform Acts. Newly defined parliamentary constituencies with greater numbers of voters meant that elections required more work. New voters had to be identified, registered and canvassed, and the financial restrictions of the Corrupt and Illegal Practices Act meant that this considerable undertaking had to be tackled by volunteers. The expansion of local government brought more elections, which added to the pressure on parties.

As we have seen, historians differ over the extent to which these developments encouraged greater political participation amongst the population at large. The effects on women with party allegiances are easier to quantify. Electoral reform and the subsequent party restructuring it prompted had had profound implications for the relationship between political parties and their female supporters. The next three chapters explore these in greater detail. Taking the Liberal, Conservative and Socialist parties in turn, they outline how established and emerging parties began to draw women into their formal organisational structures long before women became part of the parliamentary electorate. Separate women's organisations built on women's work in previous non-party groups, and legitimised it within the predominantly masculine world of party politics. Women were thus able to speak and act on behalf of parties, albeit in controlled and defined circumstances, many years before they were able to vote for them at national elections.

The formation of the Women's Liberal Federation

The history of British feminism is closely associated with that of nineteenth-century liberalism and the articulation of women's rights within this presented by John Stuart Mill. More recent feminist interrogation has suggested that the fit between Mill's concept of equal rights and the aims of many Victorian feminists was not quite as comfortable as has been thought, pointing in particular to his willingness to accept prevailing sexual divisions of labour. Nevertheless, the 'sweeping generalization' articulated by Juliet Mitchell remains useful: 'after Mill ... the feminist struggle move[d] from being predominantly the utterances of individuals ... to being an organized political movement'.[1] Most accounts of the British suffrage movement take Mill's election to Parliament in 1867 as the starting point. After his election a number of suffrage groups emerged, as has been shown, offering women opportunities to organise collectively around this issue. But at the same time, other political activities were becoming available.

Given the extensive links between liberalism and feminism in the mid-nineteenth century, it is not surprising that the Liberal Party developed a strong women's organisation as the Party sought to formalise women's involvement in its work. What is unexpected is that it did so slightly later than the Conservative Party. Conservative women could join the Primrose League from 1884, as will be seen, whereas Liberal women had to wait until 1887 before a national Women's Liberal Federation (WLF) was established. This three-year delay may have been due to Liberal women's involvement in other organisations. Sandra Holton's study of the early suffrage movement suggested that pressure for a Party organisation for Liberal women came from its radical wing, prompted by women's concerns about the over-cautious approach of their suffrage colleagues and the sense that many Liberal Party men were becoming increasingly hostile to feminism in general and suffrage in particular.

Anna Maria Priestman, who formed one of the earliest Women's Liberal Associations (WLAs) in Bristol in 1881, exemplified this point. She wrote of a 'disgraceful' degree of inertia in her local suffrage society, and saw the WLA as a means of solving this.[2] Priestman's hope was that Party women would give a sharper political edge to suffrage work while simultaneously keeping the Party alert to women's issues. Holton is right that suffrage persuaded women Liberals in Bristol to form their own association, but women elsewhere had different reasons. In Wales, for example, Ursula Masson found that the WLAs emerged as electoral reform and boundary changes had led to an upsurge in Welsh nationalism. Religion, land and language were more important to Welsh women Liberals than promoting their own political claims, particularly towards the north, where old dynastic Tory seats were being lost to MPs like Thomas Edward Ellis and David Lloyd George. Masson found suffrage was only an issue for women Liberals in South Monmouthshire and in Newport, where the WLA had strong British affiliations.[3]

Liberal women may have had different motivations for collective organisation, but they shared adherence to a radicalism which took women's participation for granted. This made setting up organisations a natural step in an era when political parties were expanding their membership and offering women a more active role. The *Illustrated London News* reported an organisation of women Liberals participating in a demonstration in Birmingham in June 1877. Two years later, in a speech during his Midlothian campaign that is often cited as 'the justification of the Women's Liberal Federation', Gladstone addressed the Party's women supporters directly:

> in appealing to you ungrudgingly to open your own feelings and bear your own part in a political crisis like this, we are making no inappropriate demand, but are beseeching you to fulfil a duty which belongs to you, which, so far from involving any departure from your character as women, is associated with the fulfilment of that character, and the performance of its duties, the neglect of which would in future times be to you a source of pain and just mortification.[4]

Following this speech, local WLAs were formed in many districts including Bristol, York, Darlington and Newcastle. The *Westminster Review* reported that over 10,000 women had joined these associations, and suggested that there was a need for the Party to respond to this, capitalising on their popularity to harness women's support for the Party.[5] Liberal men were aware that their Party needed to reshape itself in response to the Corrupt and Illegal Practices Act. Writing in 1912, Millicent Fawcett noted that it did not take long for the example of the Primrose League to convince leading Liberal men that 'if the Conservatives could make good use of women for electoral work Liberals could do so also and would not be left behind'.[6]

Liberal men were broadly supportive, but the initiative for more formal organisation came from women working at the grass-roots of Liberal politics. In 1886 Sophia Fry tried to draw the recently formed groups into a single, affiliate organisation. Fry was typical of the WLF's early leaders. As a young Quaker woman she had started philanthropic work which developed a political edge following her marriage to Theodore Fry, an active Liberal. When Theodore stood as a parliamentary candidate at Darlington in 1880, Sophia campaigned for him and set up the Darlington WLA in the process. Her extensive correspondence networks alerted her to similar groups of Liberal women in other parts of the country. Sophia felt that the disparate groups could work more effectively together and that questions about whether women should be in single or mixed-sex groups or where to peg the level of subscriptions would be better decided at national level.[7] She invited representatives of 16 local WLAs to a meeting to devise a way of improving their efforts through better communication and develop a more formalised structure. After a period of discussion the WLF was formally inaugurated the following year, uniting 40 WLAs and with the prime minister's wife, Catherine Gladstone as its figurehead president. The Federation's Annual Reports show a rise in membership to 75,000 in 1892, peaking at 133,215 women in 837 local associations in 1912.

The women behind the WLF wanted an autonomous all-female organisation. Restricting formal membership to women meant that those who joined did not have to compete with men for positions on its governing bodies. The WLF offered women unprecedented opportunities for gaining party-political experience. Its structures enabled its elected leaders to exercise varying degrees of power across a number of levels. All members in affiliated local associations elected representatives to a large ruling council of 500 women. The ruling council was in turn responsible for electing the Executive Committee which oversaw the Federation and decided its policies. The Executive was based in London, and included women from prominent Liberal families who were uniquely placed to press claims on MPs and to shape the Federation. The Executive led in practice, but encouraged the autonomy of branches and evolved a large degree of decentralisation across the nations and regions of Britain. It supported the setting up of a Scottish Women's Liberal Federation and a Welsh Union of Women's Liberal Associations in 1891. There were also several English federations coordinating work across Lancashire and Cheshire, Sussex, the Metropolitan Counties and elsewhere. Decentralisation did not preclude local associations from engaging with the national body and shaping its policy. They discussed Council agendas in detail, receiving reports of proceedings and recommending actions for their delegates. It did, however, free them to plan their own activities and determine specific policies on a range of issues. Topics chosen for discussion exceeded those deemed to have special interest to women, and emphasised the political rather than the gendered dimension of WLA membership, ranging from municipal affairs through to the crisis in the Transvaal.

The WLF aimed to be inclusive. Fry had hoped to 'secure the cooperation of all Liberal women of all classes of society', and the inaugural meeting exceeded her expectations, bringing together the various 'ladies of rank and wealth ... factory hands, board school teachers ... .and women of all grades in society' who had been chosen as delegates by their associations.[8] Associations attempted to adhere to Fry's vision and attract a diverse membership. Local branch subscriptions were kept low and could be waived for less affluent members, and there were not different categories or tiers of membership as there were in the Primrose League. These measures may have attracted some working-class women, although their presence could also be explained by a lack of direct competition; WLAs became less diverse by the 1890s when the Independent Labour Party offered an alternative for politically radical women. Local studies of WLAs have challenged the Federation's claims for success in this area, suggesting that even in urban centres where WLAs tended to be stronger and more numerous they did not necessarily unite women across class divisions. In Liverpool there were six WLAs by 1893, all dominated by women from the city's prominent middle-class Liberal families. Women with more radical beliefs and working-class activists were not tempted to join as they had the option of working in a number of successive local socialist groups which ran from the 1880s.[9] Similarly, in Aberdare, Ursula Masson found little evidence to support the local WLA's own claim that it represented women of all classes. Local working-class women there too looked towards socialism despite the WLA's strong feminist stance on many issues.[10]

Philosophy and activities

When Catherine Gladstone accepted the WLF presidency she explained that Federation members were there 'to help our husbands'.[11] Her familial interpretation of political activism reflected the preponderance of wives, sisters and daughters of Liberal MPs amongst the first WLA recruits. However, many of these women held expectations of the organisation which exceeded the notion of supporting male relations. The early historian of British feminism, Helen Blackburn, who knew several WLA members, explained how although:

> Many ... passed into the political work offered for the pleasure of helping their fathers, brothers and husbands ... very many also came to work in real earnest for underlying principles in which they firmly believed, and for which they rejoiced to work hand in hand with men.[12]

This Liberalism was strongly articulated at the Federation's inaugural meeting when it committed itself to 'promote the spread of Liberal principles throughout the country' and remained central to its work. In its early years the priority was very much on education, aimed at raising 'an intelligent interest among women in political questions and to enlist their sympathies on the side of Liberal principles'.[13] This was more difficult than it sounded, and the founders of local associations throughout Britain frequently remarked on the low levels of political knowledge amongst their early members.[14] As Mrs Byles from Bradford WLA noted, many women 'frankly acknowledged themselves to be students of politics' who needed to 'begin at the beginning'.[15] In response the Federation developed a wide range of educational literature, and facilitated a network of speakers to address meetings in areas where the local association did not yet have a sufficiently confident member available.

Liberal women developed a distinctive concept of their political role, which they often expressed in terms of their 'double duty'. This recognised the existence of separate spheres and acknowledged the particular role of women within a family, but did not stop there. As Nora Phillips, one of the leading lights of the Welsh Union, told the members of Aberdare WLA, women Liberals believed that:

> women had a work to do in politics ... it was a womanly as well as manly duty to encourage just laws .... Both men and women had duties to perform within the homefold and outside of it ... woman did only half hers if in making home happy she is blind to the needs of the orphans outside.[16]

The notion of duty expressed by women Liberals was presented as an inevitable consequence of an expanding state which interested itself in areas previously considered private or domestic. Women could no longer avoid politics, it was argued, when things which affected them directly, such as the vaccination, schooling and health of their children, had become politicised. The idea that women were particularly affected by aspects of the law was mobilised in support of calls for their greater participation in politics. Another national speaker, Eva McLaren, explained to St Helens WLA:

> Woman had been almost of necessity called into the field of action because politics were interfering very much with them and they were obliged to learn something about this in order to defend themselves against laws that might be prejudicial to their interests.[17]

Through adhering to this analysis, Federation members forged a vigorous political role. They began with the arduous clerical work an expanded electorate required, going from house to house in electoral wards to register, and then to leaflet voters. The Federation's education programme equipped women for more active engagement, teaching them salient points of party policy, economics and legislation. This was most evident in local government, where a focus on issues such as education, health and the local environment corresponded to its arguments as to why women should be active in politics. WLA members began to canvas and to initiate their own political discussions. They encouraged all eligible women to register and vote in local elections. They also pushed for greater representation by women on the elected bodies where this was possible.[18]

The move from canvasser to candidate was not a straightforward one within the Party. Many Liberal men who praised the qualities women offered municipal politics were less ebullient when it came to getting them elected. WLA members often had to fight their way onto a Party ticket against men's claims that this was unseemly. When Georgina Hubback, widow of a Liberal alderman, was proposed as a Poor Law guardian in Liverpool, local Liberal men debated whether it might be better if one of their number resigned his seat to spare her the indignity of a public election.[19] Party loyalty often asked more of women than it did of men. Caroline Kenrick in Birmingham had to wait until men could find room for her on a predetermined slate and promise not to stand as an independent in the meantime.[20] Kenrick complied, but many other Liberal women opted to stand as independent candidates. The autonomous structure of WLAs left them free to decide whether to support any members who did this, and independent women candidates were often elected with the help of WLA workers. Their successes persuaded local parties to reserve at least one place for women on the Party slate when elections to the boards came round.

As we have seen, it was not that difficult for women to access school boards and Boards of Guardians, where their position could be justified in terms of the feminine nature of much of the work. There was less of a consensus as women began to pursue their expanding rights to be active in other areas of local government. The Liberal Press in Liverpool was vitriolic when a local WLA member, Bessie Shilston, stood as an independent council candidate in 1898, opining that whilst 'a lady may do duty as a Poor Law guardian and be a useful woman to the community ... she would be lost if deliberating with men about gas, water, sewerage and other public works'.[21] It was not just male hostility which complicated women's election to councils. As Patricia Hollis has noted, a combination of circumstances including complex candidates' property qualifications, the triennial electoral system and a lack of municipal women voters combined to make women councillors a rarity before 1919.[22]

Securing Party approval would have significantly enhanced women candidates' electoral chances, but Liberal women soon found that this was not as straightforward as they would have wished. Women became eligible to stand for election for city councils at precisely the point when the militant wing of the suffrage movement was stepping up its campaign against the Liberal government. Women candidates found that they were automatically associated with suffrage in the public eye. This made many Party men wary of them even if they were personally opposed to militant tactics. The example of Margaret Ashton, a WLA member from Manchester who was elected as the city's first woman councillor in 1908, shows how suffrage could impact on the Party and on its women. As well as being active in her local WLA, Ashton had served as president of the WLF's Lancashire and Cheshire Union. She was experienced in local government, having served on Withington Urban District Council and on the local education committee. When women became eligible for election to city councils in 1907 she stood unsuccessfully as a Liberal candidate in a strongly Conservative seat. The next year she opted to stand as an independent, having resigned from the WLA over the Liberal Party's lukewarm stance towards votes for women. This time she won, but wrote anxiously to Millicent Fawcett that her campaign made her aware of how a 'few violent women' had 'injured the reputation of women politicians in Lancashire'.[23] Suffrage forced Ashton to stand aside from her Party loyalty, but simultaneously affected public perception of her work regardless of the nuances of her own suffragist beliefs.

Liberal women and suffrage campaigns

The WLF saw itself as a party political organisation for Liberal women rather than an auxiliary group grafted onto the Party with the intention of advancing the careers of Liberal men. Hollis has suggested that the WLF developed a 'parallel liberalism', prey to the schisms that beset the parliamentary Party as it attempted to work out its stance on the difficult political questions of the day.[24] The first major friction occurred when the Liberal Party split over the issue of Home Rule for Ireland in 1886. A group led by Kate Courtney left the WLF in

May 1888 to form the Women's Liberal Unionist Association (WLUA), which had 30 branches by 1890. The WLUA recruited some Conservative Unionists, combining Unionists from both parties with limited success. Courtney's biographer described how her enthusiasm for her organisation waned when she began to find it 'distasteful' to work with Conservatives, and she finally resigned from the Association after it came out in support of the Boer War, which she strongly opposed.[25] Other WLUA members who retained strong Liberal values returned to the WLF over the next decade; a minority stopped political work altogether. This facilitated a further drift to the right by the remainder of the WLUA, which was finally absorbed into the Women's Committee of the Tariff Reform League in 1906, to become the Women's Unionist and Tariff Reform Association, a Conservative Party group.

A deeper and more serious split occurred over the question of women's suffrage in 1892. As Linda Walker has pointed out, although suffragists were in a minority on the Executive, 'they were a vocal minority' who were increasingly prepared to put women's enfranchisement before their work for the Liberal Party.[26] Suffragists drew significant support from the local associations. An early survey of branches mentioned in the Federation's *Annual Report* for 1888 found 'a majority in favour of women's suffrage'. Many Federation women saw political equality as an essential part of their Liberal principles and could not understand why Party demands conflicted with this. As Nora Phillips explained in 1891:

> If we are Liberals at all, we should be everything that springs out of Liberalism ....
> I am a strong Suffragist because I am a strong Liberal ... and I say that we women
> want the keystone of the vote as men did.[27]

None of the WLF Executive opposed votes for women but they differed over how far to prioritise this. The Liberal Party remained unwilling to commit itself to suffrage as a Party question. Walker's research has outlined how the WLF's first five years witnessed increasing divisions between 'Moderate' and 'Progressive' groups on the executive. The Moderates, who included the Federation's founder Sophia Fry and her biographer Eliza Orme, were keen to emphasise the Federation's Party identity and remain neutral on questions that were not considered to be Party issues. Moderates argued that there were already several suffrage societies, whereas the Federation was Liberal women's only Party organisation. They wished to protect it from in-fighting with regard to what franchise measure to argue for, and to avoid putting further pressure on their Party during the conflict over Home Rule. Moderates also saw the gulf between suffragists on the Executive who were experienced political workers, and the average WLA member who was new to the world of politics and uncertain about suffrage, 'apathetic' in the words of Kate Ryley of Southport WLA, 'in the matter which of all others concerns [her] most vitally'.[28]

The Progressives, whose leaders included Eva McLaren, Nora Phillips, Jane Cobden and Rosalind Howard, the Countess of Carlisle, wanted the WFL to take a leading position in the national suffrage campaign. Their Liberalism was inseparable from a commitment to feminism, and they attempted to mobilise the WLF around a broad range of themes aimed at improving women's social position, which Moderates felt were not party political. Rosalind Howard, who was also the president of the British Women's Temperance Association, was particularly voluble around the drink question, which she believed to have special relevance to women, and lost no opportunity to attempt to bring the WLF in line with her views. Walker has argued that a preoccupation with such concerns stemmed from the Progressives' conceptualisation of women as a class. This led them to suspect the motives of politicians, who they feared viewed them only as party workers. Mindful of the low political level of many Federation workers, Progressives worked hard to bring individual local associations round to their point of view. In Wales, Nora Phillips and Eva McLaren went further, and campaigned to develop new associations whose delegates went on to support the Progressives' cause at Council. Rosalind Howard enlisted McLaren and Bertha Mason to undertake similar work in the North West, and was even prepared to establish alternative branches in districts where when an existing branch appeared less committed to her ideas.[29]

The tensions between Progressives and Moderates peaked in 1892, provoked by Gladstone's exchange with Samuel Smith MP, who was working on a franchise bill. Gladstone's rejection of women's suffrage in his letters to Smith complicated things for WLF Moderates, as most of them were Gladstonians. The 1891 Annual Council meeting had narrowly rejected a move by Rosalind Howard to oblige the Executive to promote women's suffrage, but the Scottish WLF made this part of its own constitution the same year. In 1892, after a stormy three-day debate, the Progressives' call for the WLF to promote women's suffrage as an objective was carried. The Moderates subsequently withdrew from the WLF and established a separate body, the Women's National Liberal Association (WNLA), under the leadership of Sophia Fry, which continued to work for the Party but did not prioritise suffrage. Despite their being rival bodies in many ways, relationships between the two groups remained cordial and they reunited in 1919. Patricia Hollis attributes their good relationship in part to the large degree of autonomy given to branches of each association, which meant that many individual branches of the WNLA came out in favour of women's suffrage while many in the WLF were prepared to be more accommodating to anti-suffrage men in the name of Liberalism.[30] There was less concern at the grass-roots about the minutiae of policy; in most instances women seemed more concerned with getting on with political work.

The establishment of the WNLA removed the strongest opposition to the prioritisation of suffrage within the WLF, but the Progressives' victory did not bring an end to all wrangling over the issue. The next problem the Federation faced was whether to make suffrage a 'test question'. This would mean that a candidate would have to support women's suffrage if he were to receive Federation support. In 1893, Anna Maria Priestman's amendment to Council that this policy be adopted was defeated, prompting her to set up the Union of Practical Suffragists. Its members remained in the WLF, where they organised around the issue of the test question. In 1902 when the Federation adopted a resolution from Cambridge WLA 'that the official organiser of the Federation be sent to help those candidates only who would support Women's Suffrage in the House of Commons', they wound up their campaign. However, as the Federation's structure left local associations free to work for anti-suffrage candidates if they wished, this negated any leverage that the WLF might have exerted over their party. The test question continued to provoke controversy within the Federation for the next decade.

Suffragists in the WLF were optimistic after their Party's landslide victory in the general election of 1906. For a decade, many of them had repeated the opinion that liberalism, if not the Liberal Party, tended towards women's suffrage, and they were confident that the vote would soon be granted now that their Party was in power. This optimism proved ill-founded, as the Liberal Party transformed itself, in Martin Pugh's words, into 'the unexpected enemy' of women's suffrage.[31] Over the next eight years, a series of pro-suffrage amendments and private members' bills were defeated or talked out. When the anti-suffragist Herbert Asquith replaced Campbell Bannerman as prime minister in 1908, suffrage campaigners were convinced that their prospects of success were significantly worsened. Suffrage now came to dominate the deliberations of WLF Council meetings and overshadow its work in many other areas. Claire Hirshfield's study of the WLF's handling of the issue has argued that this emphasis was heightened by external factors. Many feminist groups felt that the WLF's connection to the government meant that it 'held the key to female enfranchisement'. WLF members with links to women's organisations beyond their Party found themselves subject to heavy expectations that they would bring pressure on the government, making it even more difficult for Council and Executive members to avoid returning to discussions of the issue.[32]

As if this were not enough, suffragists in the WLF were also affected by the WSPU's activities. Asquith's antipathy personalised the militant campaign, which became aimed directly at Liberal MPs, to the irritation of most Liberal suffragists who repudiated militancy. Some WLF critiques also suggested class-based opposition to militancy. An article in the *Women's Liberal Federation News* in April 1906 criticised Annie Kenney's actions on a recent deputation to the prime minister, asking whether she was right to believe that:

> shouting at a gentleman from a long gallery ... will incline him to look with favour on her request? Or that making a scene in the street will recommend her cause to the public?

A handful of WLF members differed, concurring with Eva McLaren's statement that militancy was 'effecting a revolution which neither the Women's Suffrage Society nor the Women's Liberal Associations have ever achieved'.[33] In 1907 McLaren formed another internal pressure group, the Forward Suffrage Union (FSU), to keep pushing suffrage. FSU members worked to win individual WLAs over to a stronger version of the Cambridge resolution, which would withdraw support from any Liberal candidate, irrespective of his position on suffrage, until the vote was granted. As this echoed the WSPU's demand to 'keep the Liberal out', that society also addressed WLAs on the issue. The WLF national position remained unaltered, but research into local WLAs suggests that members were being convinced on the ground.[34]

For many Liberal women the government's handling of the Conciliation Bill proved the final straw. Before the unexpected general election of January 1910 the WLF was heartened by what appeared to be concessions from Asquith, and worked hard for the Party. When the Liberal Party was returned with a reduced majority it became clear that cross-party support would be required for a suffrage measure. An all-party Conciliation Committee, with Lord Lytton as chair and H. N. Brailsford as secretary, was set up to draft a measure. Conciliation Bills were brought before the House in 1910 and 1911 (and suffrage militancy was suspended in support of them). They passed their second readings but were thwarted when the government refused to grant time for further debate. A third Conciliation Bill was defeated in 1912.

Some historians have blamed this on an increase in suffragette militancy. Others such as Rover have linked the Bill's failure to a government announcement that a separate Reform Bill would shortly be introduced which would propose a further extension to the male franchise, with no mention of votes for women.[35] When these proposed terms became public there were large numbers of defections from the WLAs, fuelled by women's sense of betrayal by their Party. Although at least one WLA secretary 'begged suffragists to consider before they stood aside from liberal work, not withstanding the bitter feeling roused by the non-passing of the Conciliation Bill', many had had enough, and an estimated 18,000 individuals resigned by 1914.[36] The remaining members continued to press for greater commitment to suffrage on behalf of the WLF. A resolution from Tunbridge Wells WLA advocating a harder line on the issue was debated in 1912 and 1913. This, if passed, would have led to an effective strike by WLAs. This was not an empty threat. The Party was worried by a reduced majority in 1910, and faced trouble over a number of other issues including Home Rule. Many MPs were extremely anxious at the thought of losing the willing body of women workers whom they had come to rely on at election time and for carrying out other constituency work.

A number of those who withdrew from the WLAs over suffrage found a natural home in the National Union of Women's Suffrage Societies (NUWSS), where they were able to continue their work for the vote. Some of them defected to the Labour Party; Hirshfield has described how ex-WLA members such as Catherine Marshall and Bertha Mason, 'were in the vanguard' of those women who sought to move the NUWSS closer to the Labour Party, working vigorously for the Election Fighting Fund and arguing that it was Liberalism itself rather than their own personal political beliefs that had changed.[37] Others attempted to retain a Party affiliation through the WLF despite their opposition to the Liberal Party's actions with regard to suffrage. This was why WLAs in some areas were prepared to work for pro-suffrage Labour candidates, although this only happened in constituencies where no Liberal was adopted.[38] A further pressure group, the Liberal Women's Suffrage Union, was inaugurated in an attempt to keep up pressure on the Liberal leaders, although it had little chance to organise effectively before the outbreak of war.

Conclusion

In the final decades of the nineteenth century the Liberal Party was seen as a natural home by many feminist campaigners. Although there were some early attempts to justify their presence in the Party through familial connections, most of the WLF's leadership were not apologetic about wanting to participate in politics on their own behalf. Nor were they concerned about identifying themselves as feminist. Conservative women might fear feminism's radical connotations, while socialist women were wary of how it privileged gender over class. Liberal women, by contrast, felt 'secure with the term', helped by their Party's long association with feminism, according to Pat Thane.[39] The WLF enjoyed rapid growth, with a larger membership than any other auxiliary political organisation by 1912.

The WLF's prominence was threatened by ongoing friction over suffrage, which reduced its size and effectiveness prior to the First World War. Many Liberal feminists found it impossible to keep on supporting their Party, and prominent supporters moved towards the Labour Party, encouraged by the NUWSS's election fighting fund.[40] The question of suffrage has also overshadowed the WLF's historiography, and further research is needed on the organisation's activities during the First World War. Recent analyses of its membership in the 1920s have suggested that there was a resurgence in the popularity of Liberalism amongst some leading feminist campaigners, as a later chapter will discuss. Yet for those women who did return, the Party's irrevocable slide offered them fewer opportunities for official positions or electoral success. To a great extent the decline in the Liberal Party's women's organisation can be said to have prefigured the decline of the Party itself.

5

Women and the Conservative Party

Introduction

From 1918 until 1979 women were in the majority amongst Conservative Party members and voters, and their support has been widely credited with the Party's electoral successes in this period.[1] Yet while political scientists have attempted to interrogate the factors underpinning this support and its later decline, historians of women's politics have shown less interest in conservative women.[2] Compared with the literature examining varying strands of liberal, socialist and radical feminism and the differences between them, 'conservative feminism' remains an under-discussed phenomenon. Olive Banks' early survey of the social origins of first-wave feminism noted an 'absence of any close tie' between the two philosophies. Banks' interpretation has proved extremely intractable leading, in Barbara Caine's words, to a scholarly tradition in which the 'very idea that feminism could be associated with some intellectual frameworks is ... hard to accept.'[3] Indeed, one rare attempt by a feminist scholar to grapple with the notion of a Conservative feminism was subtitled 'Why do women vote Tory?' suggesting that such an allegiance was best viewed as a problem which required investigation.[4] Beyond feminist history the scant attention paid to women and the Conservative Party in political histories of the inter and post-war periods has replicated this position, presenting female conservatism as unexpected and perplexing.

Recently this has begun to change. The extending chronology of the history of feminism moved the search for its origins beyond Mary Wollstonecraft to consider earlier figures such as the more conservative Mary Astell. Elsewhere, political historians such as G. E. Maguire have cautioned that the history of feminism ought not to be 'the history of left-wing feminism' alone.[5] And while historical interpretations of early feminist bodies such as the Kensington Society and the Langham Place group still situate these within the trajectory of progressive, radical or Liberal politics, biographical studies of their membership have recognised the conservatism of women such as Emily Davies and Frances Cobbe.[6]

Investigations of 'conservative feminism' have gone some way to suggesting why the term is so problematic. One key issue, identified by Beatrix Campbell, has been to determine 'why a political tradition so little associated with the emancipation of women should be so strongly rooted amongst women'. Beyond their professed support for the Conservative Party, it is difficult to identify a distinctive set of beliefs that separate the political positions adopted by mid-nineteenth century women such as Frances Power Cobbe and Emily Davies, who identified themselves as conservative from those who called themselves socialist or liberal. The rarity of specific articulations of party-political philosophy amongst Conservative women has encouraged historians to approach the issue from the other side, examining the attitudes of the Conservative Party towards women, particularly after franchise reform.[7] Janet Robb's early study of Conservative women suggested that there was much within late nineteenth-century Tory politics that was designed to 'appeal to the untrained feminine mind … because they were more closely intertwined with the roots of women's emotions', citing particularly the 'romantic symbolism of imperialism' and an adherence to 'a mother's right to have her children given religious training' as examples of conservative political thought which would attract women.[8]

While few women's historians today would agree with this rather simplistic and essentialist analysis, Robb does succeed in conveying a sense of the rather vague values and beliefs which appeared to unite conservative women, particularly those from aristocratic or upper-middle-class backgrounds, in the early years of their organized participation in politics. G. E. Maguire, author of the only full-length study of women in the Conservative Party, has found that adherence to such sentiments persisted into the twentieth century, and was thought to be the way to attract women's support, particularly in conservative articulation of a domestic and maternal female role. David Jarvis found that this persisted in the inter-war period, with an assumption that women would favour 'domestic' issues and 'have a high moral stance politically'.[9]

Women's own promotion of such issues within the Conservative Party provoked contradictory rhetoric and behaviour. They sometimes attempted to justify taking on an increasingly public role in terms which would seem to point towards restricting rather than expanding their activities, particularly at the point when they were not entitled to full citizenship. The greatest paradox, summarised by Joni Lovenduski, Pippa Norris and Catriona Burness, is that most active women Conservatives 'were wary of feminist strategies and reluctant to be thought of as feminists', even when their actions and demands suggested that that was what they were.[10] Conservative women's fear of the radical dimensions of feminism is borne out by Caine's interpretation of Davies and Cobbe. Caine suggests that the most discernibly conservative feature of their political thought is displayed in their attitudes to how women should go about organising political campaigns. These pointed more to 'conservative' with a small 'c' than to specific Party policies; both women preferred to arrange quiet and controlled lobbying amongst influential people rather than open public meetings aimed at initiating mass organisations.[11] This may explain why, in the years before the First World War, it was for their skill in organisation that the Conservative Party's women became best known rather than for their development of a distinctive philosophy of feminine Toryism.[12]

The Primrose League

Much of the organisation of Conservative women occurred under the auspices of the Primrose League. At a point when women were excluded from formal membership of the Conservative Party, the Primrose League offered them the opportunity for direct engagement in politics. It also formalised activities that women from political families were already undertaking. Consequently the League has attracted a good deal of attention amongst historians as an organisation available to Conservative women seeking to engage in party-political activity. Characterised by Martin Pugh as 'a party within a party', it was founded in 1883 in England and Wales and 1884 in Scotland, as Conservatives sought to recover from the Liberals' landslide general election victory of 1880.[13] Although a National Union of Conservative and Constitutional Associations was formed in response to the 1867 Reform Act, there had been little in the way of tangible modernisation of the Conservative Party, as the 1880 defeat demonstrated. The Reform Act of 1884 threatened to make further inroads into traditional Conservative areas; Lord Curzon lamented that his South Derbyshire seat now had '7,000 new voters ... between 4,000 and 5,000 are colliers and manufacturers and I haven't a chance with them .... So certain am I to be beaten that I am planning a tour round the world'.[14] Curzon's pessimism was increased by the 1883 Corrupt Practices Act, which placed further restrictions on previous electoral practices.

At first glance the Primrose League appeared an unlikely champion of political modernisation. It had no detailed policy on the pressing economic or social questions of the day. Instead it stood for a rather vague ideology of defending broad notions of 'tradition' which focused around Church, Crown and Empire. The League's rhetoric shunned modernity and hearkened back to a romanticised medievalism, which was replicated in its structure and terminology. League branches were known as 'Habitations', and members were 'Knights' and 'Dames'. The League was ruled by a Grand Council to which members paid an 'annual Tribute' rather than a membership fee. Yet such anachronisms were also present in the rhetoric of the radical politics the League sought to combat, most notably in the socialist periodical *The Clarion*'s appeal to 'Merrie England', and as several historians of the League have pointed out, its tendency to look back did not preclude it from making 'an effective contribution to the modernization of right-wing politics in Britain'.[15]

This modernization proved attractive. By the early twentieth century League membership exceeded one million, including 94,000 Scottish members organised through an autonomous and financially independent Scottish Grand Council.[16] It was less strong in Wales, although several large branches were established in more Anglicised areas and along the coast.[17] For many historians, though, the most striking facet of the League's modernity was in its attitude towards women. As its paper, the *Primrose League Gazette*, was fond of reminding readers, the Primrose League was 'the first body to recognise the usefulness of women in politics', and it admitted them to membership almost immediately.

The Primrose League's organizers originally intended to restrict women to honorary membership, but this was swiftly revised, and by 1884 Dames could become full members. A separate, financially autonomous Ladies' Grand Council was then set up, although the additional cost of joining this body – a guinea, which doubled the habitation fee already paid by Dames – meant that most women only joined their local habitations.[18] Women enjoyed a remarkable degree of success at this level. Martin Pugh's detailed study of the membership registers of 11 habitations in England, Scotland and Wales shows female membership at 48.7 per cent.[19] Some districts started separate 'Dames' habitations' which catered exclusively for women. In other areas they worked with men, but not necessarily subserviently. Many mixed-sex habitations were led by women, and those that were under male control often also appointed a 'dame president' as deputy.[20]

The League pioneered the use of social activities to achieve political ends. This meant that it organised a formidable range of entertainments: fêtes; garden parties; magic lantern shows and dances, to extend Conservative values across a range of social classes. These took place in urban and rural habitations, and were designed to have a broad appeal – since 1885 the League had admitted a new category of associate members on a lower subscription rate, and their numbers had rapidly outstripped those of Knights and Dames. In habitations all were welcome, particularly at the social occasions, which could be extremely large. Sir James and Lady Colquohoun of Luss organised special trains and steamers to convey the 3,000 members from three local habitations to their Primrose League garden party in the summer of 1895.[21] Women took the lead in many of the League's social activities. One Primrose Leaguer, Arnold Statham, wrote in the *Primrose League Gazette* in December 1895 of his conviction that '[t]he political genius of women' was to be found their ability to enact the 'cementing [of] all classes in the bonds of a common brotherhood' through arranging or hosting such events. Pugh's analysis of the League agrees, suggesting that the work of promoting associational political culture through the organisation of social activities was seen as an ideal role for Conservative women, as it replicated their acknowledged skill as political hostesses, while Robb goes further to suggest that attendance at such events was more attractive to women, particularly in rural areas, where there was little competition for their free time.[22]

The fact that Primrose League women embraced the social role offered to them should not be interpreted as their accepting a restricted role for women in politics. There are many examples of League women attempting to extend the boundaries placed upon their work. The men who made up the League's Grand Council had a very particular view of what women should do. The League's vice-chancellor, George Lane-Fox, was quite happy to declare that 'women possessed influence which men did not', but did not wish to see them utilising this through canvassing. His opinion was endorsed by Lord Hamilton, who felt that they were not expected 'to take part in the rough and tumble of the contest' at election time, but not all Conservative men agreed.[23] One Banffshire candidate was so enthused by women's work on his behalf that he declared that he 'would be glad to see it extended to the exercising of votes as well as canvassing for votes'.[24]

Many women felt that they had much to offer, and Primrose League Dames along with female associate members soon became an established feature of elections. The *Primrose League Gazette* reported impressive statistics which testified to their efficiency, including 10,000 voting cards 'written, directed, stamped and posted' in the space of 24 hours in South Kensington in 1887, and 26,000 addresses and polling cards sent out in one week in Shepherd's Bush.[25] Pugh has described how Dames began such work with extreme caution, at pains to 'act with complete propriety' in order to win approval for this new step. Although women had electioneered with enthusiasm in previous eras, he surmised that by 1885 anyone who could recall 'the duchesses who had kissed butchers in aid of ... Fox's election at Westminster in 1784 ... would doubtless have considered it an eighteenth century vulgarity mercifully extinct in the Victorian age'.[26] Nevertheless many observers did recall this; an article in *Myra's Journal of Dress and Fashion* drew a direct comparison with the earlier event, remarking that the only change was that 'the habits of the country [now] require that instead of a kiss there should be a smile'.[27] Considering campaigning at Woodstock in the same year led Beatrix Campbell to rather different conclusions. For her, the work of Jennie Churchill, who toured the constituency with her friend Lady Georgina Curzon on Lady Curzon's tandem, begging voters to 'please vote for my husband; I shall be so unhappy if he does not get in', was 'revolutionary' adding 'eroticism to the political frisson' in a manner that was previously unthought of.[28] The fact that fashion journals saw fit to comment on electioneering tactics demonstrates the remarkable effect the Primrose Dames were having on perceptions of political campaigns.

Churchill and Curzon were wealthy women whose aristocratic assuredness could place them as extreme or atypical examples, had not many other Primrose League women replicated their work in other constituencies. This developed at an uneven rate. There was uncertainty at first as to whether women should be restricted to quieter clerical duties or be allowed to speak. 'Public speaking is manifestly out of our province, so far at least, as the addressing of very large meetings is concerned', Mrs Courtney Lord, wife of the ruling councillor of a Birmingham habitation, told the *Gazette* in November 1887. Many concurred that League women wishing to speak in public should restrict themselves to the organisation's smaller meetings. Meetings held in private homes by invitation 'in the afternoon when a few mothers could meet and bring their babies' were suggested by the *Primrose League Gazette* as ideal venues. Events of this sort were also considered to be the ideal way of reaching the wider audience that the League sought, attracting women who would not dream of attending a political rally. Jessie Boucherett , writing in the *Englishwoman's Review* in December 1897, described the 'invaluable' work performed by 'many a lady ... who has spoken at meetings, chiefly of friends and neighbours, who have surrendered to the expressions of heartfelt conviction'.

Women involved in organising afternoon meetings in each others' homes did not consider these as secondary or merely social occasions. They prepared speeches diligently, recognising the importance of educating their own membership to the point where more women could take active roles. Speakers' classes were held in several of the League's Habitations. The *Gazette* advised that, as 'Women's success in political discussion depends principally upon their ability to shatter the delusions and sophistries which form so conspicuous a portion of the Radical's argumentative stock-in-trade', they ought to 'keep well posted up as to the chief speeches of the last Session', and to 'arm themselves with hard facts' so as to achieve this.[29] League women were thus expected to become informed on a variety of political matters, and not to restrict themselves to 'women's issues'.

Once the principle of woman as speaker had been established, the distinction between participating in large and small meetings began to blur. Itinerant propaganda has been strongly associated with the spread of nineteenth-century socialism, but by 1892 the Ladies' Grand Council of the Primrose League had established its own touring propaganda van. This took speakers and literature out to areas which were quite difficult to access during the normal course of an election, and had great success in rural constituencies. The Primrose Cycling Corps enabled women to undertake mobile propaganda closer to home. The Corps was mixed-sex but female membership rose after a 'safety' bicycle was patented. This enabled riders to cycle in long skirts, thus retaining feminine propriety. Members wore the Corps' uniform of yellow and blue, and sported distinctive cycle badges. The Corps enhanced the League's social programme through events such as cycling gymkhanas and social outings. Its branches also involved themselves in propaganda and election work. Again they were most effective in rural areas, with one report from Scotland extolling 'the advantages' of 'the use of the cycle in spreading the principles of the League in country districts'.[30] In 1898 League members were given a description of one election which featured 'the recalcitrant voter being tracked to his lair by bands of enthusiastic and athletic Primrose Dames mounted on bicycles'[31]

Women could draw less attention to themselves through helping with the vast amount of clerical work that late nineteenth-century elections required. They proved particularly adept at these jobs, furnishing an indefatigable contingent of willing volunteer workers. Younger women enjoyed the camaraderie of collective work, and their enthusiasm prompted Walker's conclusion that electioneering had become 'the fashionable thing to do' amongst debutantes by the Edwardian era.[32] Older women were less motivated by concerns of modishness, but drew on more established roles, reflecting their work within the community, and often pushing into quite public roles. One Dame, Meresia Nevill, felt that women made 'the best canvassers, in as much as they are used to district visiting. They have the habit of going among the poor, and speaking to them.'[33]

Robb's study found these connections to be strongest in rural constituencies. Dames in the countryside looked on political work as 'an outgrowth of [their] normal social life in the village', and could propagandise and canvass via 'intimate knowledge of the families ... gained through years of church visiting and household shopping and the like'.[34] More recent studies of the League's urban activities show that its women did not shy away from working in more difficult city constituencies. Meresia Nevill worked in 'the most degraded holes and corners of the old Chelsea slums', where she had 'dust thrown at [her]', and in Kirkdale in Liverpool the League's women were said to have played a key role in securing a Conservative victory in a district that was 'densely and toughly peopled, [its] low life very low'.[35] In urban districts Dames spoke to the wives of newly voting men, popularly believed to hold much influence with their husbands. They presented a non-threatening façade. Jeannie Churchill explained that 'the fact that women have no vote should help ... to contribute to their influence in canvassing by proving their disinterestedness'.[36] When dealing with women, Primrose Dames would not play down their politics but would speak to them of the benefits of Conservative policies on equal terms.

There were limits to what women could do within the League. It retained separate organisational structures for men and women, with the real power residing amongst the men. League women expanded their role, but they and Conservative men drew distinctions between the 'truly feminine' work done by Primrose Dames and 'Lady Associates' in support of the Conservative cause, and the 'unattractive pressure exerted' by Liberal and socialist women. Women of the League were reminded that they 'ought not to try to emulate man', but to 'excel as woman in all that is most feminine and womanly'.[37] Most Primrose League women were not seeking full equality in all areas of political work, and wished to retain gendered restrictions on their behaviour. They placed great value on the fact that women possessed 'influence' in politics. 'We don't wish to govern the country', Lady Jersey reminded the Grand Council, 'we want to assist in placing men in government'.[38] Accepting limits prompted the Ladies' Grand Council ruling that discussion of contentious issues was beyond its scope. Meresia Nevill explained how Grand Council Dames would not 'wrangle … on … Female Suffrage and other topics concerning which there is such diversity of opinion'. When the Conservative suffragist Frances Power Cobbe wrote a letter to the Ladies' Grand Council attempting to open up a debate on this topic, she was rebuffed on the grounds that it was not their intention to 'enter into contentious politics'.[39]

As momentum built up around the suffrage question in organisations outside the League, this restriction began to irk some Conservative women. A few local habitations held one-off suffrage meetings from the late 1880s.[40] Others, along with the Scottish National Habitation, passed resolutions in favour of giving parliamentary votes to women despite the League's official position that this exceeded its remit. It soon became difficult for the Primrose League to avoid the issue. Some Dames took out joint membership with suffrage societies, and two from the Streatham Habitation were arrested on a militant suffrage demonstration. Externally suffrage societies looked to the League to take a view on the issue as a political organisation of women. The Grand Council recognised that divisions in the League ran deeper amongst Conservative women. The WLF had divided over how best to achieve suffrage, but not all members of the League wanted votes for women despite the fact that they were engaged in extremely public political activity. The Grand Council counted some of the country's most vociferous female anti-suffragists amongst its members, and at grass-roots level too not all Primrose League women were anxious for a parliamentary vote.

Other Conservative women's organisations

Philippe Vervaecke's thoughtful study of the Primrose League's attitude towards women's suffrage suggested that the polarisation of opinion around this issue was one of the key factors contributing to its decline. This may well be the case. As a mixed-sex organisation it was easy for the League to argue that it had no reason for considering suffrage above any other political issue, but this over-looked the fact that the political landscape was changing. By the start of the twentieth century the Primrose League was no longer the sole outlet for women seeking political involvement whose beliefs tended towards the conservative – with a large or small 'c'. A number of propaganda societies such as the Victoria League had strengthened the international networks of many elite women imperialists from both the Liberal and Conservative parties, while offering them the opportunity to engage in predominantly masculine debates regarding the future direction of the Empire.[41] Women whose political orientation was more strongly inclined towards the Conservative Party were also drawn to another auxiliary organisation, the Women's Unionist and Tariff Reform Association, which was rapidly gaining ground in the constituencies. A Women's Committee of the Tariff Reform League, set up in 1904, organised numerous constituency branches. In 1906 this amalgamated with remaining members of the Women's Liberal Unionist Association and became the Women's Unionist and Tariff Reform Association.[42] In 1909, in a move which predated the eventual merger of the Conservative and Liberal Unionists by two years (three in the case of Scotland), the remaining Women's Unionist Associations merged in to form the Women's Amalgamated Unionist and Tariff Reform Association (WAUTRA).

From the first signs of women's organisation in support of tariff reform, some Primrose League leaders felt threatened by its potential to draw women away from League work. Constance Davenport warned readers of the *Primrose League Gazette* of the 'danger in this new movement', which threatened to ignite feelings around a single issue to the extent that 'members may become isolated from their habitations'.[43] These fears were not misplaced; Conservative agents in Scotland reported a drift of female members into local branches of the Women's Unionist Associations, a trend replicated in England.[44]

As the national membership of the newer organisations increased, that of the Primrose League began to fall. It is also worth noting that, as these new groups did not admit men, their growth moved Conservative women to a model of organisation closer to that of the Women's Liberal Federation. Mitzi Auchterlonie has suggested that as well as the greater range of autonomy offered by single-sex organisations, the drift from the Primrose League was prompted by the 'more overtly political setting' offered by the newer groups, where controversial issues could be discussed more freely.[45] This may well be true. Although there is little research available to date on the membership activities or policies of the WAUTRA, it was clearly regarded as an important organisation by the Conservative Party. It was to this group rather than the depleted Primrose League that the Party leadership turned in the closing years of the First World War, when it became clear that women's suffrage was about to become a reality.

In its early years the WAUTRA was not an obvious supporter of women's suffrage. Anecdotal evidence suggested that pressure was being brought to bear on suffragists within the Association to drop their campaign for the vote if they wished to remain active members, while some of its prominent pro-suffrage members such as Lady Jane Strachey resigned in frustration at the Association's failure to take a public stand on the issue.[46] This posed problems for Conservative women who wanted to involve themselves in suffrage. The Primrose League was equally loath to commit itself on the issue, which left Conservative women with no option other than to join one of the existing non-party suffrage societies. Many had already done this. Lady Strachey, Lady Louisa Knightly and the Countess of Selbourne were active supporters of the National Union of Women's Suffrage Societies (NUWSS), and much of the leadership of the London Society for Women's Suffrage leaned towards the Conservative Party.

Militant suffrage too had its followers amongst Conservative women. Its most prominent advocate was Lady Constance Lytton, who served prison sentences and worked as a paid organizer for the Women's Social and Political Union. Other women with strong party identities found the politically neutral stance of both the constitutional and militant wings of the suffrage movement unsatisfactory. They also recognised that external organisations could not bring pressure on Conservative men through the mechanisms of party, as Liberal women tried to do through the WLF. In 1908 a group of Conservative suffragists proposed a solution to the problem by starting a Conservative and Unionist Women's Franchise Association. Their idea was to set up an organisation that would campaign specifically for votes for women but would do this within the context of Conservative politics. This would allow Conservative suffragists to sidestep the prevarication of both the Primrose League and the WUTRA on the issue without compromising their party loyalty through working in an apolitical suffrage group.

The Conservative and Unionist Women's Franchise Association

Several factors explain why the Conservative and Women's Franchise Association emerged when it did. Most accounts of its formation agree that Conservative suffragists were concerned by the formation of a Women's National Anti-Suffrage League in July 1908.[47] Both this and the Men's League for Opposing Women's Suffrage, which was formed the next year, had many Conservatives among their leadership. The Women's League was led by Lady Jersey, president of the Victoria League and a former president of the Primrose League's Ladies' Grand Council, who was 'thoroughly at home within the inner circles of the Conservative Party'. Conservative suffragists feared that much of the ground they had recently made within their party might be lost under pressure from the new organisation.[48]

The CUWFA adopted a style of presentation which aped that of the Anti-Suffrage League, particularly through its emphasis on promoting the names of its titled or aristocratic supporters.[49] As well as reacting to the consolidation of Conservative opposition to suffrage, the CUWFA was also responding to the possibility that votes for women were becoming imminent. Martin Pugh in particular has noted how Tory anxiety about the likelihood of the Liberal Party initiating further franchise extension via adult suffrage was now harnessed to calls for limited women's suffrage. This was seen as a more controllable measure which could be presented as conservative in both senses of the word.[50] A further trigger for the CUWFA's formation, although less easy to quantify, may be seen in some women's desire to adopt the dual public identity of Conservative and suffragist, as Liberal women did through the Forward Suffrage Union. There was also the question of the political leanings of other available suffrage organisations. Auchterlonie's study of Conservative suffrage noted increasing dissatisfaction with the NUWSS leadership's continued association with Liberalism, evidenced by Lady Knightley's appeal for Conservative suffragists to 'organise ... on party lines' to combat this.[51] Such discourses emboldened those inclined to take a more public stand, and in June 1908, before the CUWFA was formed, a group of Conservative suffragists accepted Millicent Fawcett's invitation to participate in the large NUWSS demonstration in London, where they marched under a party banner.

The CUWFA struck a chord amongst Conservative women. Membership grew rapidly – over 1,500 were enrolled by July 1909, according to its newspaper, the *Conservative and Unionist Women's Franchise Association Review* – and what had begun as a metropolitan committee developed into a network of branches throughout Britain. These extended from Glasgow to Bath, and had reached over 70 in total by 1914. The CUWFA made no attempt to duplicate the activities of other suffrage societies, or to take members away from these. Its distinction lay in its identity as a Party organisation where Conservative suffragists could convince other Conservatives of their cause. Lady Knightley explained in a letter to *The Times* that members would:

> Work on constitutional lines and will organize meetings and give lectures, by means of which they hope to convince and educate, without attempting to use coercive methods of any kind ... every effort [will be] made to have a large and representative body of Conservatives and Unionists pledged to assist their leaders, and to influence the Conservative party to extend the franchise to duly-qualified women.[52]

Party orientation was further emphasised in the Association's official objects, which were printed each month in the *Conservative and Unionist Women's Franchise Review*. These expanded Lady Knightley's vision for how the Association would target the Party, by suggesting that the Party would also impact on the Association. CUWFA members were expected to 'maintain the principles of the Conservative and Unionist Party with regard to the basis on which the Franchise should rest'. Much was made of women's supposedly innate Conservative tendencies, which would further the Party's fortunes if they were enfranchised. An insistence on constitutional methods was iterated, but only within the organisation itself. The Primrose League's Grand Council demanded the 'immediate resignation' of the two members of the Streatham Habitation who were arrested during a militant suffrage demonstration.[53] The CUWFA took quite a different approach to such actions on the part of its membership. It was prepared to tolerate low-level militancy by some of its members – indeed it supported the tactic of tax-resistance. There was no official prohibition on CUWFA members holding joint membership with the WSPU, although in practice the latter's insistence on an apolitical stance meant that few chose to do this. The majority of CUWFA members favoured constitutional suffrage, and thus the organisation was able to benefit from the NUWSS's growing association with the Labour Party, offering an alternative for Conservative women. Emily Davies resigned her membership of the NUWSS over this issue, to channel her suffrage campaigning into the CUWFA where she could work openly as a Conservative.

Although the CUWFA's main focus was on the vote, it could sometimes be seen engaging in broader considerations of the conditions surrounding women's social inequality. Auchterlonie's study of the organisation has suggested that contributors to the *Review* could be seen arguing in quite feminist terms on occasions, particularly when they were claiming to speak on behalf of working women, although their primary loyalty remained to their party rather than their sex.[54] Not all Conservative women wished for greater equality, however. Julia Bush's recent study has demonstrated how some held a very different view, which led them to take a prominent part in the anti-suffrage movement.[55] They maintained that further franchise reform was neither necessary nor desirable, and that women's participation in local politics should be considered sufficient.

Conclusion

Although conservatism and feminism are not usually connected, not all of the women who sought greater social and political equality for their sex in the nineteenth century were Liberals or socialists. The Conservative Party had benefited from the work of women as political hostesses from the eighteenth century, as had its Whig opponents. When political reforms demanded modernisation on the part of parties, the Conservative Party was slightly quicker to recognise the potential of women activists to help shape its response. Through their work in the Primrose League, Conservative women were able to build on the earlier role of the political hostess and develop political sociability into a strong associational culture. As in the Liberal Party, many entered the League through familial connections, but its popularity soon expanded beyond this to recruit a new generation of activists who were motivated by conviction rather than expectation.

Primrose League women were quick to push at the boundaries surrounding their work to take on a more public role. This was not restricted to propagandising, but expanded to include the task of providing political education for other women, sometimes covering topics that went beyond obviously 'women's issues'. Although the League could appear old-fashioned in its language and structures, it could also be self-consciously modern, and offered women some novel opportunities for political work through initiatives such as the cycling corps.

Although not all Conservative women supported the demand for parliamentary suffrage, they managed to avoid a damaging split on this issue through the CUWFA. This enabled Conservative women to campaign for the vote in a Party context rather than attempting to alter the policy of existing organisations. Their task was arguably easier than that of Liberal women, as the question of militancy did not threaten to undermine the Conservative Party in the same way as it did the Liberal government. The CUWFA's thriving network of branches shows that the pre-war decline in popularity of the Primrose League was not matched by a similar reduction in support for the Conservative Party amongst women. At the end of the First World War, the Party recognised this and responded to women voters as quickly as it had recognised their potential as Party workers in the previous century.

6
Women and Socialism

Introduction

From the 1890s, women who wanted to work through political parties no longer faced a stark choice between Liberalism and Conservatism. A growing socialist movement drew in many women members, particularly at local level where they became active in party branches and participated in a wealth of cultural organisations. For women on the left, the newly emerging socialist parties offered full membership and distinctive opportunities. The Independent Labour Party (ILP) took self-conscious pride in its ability to attract and retain women members. Women were also active in the Social Democratic Federation (SDF) and, from 1906, in the Labour Party. The latter's commitment to women's suffrage encouraged the development of the National Union of Women's Suffrage Societies (NUWSS) Election Fighting Fund, which established a formidable alliance between suffragists and Labour before the First World War. In more recent years, the interplay between labour history and women's history has encouraged research on socialist women. Thus we have more information about their political work before the First World War than exists for their liberal or conservative contemporaries.

The analyses of women's political participation that emerged from the Liberal and Conservative Parties were formed within national boundaries in response to women's attempts to move into party activity. Socialists' views were shaped through international discourses on what became known as the 'woman question'. The woman question was actively debated across different organisational levels. Discussions took place in local branches and regional and national party councils, but they also went beyond Britain. British delegates participated in the congresses of the Second International (1889–1914). There, they learned how different European socialist parties were providing space for women members and responding to their priorities. This knowledge circulated through discussions, pamphlets and socialist newspapers to reach all levels of membership. Such debates were not theoretical abstractions, as a number of studies have demonstrated. In Scotland, Eleanor Gordon has described how the definitions of sexual equality arrived at by the Independent Labour Party and the Women's Labour League impacted directly on what women were expected to do within these groups.[1] Karen Hunt's work on the Social Democratic Federation has similarly shown how its conceptualisation of the woman question influenced the range of organisational practices it developed, thus determining the roles women could take on within the Party.[2]

As we have seen, Conservative Party women did not produce a highly developed discourse outlining a philosophy of conservative feminism. Women in the Liberal Party were more productive in explaining their role and less concerned about being associated with an emerging women's movement, but it was socialists who produced the most detailed articulation of women's role in politics. Those with Marxist leanings (which included many in the early ILP) formed their arguments with reference to two key texts; August Bebel's *Women Under Socialism* (popularised by appearing as a précis in a series of articles by Eleanor Marx and Edward Aveling in the *Westminster Review* prior to the book's translation) and Frederick Engels' *Origins of the Family, Private Property and the State*. Both texts responded to socialists' fears about the effect a growing feminist movement might have on their parties. Feminist arguments about equality shared much with socialist thought, while the sense of urgency they brought to issues such as suffrage attracted many socialist women. At the same time, feminism downplayed socialism's concern with class differences, and argued that women had more in common with other women than with men from their own class. Bebel and Engels countered feminism through emphasising the role of class in women's oppression, and arguing that the abolition of class society was the way to end this, but had little to say about those problems that affected all women. The result, as Karen Hunt has described, was a degree of ambivalence towards the importance of the woman question which resulted in a variety of approaches, both theoretical and organisational.[3]

Recent research has drawn attention to the role that socialist women's own writings played in developing theories of women's political participation. Local and national socialist newspapers carried women's columns which were able to discuss issues deemed to have special interest to women. June Hannam and Karen Hunt have suggested that these columns represented an important space where women developed their own slant on socialism. Columns discussed women's role in political parties and the relationship between socialism and women's emancipation. They also tackled less obviously political issues. Katharine Bruce Glasier wrote about housework in the *Labour Leader*. She defended her decision on the grounds that this was also a class issue, and one that affected working-class women far more than the middle-class critics of the topic, who could 'place upon others the drudgery of cooking and looking after babies'.[4] In *The Clarion*, columnists Eleanor Keeling and Julia Dawson extolled the virtues of dress reform, and Dawson provided readers with a pattern for a gown without corset or stays.[5] Such discussions by socialist women did not completely reject contemporary gendered divisions of labour. Writings on housework praised the benefits that labour-saving devices or communal schemes offered women rather than critiquing the sexual division of domestic work. They also used women's maternal potential to justify their presence in politics, countering opponents' claims about women's innate conservatism on the grounds that their caring nature made them natural socialists.

Socialist women demanded inclusion in politics in more radical terms than those used by Conservative or Liberal women. They were less apologetic over wanting a role in their party, and less inclined to justify it in terms of their 'influence'. Although most socialist women embraced ideas that historians have described as 'feminist', they tended not to describe themselves in this way, as they saw feminism as a bourgeois movement and were wary of its aims. They were, however, less threatened than women in other parties by the figure of the 'New Woman'. While Conservative women refuted accusations that their political work made them 'New Women'; socialists like Eleanor Keeling happily defined a 'New Woman' as 'one who has high ideals on what life should be and … is determined to think for herself to use her newly discovered reasoning powers'.[6] Not all socialist men agreed, and the socialist press could caricature the 'New Woman' in vicious terms, prompting women socialists to demand 'an end to this silly sneering'.[7]

Socialist women and party organisation

In 1913 the ILP leader Keir Hardie proudly explained how his Party was:

> the one political organisation wherein women stand on terms of perfect equality with men. Women are eligible for election to the National council of the Party, and to the various offices on the same terms as men. From its earliest inception the ILP has taken a decided stand on the side of women's claim for political equality.[8]

Women's status as equal members in the ILP has led many historians to present the Party as the undisputed champion of women before the First World War. Olive Banks described it as 'feminist from its inception', while for Jill Liddington and Jill Norris, 'more than any other party [it] was sympathetic to the aspirations of feminism'.[9]

Against this optimistic picture, recent work has suggested that the ILP's theoretical desire for sexual equality at all levels of its organisation was harder to achieve in practice. While the Primrose League and the Women's Liberal Federation strove for an eclectic class mix in their local branches, socialist parties addressed a more restricted audience. They accepted middle-class applicants but their ideology and rhetoric focussed on recruiting a working-class membership, which had implications for women's recruitment. Few working-class men in nineteenth-century Britain enjoyed unlimited leisure time, but women were in a worse situation. Wives, mothers and older daughters frequently worked outside the home. Their work was usually demanding and low paid, and did not finish at the end of the working day, when they returned home to domestic chores. The ILP recognised what it described as the 'double burden' facing women in balancing paid and household labour. One of its pamphlets admitted that 'For a wife and mother to work all day and then to be called upon to do her housework at night is sufficient to drive one to revolting point.'[10] But noticing the problem was not the same as solving it, and many women who were drawn to socialism discovered that becoming politically active increased the amount of work that they were expected to do. Hannah Mitchell, whose political activity eventually broke her health, described how for married working-class women, embarking on political activism was like having to 'work with one hand tied behind us, so to speak'.[11]

Mitchell's comments may explain why many active socialist women agonised over whether to marry at all, and why those who did often ended up in political partnerships.[12] Some believed that a socialist marriage could enhance the work of both partners. 'You might be more useful together', Eleanor Keeling's friend wrote to her when she was debating a proposal from the editor of the *Labour Annual*, Joseph Edwards.[13] Katherine and John Bruce Glasier, Enid Stacy and the radical cleric Percy Widdrington, and Ada and George Nield Chew offered examples for less prominent socialist women to aspire to, and local branch records reveal many hitherto overlooked partnerships at the grass-roots. These differed from the familial politics of Liberal and Conservative women; socialist women were independently active in politics and met their husbands through shared political work.

Not all the partnerships succeeded. Annot Robinson's daughter believed that her father's jealousy over his wife's greater popularity as a speaker was a factor in the breakdown of their marriage. Socialist men who prided themselves on their advanced views with regard to women's participation in politics felt differently about their own homes. A correspondent to the Glasgow socialist paper *Forward* observed that although socialist men espoused sexual equality, many would 'shed … that belief along with the mud from his boots when he crosses the threshold of his own door'.[14] The difficulty women could face in taking an active role in socialism was reflected in the movement's language. British socialists often addressed each other as 'comrade'. This was supposedly a gender-neutral term, but the frequent awkward references to 'women comrades' in the socialist press suggest, as Karen Hunt has noted, that when parties spoke of 'socialists' they were referring almost exclusively to men.[15]

Socialist women directed much of their political energy into persuading men to develop an atmosphere that would encourage women's participation. Some branches held their main meetings on Sunday afternoon, with a Socialist Sunday school at the same time so that parents could attend together. Many socialist parties had their own premises with club rooms, and there were frequent debates over whether they should be licensed or not, some activists arguing that this would deter women from attending. Women rarely took on the key branch positions of secretary or treasurer, but were much more likely to involve themselves in the social side of the movement, organising entertainments, providing refreshments for meetings or clearing up at the end. This prompted some resentment; Hannah Mitchell's autobiography recalled how 'capable women [would] sit by with folded hands until a social or tea party is needed', when they would take a greater role.[16] However, some historians have argued that social roles were not necessarily marginal. David Clark's study of socialism in the Colne Valley found that organising 'teas and socials … stimulated the involvement of women in the working of the Labour clubs and the Labour Union'. Clark believed such activities were essential to promoting the distinctive socialist culture which sustained the movement in certain parts of Britain before the First World War.[17]

There were also local variations in attitudes towards women's participation. Katharine Bruce Glasier found that the ILP branches of the West Riding of Yorkshire displayed a more 'fruitful attitude to women' than those she visited in London and Glasgow, while another unnamed correspondent to the *Labour Leader* praised Northern socialists over those in London, who expected women to take a more subservient place.[18]

Few socialist women took on non-social roles, and even fewer managed to do so at national level. Most discovered greater autonomy when addressing problems faced by specific groups of women in their locality. Although socialists were wary of concentrating too much on issues that affected women as a sex, there was less concern over approaching women workers who were grouped in sex-segregated trades. In regions with high levels of female employment, socialist women organised working-class women into trade unions which they linked into the broader labour movement. Organisers such as Enid Stacy and Isabella Ford were often from more middle-class backgrounds, but were tireless in the efforts on behalf of working women. There were some exceptions; Ada Nield, who had worked as a tailoress in a Crewe factory, met the ILP when she attempted to unionise her co-workers, and went on to become a national ILP speaker and a local Poor Law Guardian. In Glasgow Fanny Abbot and Jane Rae joined the ILP as strikers at the Singer manufacturing works, but remained in the Party to play a leading role in Clydeside politics in later years.[19]

Itinerant propaganda helped spread socialism throughout Britain before the First World War, and offered a role for women. The most frequently mentioned women speakers are Caroline Martyn, Enid Stacy, Katharine Bruce Glasier and Margaret Macmillan, the 'famous four' whose names recur as examples of the ILP's progressive stance on women.[20] Hannam and Hunt have queried the emphasis on this group, which they suggest 'obscures the range of women who contributed to socialist politics' locally and also in other organisations such as the SDF.[21] Although not all women made national names for themselves, many had opportunities to propagandise beyond their local areas with the Clarion Van, which had at least one woman present on most of its tours. Socialism placed great emphasis on outdoor propaganda as the best (and cheapest) means of reaching large groups of apolitical listeners. This gave women further opportunities in their own districts. Some, including Emmeline Pankhurst in Manchester and Elizabeth Turner in Liverpool, even ended up in court for persisting in holding open air meetings in the face of opposition from local authorities.

Women's sections

Most of the socialist parties affiliated to the Second International discussed whether women should be organised in separate groups. Many socialist women in Britain felt these were unnecessary when they had equal membership with men. They feared that women's organisations could reduce their role to an auxiliary one. Others took the opposite view, and argued that for working-class women especially, a separate space where they could develop their confidence was an essential prerequisite to their taking a more equal and active part in Party life. Women's groups began to attach to local branches of the ILP and SDF and to local socialist societies in the 1890s. Their strength and success was very much dependent on who they managed to attract. In Scotland, the Glasgow Women's Labour Party, which included Isabella Bream Pearce and Lizzie Glasier, was a thriving body which sent delegates to the ILP's annual conference and devised its own election manifesto.[22] Elsewhere most groups restricted their activity to a weekly meeting rather than attempting to organise on a larger scale.

The ad hoc development of local socialist women's groups gave way to more systematic forms of national organisation from the early twentieth century. The Social Democratic Federation approved the establishment of women's socialist circles in 1904. These were coordinated by the Federation's National Women's Committee (later the Women's Education Committee), and 30 were formed within five years. Like other Party auxiliaries, women's circles started with the aim of reaching the 'wives, daughters and sisters' of SDF men who were already on the periphery of the movement.[23] Karen Hunt has argued that their formation implied that branch meetings were recognised as being less appealing to women, and shown how they strove to make women comfortable, meeting in members' homes and including music and refreshments.[24] Women's circles were involved in educational work. A Women's Education Committee drew up a national syllabus and provided specially commissioned essays so that all Circle members could participate in the weekly discussions. Unfortunately the circles did not survive the SDF's move into the British Socialist Party in 1911. The British Socialist Party developed no separate women's organisations, although small networks formed around individual branches.

A more successful model numerically was achieved by the Women's Labour League (WLL), which had 100 branches by 1911. The WLL was formed on the initiative of Mary Fenton MacPherson. MacPherson was active in the Railway Women's Guild, an organisation for the women relatives of unionised railwaymen, and wrote a woman's column for *Railway Review*, a union journal. She wished to see a Labour women's organisation on similar lines to the Guild, autonomous but integral to the overall movement, which would appeal to Party and trade union women. MacPherson convinced the Labour Representation Committee to take up the idea, and the League was formally inaugurated in 1906. Margaret Macdonald, wife of the Labour leader Ramsay Macdonald, was its first president, and Mary Middleton, wife of his assistant James, was the secretary. Sylvia Pankhurst believed that the League grew from a concern amongst men in the Labour movement that the activities of the militant wing of the suffrage movement were drawing women away from their ranks, although as Macpherson first approached the LRC in 1905 this seems unlikely.[25] It is more plausible that it responded to increasing pressure from Labour women seeking an autonomous space.

WLL branches formed throughout the country, but mainly centred on urban areas and industrial districts. It employed a small number of organisers, usually on a part-time basis, including Lisbeth Simm in the North East, Annot Robinson in the North West and Agnes Brown in Wales. WLL branches ran on similar lines to the SDF's women's circles. Afternoon meetings were experimented with as a means of maximising attendance. Their content aimed to balance political instruction, education and recreation. Many League members were socialists, but its broader Labour identity enabled it to work closely with other groups such as the Women's Industrial Council, with which it cooperated in investigating married women's work in 1908. It also attracted large numbers of ILP women, as this Party still offered no separate spaces for women members aside from those established through local initiatives. Christine Collette has argued that the WLL evolved an autocratic model of leadership which reduced initiatives by its branches.[26] Yet this does not appear to have prevented it from involving itself in a plethora of grass-roots activities including running candidates for local elections, as she herself observed.

In common with other women's auxiliary groups, the League believed that women had particular skills to bring to the political arena. This was most noticeable in the work it did in support of its candidates for Poor Law boards. An early League leaflet compared board work to 'housekeeping for a very big and very difficult family', where 'all sorts of questions arise which a woman knows more about, or can tackle better than a man'. The League organised national campaigns around issues relating to child welfare, especially the feeding of school children. Leicester WLL persuaded the local town council to form a charity to provide school meals. Branches in other areas lobbied their local authorities on the issue, and the League organised a national petition. WLL members also involved themselves in campaigns against the employment of women in sweated industries. During the wave of industrial unrest that covered Britain in 1911 they provided food and clothing for strikers' children. Such issues were typically left to women in politics, and were often presented as a 'softer' alternative to the more serious preoccupations of state or economics. Yet as Christine Collette's research has shown, League women worked hard to overcome hostility around their determination to shift responsibility for school meals from the hard-pressed working-class mother to the ratepayer.[27] The work of the League politicised the difficulties faced by many working-class wives, although it did so in a way that reinforced rather than challenged sexual divisions of labour.[28]

Socialist women and suffrage

At first the emergence of a strong, autonomous suffrage movement was less threatening to socialists than to members of other political parties. The ILP had repeatedly passed motions in favour of women's suffrage, including support for a limited equal suffrage measure, and the Labour Party had come out in favour of votes for women by 1912. This put socialist women who wanted the vote (the overwhelming majority) in a more comfortable position in relation to their Party than Conservative women, who were still attempting to wrest a commitment from Bonar Law. They were also spared the embarrassments faced by Liberal women when a government bearing the same Party name refused to move on the issue. Where women did have the vote in the field of local government, socialist groups encouraged their participation, leading John Bruce Glasier to suggest that the ILP was 'the first political party to promote the candidature of women for election onto public bodies'.[29] Liberal and Conservative women were not Party members, so they had to seek official endorsement as loyal supporters. ILP and SDF women were, so could argue alongside men for their inclusion on Party slates at selection meetings. Over a dozen socialist women were elected to various local bodies before the First World War.

The optimistic picture of a mutually supportive relationship between socialism and suffrage has been furthered through the work of historians such as Jill Liddington and Jill Norris, who suggested that the ILP and Labour Party's approach to suffrage was critical in enabling it to retain the support of large numbers of working-class Lancashire women working through the constitutional suffrage movement.[30] Yet, as Hannah Mitchell discovered through her own work for the ILP, 'Socialists were not necessarily feminists', and many socialist suffragists came to suspect the extent to which Labour men were prepared to push to deliver on their commitment.[31] The much-quoted remark of ILP leader John Bruce Glasier that he was forced to endure 'a weary ordeal of chatter about women's suffrage' from Christabel and Emmeline Pankhurst at one ILP meeting offers an example of the resistance that could be encountered.[32] Not all socialist women wanted to prioritise suffrage either, and some, like Julia Dawson, paid it little attention. Such attitudes persuaded Mrs Pankhurst to form the WSPU to work for suffrage within the ILP. Rachel Scott, the WSPU's first secretary and herself an active ILP member, explained to readers of *The Clarion*:

> As in the other political parties, so in the Labour Party, the help of women is welcomed in the work of elections; but when leaders and men members of the party are asked for efforts to be made to secure the enfranchisement of women, they express, at the best, vague sympathy. Every reform is considered more vital and more urgent than the removal of the unjust disability put on women.[33]

The WSPU did not immediately compromise other organisations of socialist women as many women worked for both groups. Teresa Billington, the ILP's first woman organiser, remained on the Party's payroll for 1905, while in Yorkshire Mary Gawthorpe was loath to leave her paid position with the Women's Labour League, explaining that at that point, to her mind the WSPU was a Lancashire organisation. Dual activity was more difficult after the WSPU altered its by-election policy in the summer of 1906. In line with Christabel Pankhurst's growing commitment to political independence, she and Teresa Billington declined to support the Labour candidate Robert Smillie at Cockermouth, working instead to 'keep the Liberal out', with the result that the Conservative candidate got in. Billington and Pankhurst were called to account for themselves at their local ILP branch, which decided not to expel them, although Christabel and her mother quietly resigned soon afterwards. From that point the WSPU was determined to be a politically independent organisation, and in theory members were supposed to stop any party-political activity on joining. There is evidence that the WSPU pulled a small number of women away from socialism. The president and general committee of Preston Women's Labour League resigned over the issue, and Nelson branch also ceded, complaining that too little attention was paid to suffrage. However many women carried on being active in both movements, suggesting that the WSPU's demand for political impartiality amongst its membership may have been somewhat exaggerated.

Women's or adult suffrage

While the Liberal and Conservative parties continued to deliberate whether they should take any position on suffrage, socialists' acceptance of the principle focused their debates on what sort of measure to adopt. Discussions centred on whether to support a limited bill or to hold out for a full adult suffrage measure. Many socialist women agreed with the view expressed by Elsie Harker from Manchester ILP, that a limited franchise for women to have votes on the grounds currently available to men would benefit middle and upper-class women whilst leaving working-class women powerless. Their interests, it was argued, would be better served by complete adult suffrage, which would simultaneously enfranchise working-class men. On the other hand, others felt that the principle of women being debarred from sharing in government was one that required challenging on equality grounds. Isabella Bream Pearce was one supporter of this view, and used her column in the *Labour Leader* to argue for it.[34] Socialist supporters of limited women's suffrage believed that sex discrimination for all women was worse than class discrimination for some.

In the 1890s there was little distinction between the two positions. No socialist woman who supported equal suffrage wished to see franchise extension stop there. They believed that in the short term equal suffrage was more achievable, but that this measure, once granted, would open the way for a full adult franchise. The ILP passed several resolutions in support of the equality principle, although these did not go through without debate. This altered as the suffrage movement became more organised at the beginning of the twentieth century. The WSPU worked hard to convince the ILP and the LRC to commit to support an equal franchise measure. In 1905, Keir Hardie, a strong supporter of the WSPU, initiated a survey which appeared to demonstrate that 80 per cent of the women who would be enfranchised under an Equality Bill would be working women. Women socialists who supported equal suffrage drew considerable ammunition from the results, although it was imprecise in its definition of 'working', and, according to Liddington and Norris, was only carried out in ILP branches thought to be sympathetic to equal suffrage demands, which called its findings into question.[35]

Adult suffragists were also sharpening their organisation. An Adult Suffrage Society (ASS) was formed in 1904, presided over by trade union organiser Margaret Bondfield. This attracted a number of women from the SDF, including one, Kathleen Kough, who turned the WSPU's own tactics against them by insisting on her right to move an amendment during a suffragette meeting in Reading.[36] The SDF's adherence to adult suffrage has encouraged historians to connect the ASS exclusively with this party, although it also recruited ILP women such as Ada Nield Chew. It was not until the SDF adopted an adult suffrage manifesto in 1907 that the two groups had become more closely associated. This link was strengthened when Dora Montefiore left the WSPU and joined the ASS, becoming its secretary in 1909. Her writings in *Justice* gave regular coverage to the society's activities, keeping them in front of the SDF's membership.[37]

Despite the undoubted commitment of women like Bondfield and Montefiore, the ASS was regarded with suspicion even by some who supported its demands. Charlotte Despard resigned from the society, claiming that it was 'not an honest movement' with 'little enthusiasm and no hope'.[38] Keir Hardie, whose sympathies had never lain with adult suffragists, dismissed it as a society which 'holds no meetings [and] issues no literature'.[39] Bondfield admitted that it had been inactive for much of 1906, but although its arguments gained ground in the WLL and elsewhere, the organisation itself remained, in Hunt's analysis, 'marginal' to the debate on adult suffrage within socialist parties.[40] A more influential organisation, the People's Suffrage Federation (PSF), was formed in 1909 by both Labour and Liberal supporters, including Mary Macarthur and Florence Balgarnie. The PSF attracted the support of a wide range of groups, including the Women's Labour League as well as a number of ILP branches, despite the Party's official adherence to equal suffrage. This brought some adult and equal suffragists closer together, although the ASS remained separate, disparaging the PSF's willingness to support some more limited suffrage measures for tactical reasons.[41]

Holton has argued that the division over limited or full suffrage was more important to the suffrage movement than that over militant or constitutional tactics. However, although the arguments were polarised, many moved between them. Ada Nield Chew, for example, engaged in a lively debate with Christabel Pankhurst in *The Clarion* in 1905, in which she strongly rejected Christabel's arguments for equal suffrage; by 1911 she was working as an organiser for the NUWSS. Others, such as the Wigan cotton worker and trade unionist Helen Silcock, moved from a strong limited suffrage position into the ASS.[42]

Conclusion

Socialist women enjoyed equal status with men in their parties. In theory this offered them opportunities to experience many forms of political activity as speakers and writers, as workers or candidates in local elections, and in a variety of official Party positions. In practice, however, as Hannam has observed, 'only a small minority of office holders were women', and the positions that they achieved tended to be closer to the grass-roots of Party activity, working as branch officials rather than on district or national committees.[43] Women were more likely to be found on committees charged with fundraising or arranging social events than those concerned with shaping Party strategies. While this work was vital for the growth and retention of Party membership, many women clearly felt the need for a more autonomous position, and pushed for separate forms of organisation within the overall Party structure.

In common with their contemporaries in Conservative and Liberal organisations, socialist women were challenged by the growing suffrage movement and the competing positions of limited and adult suffrage. They also differed in their attitudes over feminism. Many socialist women developed a gendered politics which suggested that working women were disadvantaged by their sex as well as their class. Others were more concerned with advancing the cause of socialism, and would not push women's issues forward if they felt that these conflicted with Party demands. Different positions on the 'woman question' were widely debated at all levels of the socialist movement, although the tensions between sex and class were never wholly resolved by socialist women before the First World War.

Postscript: women, political parties and the First World War

The outbreak of war in August 1914 disrupted the normal political processes. A coalition government was set up, elections suspended and a combative model of politics replaced by one of cooperation and party truce. This diminished political activity for a number of reasons. Without elections, there was less need to canvass or engage in propagandising. Many contentious political issues were put on hold for the duration of the war, or at least for its early years. The auxiliary organisations and women's sections of political parties reduced their activity in line with a general downturn in levels of activism.

The Women's Liberal Federation and the Conservative and Unionist Women's Franchise Association put much of their energy into the sort of low-level war work favoured by the NUWSS, which focused on relieving the worst effects of the war on women. They involved themselves in a variety of welfare work, often at branch level, although the CUWFA did sometimes join in other suffrage groups in speaking of the need to 'keep the suffrage flag flying'. For socialist women the position was slightly more complex. The Women's Labour League had always been committed to internationalism, and had sent delegates to the congresses of the Second International. The League's publication *Labour Woman* reported international events, and in common with other socialist publications adopted an anti-militarist tone before the war. Some League members were overt pacifists, including the South West organiser Bertha Ayles, whose husband Walter was one of the founders of the No Conscription Fellowship. The League sent a small number of delegates to the 1915 Labour and Socialist Women's International which Clara Zetkin organised in Bern. The meeting sent its greeting to the Hague conference at which the Women's International League for Peace and Freedom was formed, but many socialist women felt that this was more of a feminist than a socialist body. A group of women socialists in Glasgow responded by setting up their own organisation, the Women's Peace Crusade (WPC), which brought class politics into pacifism. By November 1917 there were almost 50 active WPC branches throughout Britain.

As well as anti-militarist efforts socialist women involved themselves in a number of other campaigns during the war. Socialists were less rigorous in observing ideas of cooperation with the war effort, as their analysis of the conflict held that bourgeois governments were responsible. There were a number of neighbourhood-based campaigns throughout Britain. In one well-known example women took an active part in the Clydeside rent strikes in 1915, while in other districts socialist women helped organise protests against unequal rationing. In addition to these oppositional politics, many socialist women found that wartime conditions brought them into a range of local and national committees dealing with issues such as food management, the welfare of soldiers' and sailors' families, and training schemes for women workers. They also kept a close eye on working conditions in the predominantly female trades such as munitions. After the armistice some socialist women argued against sacking women to make way for a returning male workforce, although the majority of trade unionists did not support them in this.

When the Representation of the People Act was passed in March 1918 Britain's three main political parties all had thriving women's organisations. Women were experienced Party activists with a tradition of involvement that spanned almost four decades. They had stood as Party candidates in local elections as well as working tirelessly for men in parliamentary contests. They had become experienced propagandists, speaking and writing on behalf all parties and often directing their messages specifically at other, less politicised women. Many of these experiences were shared by women across all parties, but there were some areas of difference. Liberal and Conservative women remained in auxiliary bodies outside of the main Party organisations. Socialist women were equal Party members, but had opted for separate sites of organisation as well. Women in all political parties were challenged by the rise of militant tactics for suffrage, although not all responded in the same way. While some Liberal women had been embarrassed by the way their Party was targeted by militant suffragettes, others found their patience with it was pushed to its limit by the attitude of men like Asquith to this question. Conservative women benefited from the anti-Liberal tone of militant suffrage but were unable to shift the men in their Party to a definite commitment on the issue. Labour women also gained when they found their numbers swelled by former Liberal suffragists encouraged by the Election Fighting Fund.

The growth of autonomous, non-party women's organisations posed further questions for women in political parties. Conservative and socialist women could both be uneasy with describing themselves as 'feminists' for different reasons. Conservative women were uncertain about feminism's radical connotations, while socialist women feared that its emphasis on gender would dilute the primacy of class in political analyses. Liberal women, who were more comfortable with the term, were disappointed by their Party's seeming inability to transform its long sympathy with feminism into concrete legislative reform. Some women chose to suspend their Party work at the height of the suffrage campaign and devote their energies to the suffrage movement. At the end of the First World War, when a partial franchise was awarded, they had to decide whether or not they would return. At the same time, Party men were thinking about how best to reconfigure their organisations to accommodate women as equal members and to attract women voters.

Part 3
Women's Politics
after the Vote

7

Women Members
of Parliament

Introduction

The Representation of the People Act of 1918 redefined the political status of British women. Their involvement in formal party-political structures had altered throughout the nineteenth century as parties responded to the demands of industrialisation, an expanding electorate and a rise in contested elections. Women had played an important role in shaping party responses through their work in auxiliary organisations, or, if they were socialists, also as equal members. The numbers of women involved in local government grew and their involvement became more formalised as the state took over many of their traditional charitable and philanthropic roles. During the First World War, government increasingly expected women to pay a role in administration and set up bodies such as the Central Committee for the Employment of Women to enable this. Yet despite suffragists' best efforts, Parliament remained closed to women.

In 1918 this changed. The Representation of the People Act enfranchised women aged over 30 provided they occupied (or were married to the occupier of) property with an annual value of not less than £5. Women graduates could also vote for candidates for the combined universities constituencies. The 1918 Act fell short of the total equality that suffragists had demanded. It did not deliver votes for women on the same terms that they were given to men. All men over 21 (younger if they had served in the war) now had a vote regardless of their property-owning status. Young women, and many older ones who were unmarried or working class, remained disenfranchised. The women's movement kept up a strong campaign for full political equality until 1928, when women were finally awarded the vote on the same terms as men. By this point there were already a small number of women sitting in Parliament as MPs. Women, in theory, were now equal citizens fully integrated into the British polity and able to become part of the party elite. In practice, feminist campaigners were to find that the transformation of British politics which they had predicted would follow the women's votes remained elusive.

This chapter describes the experiences of women MPs in Parliament. It explores selection procedures and party attitudes to question why so few women succeeded in being elected, as well as considering whether those who did considered themselves to be representing their sex as well as their chosen party.

The first election attempts

It was not immediately clear that the Representation of the People Act allowed women to stand as parliamentary candidates. When the question was raised, responses were as strongly polarised as they had been over women's suffrage. Anti-suffragists had long argued that women MPs were the logical conclusion to women's votes, and had predicted that dire consequences would follow from any feminisation of parliamentary systems. The prime minister denied that the Act changed anything in regard to women's candidacy. This worried feminist observers who had always wanted to see women representing women. Eleanor Rathbone feared that the government was appeasing anti-suffrage opinion by delaying women MPs, so that full political equality 'would probably be a generation in coming'.[1] Others were not content to accept this. Nina Boyle of the Women's Franchise League (WFL) forced the issue by standing herself at the Keighley by-election in May 1918. She was disqualified because of irregularities in her nomination papers, but the returning officer was adamant that his decision had nothing to do with her sex. Qualification, he explained, was to be determined elsewhere. Had her papers been in order, he would have been happy to accept her. This was enough to persuade both the Independent Labour Party and the Labour Party to endorse women as prospective parliamentary candidates. The ILP put a small number of women including Margaret Bondfield and Ethel Snowden onto its lists, and the Labour Party adopted Mary Macarthur as its candidate for Stourbridge.

In its final days the coalition government ended the confusion around women's status as candidates and allowed a free vote on the issue. The Parliament (Qualification of Women) Bill was introduced by the Liberal MP Herbert Samuel in October 1918. The bill made women eligible to stand for Parliament on equal terms to men, ironically allowing women between 21 and 30 to stand for a Parliament that they could not elect. The women's movement geared itself up for a strong campaign in support of the bill, but this proved unnecessary. Edith How Martyn and other ex-suffragettes who had gathered in the Ladies' Gallery for the debate heard the opposition collapse. Herbert Asquith, a long-standing opponent of women's suffrage, now declared himself broadly in favour of women MPs. Arnold Ward announced that his National League for Opposing Women's Suffrage (which had more or less disbanded anyway) would offer no opposition. Only one MP, Admiral Sir Hedworth Meux, the Conservative member for Portsmouth South, fought against the proposal. Meux claimed that Parliament, with its late hours, was no place for a respectable woman. Rather than the familiar cry of 'Who goes home' to signal the end of a debate, he suggested, 'It will be a question of who will take me home?'[2] Meux's pseudo-chivalrous thoughts were out of step with the overall mood at Westminster. The bill was rushed through, passing into law on 21 November 1918, just in time for women to stand as candidates in the first general election since the war.

Scarcely three weeks remained between the bill's passage and the election date of 14 December. Having won the right to stand, women now faced the far greater hurdle of finding a seat. The suffrage campaign had politicised many Edwardian women and given then a valuable grounding in public life. What it had not done was prepare them to secure parliamentary nominations at short notice, in a party-dominated system which remained overwhelmingly male. As Elizabeth Vallance observed, the Edwardian women's movement was at heart a non-party affair, a stance which put it at odds with the organisation of Parliament as well as the processes through which would-be MPs were selected.[3] Many women had stepped aside from party activism to put their energies into suffrage; not all wished to return. Those who did found their re-entry complicated by the circumstances of this particular election, especially if they were Liberals or Conservatives. Although Lloyd George led the coalition government, he did not enjoy the support of the entire Liberal Party, many of whom remained strong supporters of Asquith. Lloyd George's coalition Liberal supporters decided to fight the election in an alliance with the Conservative Party, endorsing their preferred candidates with a 'coupon' or letter of approval from Lloyd George and Bonar Law. As coupons represented the government's seal of approval they increased a candidates' chance of getting elected. As a result they were much sought-after, and had been allocated in most constituencies before November. Thus, the generation of women who had fought hardest for the vote were not necessarily in the best position to capitalise on their new political equality. Only 17 women stood as candidates in December 1918, and of these only nine were adopted by the three main political parties. Sinn Fein provided a further two women candidates for seats in Northern Ireland. The remaining six (with the exception of Christabel Pankhurst, who represented the Women's Party) stood as independents, backed by existing feminist organisations such as the Women's Freedom League. Pankhurst was the only woman candidate with a coupon.

Not all feminists looked to political parties at this time. The strength and coherence of the Edwardian women's movement convinced some women that their interests would be better served by a completely different political model, with women representing themselves. In November 1917, Emmeline and Christabel Pankhurst transformed the WSPU into the Women's Party, which would replace 'men's political machinery and traditions, which ... leave so much to be desired' with a new party that determined its policies on gendered interests.[4] Its programme was an odd mixture. The anti-Bolshevism Christabel and Emmeline Pankhurst had developed during the war was combined with ideologies inspired by their much earlier affiliation to socialism, hence its call for a variety of social improvements which would benefit working-class women such as forms of communal housekeeping.[5] The Women's Party agreed with the established parties that there was a 'woman's vote' which would be secured through appeals to gender rather than class or party. When the Parliament (Qualification of Women) Act was passed, the Women's Party announced that

Christabel Pankhurst was its sole candidate, and put all its efforts and resources into her campaign.

Lloyd George agreed to help Christabel find a suitable seat. It was announced that she would be standing for Westbury, in Wiltshire, but she soon renounced this constituency in favour of the newly formed one of Smethwick in the West Midlands, where she persuaded Bonar Law to convince the couponed Conservative candidate to stand aside. The decision, which Martin Pugh believed was prompted by her drift to the right, as it offered the chance of defeating a Labour candidate in a two-way fight in an industrial constituency, cost her the election.[6] The Westbury seat she had declined was comfortably won by the replacement couponed candidate, but Smethwick proved much more difficult, and after a recount she conceded that she had lost by 775 votes. Pankhurst subsequently left politics, devoting her remaining campaigning energies to the cause of Second Adventism.

Most of the other women candidates did no better, making the first election a disappointment for the women's movement. Only Constance Marcievicz was elected, but as a Sinn Fein candidate she did not take her seat. The 'constitutional experiment', as *The Times* dubbed it, made no difference at all to the gender of Parliament. The women's movement, both within and outside political parties, attempted to analyse the reasons for its candidates' failure. Its evaluation of the experiences of the nine women who had stood as party representatives made much of the timing of the election, which had made it very difficult for women to secure such nominations. Male candidates had been 'nursing' constituencies for several years if they were not already representing them, making it difficult for women to compete or to present themselves as anything other than outsiders to a local electorate.

Other particular circumstances attached to this election militated against several of the women candidates. The coupon was one, although women trying to get into Parliament continued to describe problems in being selected for winnable seats up to the 1980s. Certain wartime experiences worked against some women. Cheryl Law's research showed how the pacifist connections of seven candidates drew accusations of pro-Germanism; Charlotte Despard and Ray Strachey both had their meetings disrupted.[7] The unpopularity of feminist pacifism was confirmed by the experience of Mrs Dacre Fox, who had been an outspoken participant in the WSPU's patriotic campaign against Germany and outpolled many better-known women candidates despite her record of suffragette militancy.

A final factor suggested was one returning officer's insistence that Mary Macarthur, who was recently married, appeared on the ballot paper as Mary Reid Anderson. Of all the women candidates, Macarthur was the one thought most likely to succeed. She had been selected for Stourbridge as part of the Labour Party's decision to endorse women candidates in advance of the Qualification Bill, which gave her time to work up a campaign in an area where she was already known through her trade union organising. Macarthur blamed her inability to translate her popularity amongst working-class women into votes on the fact that she had been 'robbed' of her name. Her biographer Margaret Cole concurred that this decision may well have cost her many votes amongst her strongest supporters, as 'illiterate women who had never voted before did not realize that the unfamiliar name signified ... their leader and inspirer'.[8] Yet it is unclear how many of these would have had a vote, and the effect of the name change is not easy to quantify. There was, after all, only one female candidate at Stourbridge. Elsewhere Violet Markham persuaded the returning officer to let her stand under her maiden name, but she still lost the contest.

The 1918 election ended the Women's Party experiment and challenged the women's movement's commitment to independence. Women's organisations worked hard on behalf of independent women candidates despite their limited resources. Many feminists had been convinced that the vote presented an opportunity to move away from masculinised party politics and develop a new feminist coalition. They expected that women would vote for women, but the results did not bear this out. Independent women candidates did badly at the polls, and three (Ray Strachey, Eunice Murray and Edith How Martyn) lost their deposits. Hence one immediate casualty of the 1918 election was the feminist hope for a regendering of British party politics. The proportion of independent women candidates dropped sharply at the next election, and remained consistently low thereafter (see Table 7.1). The WFL and the National Union for Equal Citizenship (as the NUWSS had become) felt that better education of the electorate might make voters more prepared to vote for women candidates as well as for independents, but few of their own members were prepared to put this to the test at election time. The WFL took a more radical position, and called for a proportion of seats to be reserved for women as a means of speeding up the process of electing women MPs, but no large campaign developed around this either. In the inter-war period, Eleanor Rathbone was the only woman who succeeded in being elected as an independent MP, and this was for the very particular and limited constituency of the Combined English Universities. The overwhelming majority of women who sought election to Parliament did so as representatives of political parties.

The first elected women

In 1919, Waldorf Astor's succession to the House of Lords caused a by-election in his Plymouth constituency. At his suggestion his wife Nancy was adopted as the Conservative candidate, and elected with a respectable majority of over 5,000. Although she declared her intention not to be 'a sex candidate', Astor's campaign paid particular attention to temperance, an issue long promoted by Conservative women in their political work. As Astor had played no part in the suffrage movement, her appointment met with mixed responses amongst suffragists. The *Women's Leader* later expressed the collective disappointment that the first woman MP was neither 'one of ourselves' nor 'a woman of tried political experience', but 'someone entirely outside our own world'.[9] Nevertheless, feminists determined to make the best of the opportunity of having a woman in Parliament. *Common Cause* noted that although Astor was not part of an organised movement, she had demonstrated her commitment to equal opportunities 'practically, and in a way which will make it easier for other women to prove theirs'.[10] Former suffragist Ray Strachey offered to act as Astor's political advisor. She did this because she believed it:

> so important that the first woman MP should act sensibly; and she, though full of good sense of a kind, is lamentably ignorant of everything she ought to know as a Member of the House.[11]

Astor accepted the offer, and Strachey worked for her until the summer, which drew the first woman MP into contact with the opinions and agendas of the main feminist organisations. Astor proved herself a quick learner; she built on her contacts and developed others, and her enthusiasm for women's organisations and issues surprised many who had been sceptical on her election. She was soon counted as a strong fellow traveller within the women's movement.

The next woman MP was a Liberal, Margaret Wintringham. She too was elected in a by-election at Louth in 1921 caused by the death of her husband, the sitting MP. Like Astor, Wintringham was a popular constituency wife. She had also been active on her own part in many local capacities, as a magistrate and a member of the Grimsby Education Committee. Because of her recent bereavement Wintringham took no active part in her own campaign, which she won with a majority of 723 votes. A third woman, Mrs Mabel Philipson, was elected in May 1923, again in a by-election for a seat formerly occupied by her husband, but in different circumstances from Astor and Wintringham. Hilton Philipson's agent had been found guilty of malpractice so he was disqualified from office, although as he had no knowledge of the fraud, his popularity in the constituency remained intact. Hilton Philipson had fought two success-ful elections on behalf of the National Liberals; his wife opted to stand as a Conservative, holding the seat for family rather than Party. She secured a majority of over 6,000, larger than that of her husband.

Thus the first three women to be elected to Parliament were not part of the women's movement, although they had political experience as party wives. The pattern was replicated in Scotland and Wales. Scotland's first female MP, Katharine, Duchess of Atholl, also took over her husband's former seat although it had briefly been held by another Unionist MP after Lord Tullibardine received his peerage. In Wales, Megan Lloyd George owed some of her electoral success to the fame of her father. Some historians have concluded that their status as wives – or widows or daughters – of successfully elected men was a significant factor in the success of early women candidates. Brian Harrison argued that this 'male equivalence' eased women's arrival into the House of Commons by allowing them to present themselves as replacements for acceptable but unavailable men rather than part of a feminist vanguard.[12] Elizabeth Vallance concurred that the 'halo effect' that derived from women replacing their husbands in seats already held by them allowed them to allay fears amongst the electorate that women seeking office would be 'too radical, brash, feministic and iconoclastic', but further argued that it had the added advantage of placing women candidates into winnable seats, a position that eluded them elsewhere.[13] According to Beverley Stobaugh's research this tendency was particularly strong in the Conservative Party, where seven of the successful women candidates up to 1935 sat in seats previously occupied by their husbands.[14] Electoral statistics support the idea that male equivalence was important, at least for the earlier period. In the 1922 election, for example, the number of women candidates was double that of 1918, but only two – Lady Astor and Mrs Wintringham, who were defending seats won in by-elections – were returned to Westminster.

Numbers of women MPs

The number of women MPs rose slowly in the inter war period. Table 7.1 shows a small but steady rise (with a slight falling back) in the number of women candidates who stood at the six general elections between 1918 and 1935. There was a much smaller rise in the number of women elected, which peaked at 15 in 1931, falling back slightly in 1935. Between 1918 and 1939 a further 31 women stood as Conservative, Labour or Liberal candidates at by-elections, with 10 succeeding in entering Parliament through this route.[15]

Women candidates increased in number after the Second World War: 127 stood in 1951, although their number then remained below 100 until a further peak of 216 in 1979. The rise in women candidates did not lead to a corresponding rise in the numbers elected, which never exceeded 29 (in 1964), and fell back slightly from this figure for much of the 1960s, to decrease to 19 in 1979.[16] Thus Britain's first female prime minster presided over a House of Commons in which only 3.0 per cent of MPs were women, a figure that barely exceeded the 2.3 per cent returned after the first election when women had voted on equal terms with men, 50 years earlier.[17]

Several explanations have been offered for the continually small numbers of women MPs. Historians have largely focused on the period before 1945, although many of their findings for this earlier period concur with those of political scientists whose attention has been concentrated on post-war elections. Women's most immediate problem, as this chapter has already suggested, was in getting selected for a winnable seat. Studies suggest that women candidates' chances did not differ significantly between parties. Labour women faced an

Table 7.1   Women Candidates in General Elections 1918 – 1935[i]

Date	Conservative	Labour	Liberal	Independent	Other	Total	Elected
1918	1	4	4	5	3	17	1
1922	5	10	16	2	0	33	2
1923	7	14	12	1	0	34	8
1924	12	22	6	1	0	41	4
1929	10	30	25	1	3	69	14
1931	16	36	6	1	3	62	15
1935	19	35	11	2	0	67	9

[i] Overall table figures are taken from Pamela Brookes, *Women at Westminster* (London, 1967). Independent candidates have been identified though broader reporting in sources such as *The Vote*.

easier task in theory, working in a Party that had been committed to sexual equality from the outset. In practice, Pamela Brookes found that the slightly higher proportion of women standing as Labour candidates often 'had to fight difficult seats' in constituencies not previously held by their Party, which gave them less chance of success than women representing other parties.[18] They were also less likely to have union support. Millie Miller, who took Redbridge North for the Labour Party in 1974, had waited 20 years for a constituency. She felt that her lack of union experience outweighed her successful work as lord mayor, as 'a trade union sponsored candidate would be a first choice' at any selection meeting, and the most powerful unions represented predominantly male trades.[19] The Conservative Party relied more on a system of self-selection by potential candidates, which many felt worked against women, who could be more diffident about coming forward.[20] This is difficult to quantify, but is supported by the work of Joni Lovenduski and Pippa Norris, who found that in the post-war period, although women comprised a small majority of Conservative Party members, they were 'less politically confident and assertive than the men'.[21] For Liberal women, securing a winnable seat was complicated by their Party's decline, which continued throughout the twentieth century.

A number of women candidates represented minority parties, although there is little research on their experience to date. The Communist Party fielded a steady stream of women, starting with three in 1929 and peaking at nine in 1950. The British Union of Fascists selected a number of women candidates, although the outbreak of war meant that the anticipated general election did not take place. Thirty-six women stood on a National Front platform in 1979. There were also women candidates in Plaid Cymru and the Scottish Nationalist Party (SNP). Elizabeth Vallance has suggested that minority parties may have been willing to risk women candidates when they felt their electoral chances were low, pointing to a rise in candidates for the Liberal Party at the point when it began to 'feel the pinch electorally'.[22] Her findings are challenged by Catriona Burness' more recent research into women in the SNP, which suggests that the high-profile by-election successes of candidates such as Winnie Ewing at Hamilton encouraged an association between nationalism and women MPs, which paved the way for greater numbers of women candidates.[23]

The cost of becoming a candidate was another factor that worked against women's selection and election, particularly before the Second World War when candidates had to pay their own election expenses. In practice Labour candidates were helped by the local Party, but Conservative candidates were expected to foot the bill themselves. This disadvantaged women candidates, who had lower levels of affluence or economic independence. Mavis Tate, an effective and popular Conservative MP from 1931, told her Frome constituency that she could not afford to stand for re-election after her divorce left her considerably poorer in 1939.[24] Economic factors worked against women in other ways. Pat Hornsby-Smith, a Conservative MP from 1950, described how expecting pre-war women MPs to bear the cost of Westminster lodgings as well as their travel and secretarial expenses amounted to giving them 'the price of admission without the price of a ticket'.[25]

Women's groups outside Parliament have made attempts to increase the number of women MPs since Astor's arrival, but with little success. The National Union of Societies for Equal Citizenship (NUSEC) and the WFL suggested many measures to achieve this, including pressing for greater female involvement in the selection process. A small number of single-issue feminist organisations formed to further this aim. In 1921 the Women's Election Committee was set up by Dr Christine Murrell, a former suffragette. This supported a number of candidates in early elections, providing canvassers and also funds, as Murrell explained to readers of *Time and Tide* that the cost of a deposit alone put a candidacy beyond the reach of most women.[26] The initiative had folded by the 1930s, 'paralysed', according to Harold Smith, by 'the conflict between new and equality feminists'.[27] After the Second World War a similar group, Women for Westminster, emerged. Unlike the Women's Election Committee this aimed to work more within parties, offering suitable names for inclusion on selection lists while simultaneously encouraging female party members to nominate them.[28] In this way they hoped to avoid accusations of outside interference, yet this initiative too had folded by 1948, partly, according to Martin Pugh, because party-political women were suspicious of externally imposed feminist agendas.[29] It was left to broader-focused feminist bodies such as the Six Point Group to continue to prioritise this issue beyond the Second World War. In the competition for securing a nomination, the backing of a feminist organisation was not necessarily a help to the would-be woman candidate. It was not until the late 1970s that this division was bridged, when a new generation of party-political women influenced by second-wave feminism began to demand the implementation of equal opportunities policies within their own parties.[30]

Party members or women MPs?

Studies of women MPs have focused on the extent to which they acted collectively as women. Women MPs were aware of both the potential and the danger of this, especially during what Stobaugh termed 'the pioneer period', the early years of women's presence in Parliament up to 1945.[31] A focus on what united women MPs as women, rather than what divided them as party members, has informed the few historical studies to engage directly with their activity. Their small numbers have enabled detailed comparison of their work in the House in investigations underpinned by the methodology of collective biography. For Brian Harrison, the 'women MPs' had more to unite than to divide them. Harrison's analysis emphasized the hostility that women faced in Parliament in the inter-war period, ranging from the misogyny of men who ignored Astor, to the more subtle 'half-conscious forms' of anti-feminism suggested by the combative, adversarial styles of debate and a late hours, drinking and smoking culture which replicated that of gentlemen's clubs.[32]

As the hostile reaction to women MPs was provoked by their sex rather than their party, it was not surprising that they developed a degree of solidarity as they attempted to format collective responses. Harrison's account explained how the spatial arrangement of the House of Commons assisted this. The first women to arrive at Westminster discovered that parts of its precincts remained closed to them. Outside the debating chamber they confined themselves to the Women Members' Room which had been hurriedly provided for Lady Astor. In 1927 eight women were still sharing its three desks, two armchairs, two sofas and one small mirror. The nearest bath stood a quarter of a mile of corridors away, and there was no dressing room until Edith Picton-Turbervill demanded one in 1931. Women MPs shared facilities until the 1970s, when separate 'sitting rooms' appeared for Conservative and Labour women, which discomfited some longer-serving members.[33] Other spaces were more difficult to access. Ellen Wilkinson succeeded in opening the Strangers' Dining Room to women in 1928, but successive attempts to allow women observers to sit in the Distinguished Strangers' Gallery or to enter the Smoking Room without male invitation were rebuffed for many years. Exclusion from the Smoking Room restricted women MPs' ability to progress beyond the backbenches. The few who were selected as parliamentary private secretaries were disadvantaged as they were less able to remain in touch with professional gossip and thus to keep their ministers adequately briefed.

All of the early women MPs found that their appearance was scrutinised. Nancy Astor determined on a plain outfit of white shirt and black suit, but found much attention focused on her trademark tricorn hat and whether she should remove it when speaking. The Speaker's ruling that women were free to make their own choice in this matter did not preclude Colonel Appelin protesting when Ellen Wilkinson spoke without a hat five years later. Wilkinson's casual style was condemned; other women were criticised for being overdressed. Lady Terrington expressed her intention to 'wear [her] best clothes' to Parliament during her election campaign in 1923, provoking a scathing headline about 'furs and pearls' in the *Daily Express*.[34] The emphasis on women's appearance continued throughout the period of this study; repeated references to 'blonde Mrs Oppenheim' in the 1970s echoed newspaper descriptions of Irene Ward as 'the only blonde in the House' when she arrived there in 1931.[35] The persistence of such attitudes led Elizabeth Vallance to conclude that clothes became an important way for men to continue to 'set the parameters and define the rules of parliamentary form', perpetuating women's exclusion.[36]

Other factors impacted equally on all women MPs. Many of those elected in the inter-war period remarked on the weight of expectations on them, which exceeded those attached to men. Thelma Cazalet believed that 'the relative rarity of women MPs in the early thirties' meant that they 'had many more calls upon [them] than the average MP' for press interviews and public appearances.[37] It was sometimes unclear whom women MPs were meant to represent. Nancy Astor's postbag regularly exceeded 2000 letters a week from all over Britain, filled with women's rather than constituency problems. The Duchess of Atholl summarised the dilemma facing women who were elected as party candidates by a mixed electorate, only to find that they were then expected to be answerable to 'the women of the country … thinking that it is they who have sent you there and that you are only responsible to them'.[38] Pressure could also be exerted by the feminist organisations that had offered women valuable help, practically and financially, in their election campaigns. This was not all one way. Many women MPs had worked in the women's movement before entering Parliament, and others such as Lady Astor became convinced feminists as a result of their parliamentary experience and worked with the women's movement once elected. Yet with the exception of Eleanor Rathbone, all were party representatives sent to Westminster by electors who saw themselves as voting for a party and not an individual candidate. This meant that women MPs could sometimes be forced to choose between competing claims on their office.

When faced with hostility provoked by their sex it is not surprising that women MPs could unite. Nancy Astor was known for her unobtrusive acts of kindness to other women MPs throughout her time in Parliament; Pat Hornsby Smith found that in the 1950s and 1960s a particular friendliness existed between women MPs across parties 'because there are so few of them', while in the 1970s the practice of attending a woman's maiden speech regardless of her party was 'almost a tradition' amongst other women MPs.[39] Nevertheless, all women MPs apart from Eleanor Rathbone were party members, and many, even those who worked cooperatively on some occasions, were at pains to refute accusations that they were in Parliament to serve the interests of their sex. There was little interest in forming a women's group. Nancy Astor set up a Consultative Committee of Women's Organizations in March 1921, building on the attempts of the NUWSS to establish such a body during the First World War. This aimed to provide a single voice for the 49 separate feminist societies that affiliated to it, although those on the left remained apart, distrusting its political leanings. The Committee's regular evening soirees, hosted by Astor, offered valuable opportunities for trans-organisational networking as well as acting as a conduit between the external women's movement and the parliamentary world of MPs. It dissolved in 1928 amidst disagreement between its equality and welfare feminists, but in the next Parliament Astor attempted to form a more coordinated bloc amongst the 14 women MPs. She was rebuffed, by Labour members in particular.[40] '[T]here's no such thing as a woman MP', Alice Bacon told the young reporter who asked her about the height of heel favoured by women entering the Commons shortly after her election. Eleanor Rathbone, who remained strongly independent throughout her political career, felt that a Woman's Party was impossible 'because of politics'.[41] Successful female candidates had often triumphed over substantial hurdles to secure the backing of their parties, and were careful to preserve their carefully cultivated image of loyal political representatives as far as possible.

Women in the House

As party representatives women were as likely to divide on political issues as men when engaged in parliamentary business. There was not even unanimity over the question of equal franchise. Brookes' account of the debate on the second reading of the amendment that was finally passed in 1928 credited Wilkinson and Astor with 'pushing forward this final stage in the enfranchisement of women', forcing the Home Secretary to pledge on the issue before the final cabinet decision had been taken.[42] Yet not all women MPs agreed with this. The government, attempting to postpone the decision for as long as possible, found a willing ally in the Duchess of Atholl. She had been a strong anti-suffragist before the First World War and had never renounced her hostility to feminism. Atholl opposed further franchise reform on the grounds that it would give women a numerical advantage in the electorate at a point when they were insufficiently politically educated. However, her contribution to the debate revealed the class bias behind her position when she complained that the bill, if passed, would enfranchise women tinkers.[43]

Atholl's decision to prioritise class over sex was not unique to Conservative women MPs. Although they were also Labour MPs, Jennie Lee and Ellen Wilkinson stood firmly on the left of the Party and felt no solidarity as women with the Minister of Labour, Margaret Bondfield, as she struggled to keep unemployment relief within affordable levels during the economic crisis of the 1920s. For Lee and Wilkinson the privations of their working-class constituents were more important than loyalty to government policy or other women MPs. As their novelty value decreased after the Second World War, women MPs divided along party lines innumerable times. This led to some criticism from feminist organisations; Helena Normanton KC delivered a strong attack on the record of women MPs at a Suffragette Fellowship meeting in 1950, criticising their tendency to put party loyalty above feminist principle.[44] Yet, given the failure of the Women's Party experiment and the demise of independent women candidates, it is difficult to imagine what other position women MPs elected on behalf of political parties could have taken.

This is not to say that women MPs never worked collectively. Brian Harrison's detailed analysis of their speaking patterns up to 1945 has found that 49 per cent of women's contributions to debates concerned welfare issues, broadly defined, with a further 13 per cent being on topics particularly affecting women, such as equal pay or women's employment.[45] Some of these discussions did see cross-bench cooperation amongst women; Margaret Bondfield's unsuccessful attempt to provide footwear for children in distressed areas in December 1928 resulted in a private members bill that was presented by all seven women MPs. Women MPs spoke up for groups of women such as the unemployed or new mothers. The exceptional conditions of the Second World War encouraged cooperation between women in Parliament, and they 'came nearest to acting as a women's party, speaking with one voice on behalf of their sex' than at any other time, as the next chapter will illustrate.[46]

The post-war era: women in the House of Lords

The House of Lords was slower to open its doors to women. Lady Rhondda's father had named her as heir in his patent of peerage, but her attempt to use the Sex Disqualification (Removal) Act to take his seat in the Lords failed on the grounds that the Act did not confer new rights on women. Women MPs made numerous attempts to challenge this, including through a Woman Peers Committee in 1929, which drew in representatives of the main feminist groups but was unable to bring about any change.

Women finally gained admission to the House of Lords in the 1950s under the 1958 Life Peerage Act. Not all women MPs supported this measure; Labour women felt that it did not go far enough to challenge the hereditary character of the upper house. After the Act was passed, four women were included in the first group of new life peers: Barbara Wootton, who sat on the Labour benches, Baronesses Swanborough and Ravensdale (cross-bench) and Baroness Elliot (Conservative). As they are nominated rather than selected then elected, women peers have not attracted the same level of attention from political scientists as their counterparts in the House of Commons. In some cases it appears that the notion of male equivalence continued in the upper house through the practice of nominating widows such as Baroness Philips, widow of the general secretary of the Labour Party. Women peers often pursued social reform or legislation that concerned women or children, but many were selected after lengthy public careers which had concentrated on similar questions. This pattern continued when women MPs began to move into the Lords in the 1960s.

Post-war women MPs

At the general election of 1945 an unprecedented 87 women stood and 24 were returned. The numbers of women MPs remained more or less stable for the next two decades, to peak at 29 in 1964. This was still a small proportion; women made up less than 5 per cent of the total of MPs in 1964, and their number reduced slightly to 26 in 1966. However the slight rise in numbers, combined with the fact that half a century of their presence had reduced the novelty value of women MPs, meant that the women who were elected were less likely to be seen as representatives of their sex and more as representatives of their party.

Unlike previous intakes, many women elected after the war were married with families, a trend which continued throughout the 1950s and 1960s. The Labour MPs Jean Mann and Agnes Hardie were among those who were happy to be described as 'housewife MPs', and spoke out on prices, rationing and the availability of consumer goods. Mann in particular often invoked her own domestic experience in speeches. Women in other political parties used similar rhetoric; Margaret Thatcher often presented herself as a housewife or mother, and continued to do so after being elected Britain's first female prime minister. Femininity thus appeared less of a common or uniting feature beyond the framework of party politics.

As the novelty of women MPs wore off they were less likely to work collectively, although some issues continued to unite them across party lines. Equal pay was one example. This had been a long-held aim for many feminists, who saw it as the most effective way of dismantling gendered notions of a male breadwinner. A feminist campaign for equal pay in the civil service led to an unsuccessful parliamentary motion in 1936 which was supported by most women MPs.[47] The issue re-emerged during the Second World War, when the Royal Commission on Equal Pay gave a lukewarm endorsement to the principle despite not being able to make any recommendations. Women MPs formed an

Equal Pay Campaign Committee (EPCC) and continued to combine to press for equal pay after the war. Demonstrations were organised, and at one point the Conservative MP Irene Ward joined Labour MP Edith Summerskill in an open carriage decorated with suffragette colours to present a petition to the House of Commons.

The post-war Labour government appeared to have accepted the arguments for equal pay in certain professions such as teaching and the civil service, but refused to prioritise the issue. The EPCC did not just campaign in Parliament. A film, *To Be a Woman*, was produced by Jill Craigie and shown nationally, supported by other feminist groups. In 1950 all three parties mentioned equal pay in their manifestos, and the Conservative government followed this up with legislation to introduce equal pay for civil servants and teachers. Historians disagree over whether this represented a victory for feminism or not. Martin Pugh suggested that the campaign was dominated by middle-class women and served a limited constituency, with little wider implications, but Helen Jones argued that it demonstrated that governments were beginning to respond to women's demands, albeit slowly.[48]

The principle of equal pay for work of equal value presented women MPs with a more difficult issue. The European Economic Community (EEC) committed its members to extend equal pay in the Treaty of Rome, and the Labour government promised it would comply as part of its application for membership in 1967. When Britain's application to the EEC failed the government dropped its commitment, but pressure began to mount outside Parliament. In 1968 a group of women sewing machinists at Ford's Dagenham plant came out on strike, arguing that their work was of equal value to that of male assembly line workers. The strike brought a more militant attitude amongst women workers, which April Carter has linked to the decision of Barbara Castle, secretary of state for Employment, to bring in an Equal Pay Bill in 1969.[49] The subsequent Act disappointed many campaigners. Despite the fact that feminists had been calling for this measure since the 1920s it still offered employers a five-year period of grace before its full implementation. It also allowed a degree of freedom which enabled many employers to subvert its intention, for example by designating male shop assistants as 'trainee managers' to justify a continued higher rate of pay.

Another significant piece of legislation was the Sex Discrimination Act which was passed in 1975, the same year that the Equal Pay Act came into force. The Act had been suggested by the Conservative government, which had set up select committees in the Commons and the Lords to draft a bill to outlaw sex discrimination. When Labour returned to power in 1974 they drafted a broader bill which supplemented the Equal Pay Act but went further in including education and the provision of goods and services. The Act was presented as a victory by women within the Labour Party who had lobbied for legislation as a means of removing gender inequalities and by some feminist groups, although Vallance found that it divided women MPs, as some saw it as a cosmetic measure in response to International Women's Year.[50] Following the Act the Equal Opportunities Commission (EOC) was set up to ensure compliance. Expectations of it were high, and many women felt disappointed by its failure to bring about large-scale change. The EOC only initiated two formal investigations between 1976 and 1978. Anna Coote and Beatrix Campbell dismissed it as 'neither representative of women, nor accountable to them'.[51] Although both the Labour and Conservative parties were now broadly supporting legislation in favour of gender equality, there was still no significant bloc of feminist opinion inside Parliament linking the external women's movement with the state.

Conclusions

There was no rapid transformation of the gendering of Parliament after women received the vote. Furthermore, some of the most visible changes had little or no impact on a broader hegemonic male power which contributed to women's continued marginalisation within Parliament or the party structures surrounding it. Sixty years after the first woman took her seat in Parliament, Margaret Thatcher entered Downing Street as Britain's first woman prime minister. Ironically, the 1979 election which brought Thatcher to power also saw the number of women MPs fall to its lowest total since 1951. Vallance ended her study of women MPs at this point, with the hope that a woman prime minister who 'wields power and dispenses patronage in a perhaps uniquely visible and dramatic way' might prompt some radical changes, although she also noted that the success of one individual was unlikely to 'produce a social revolution'.[52] This optimism proved to be misplaced. As prime minister, Thatcher did little to alter the gendering of the house. She promoted very few women to cabinet office, and introduced a wide range of policies that undermined feminist achievements in community politics, including scrapping the metropolitan authorities along with their women's units. As Harold Smith has noted, she 'distanced herself from the women's movement', and the Conservative women's vote declined during her premiership.[53]

At the same time, the presence of even one woman at head of the British political elite draws attention to how much had changed since 1918. As Pat Thane has noted, the sixty years that separated the first women's votes from this point was not a long time within the context of the longer history of Parliament.[54] Much had changed, albeit at a gradual (and sometimes almost glacial) pace. All women could vote, become MPs or sit in the Lords, and enjoy equal membership of all political parties. They could enter professions on the same grounds as men. They had equal access to education, and had benefited from a number of legal reforms which had advanced their social status. The rise of the WLM movement in the 1960s shows how many of these advances would eventually feed back into politics as a new generation of educated young activists began to lobby for further improvements from a stronger starting point than their Edwardian predecessors.

Many men feared that women would act for their sex in Parliament rather than becoming loyal party members. Whether women sought to represent women or their parties remains difficult to prove, and remains a key question for feminist political scientists.[55] There were clearly some issues that all women felt strongly about, and on which they would combine across party lines, but these were not easy to predict and did not result in a sustained women's group at Westminster. It was not until the 1990s, beyond the period of this book, that political parties began a series of internal reforms aimed at increasing the numbers of women in Parliament. Although the numbers of women MPs increased dramatically as a result of this, there is still no consensus as to whether this rise has amounted to a feminisation of the British polity.

8
Women in Political Parties, 1918–45

Introduction

After the Representation of the People Act (1918) political parties were swift to take account of a new female constituency. While no party sought to promote women MPs, all assumed that women would vote as a bloc for the party that represented their interests. Politically active women noticed a change in attitudes, as Ray Strachey recalled:

> The [1918 Act] had not been on the Statute Book a fortnight before the House of Commons discovered that every Bill … had a 'women's side' and the Party Whips began eagerly to ask 'what the women thought?' … Letters from women constituents no longer went straight into wastepaper-baskets … and the agents of the women's societies were positively welcomed at Westminster.[1]

Governments set about winning the supposed 'woman's vote' with a number of reforms. The Sex Disqualification Removal Act (1919) was followed by measures to equalise divorce law, offer wives maintenance, and raise the age of consent to sixteen for girls. There is some debate over what prompted these moves. While feminist analyses saw them as 'a significant extension of women's rights', Harold Smith cautioned against interpreting them as major achievements for feminism.[2] Smith felt that much of the legislation fell short of what feminist campaigners demanded; the Sex Disqualification Act, for example, failed to stop employers using the marriage bar to remove married women from professions such as teaching in the 1920s. Whilst this is correct, the changes went some way towards meeting feminist demands in the 1920s, and Millicent Fawcett claimed they showed 'the difference the vote has made'.[3] It is unlikely, as Pat Thane has observed, that feminists expected wholesale immediate change after their lengthy experience of working for the vote.[4] They welcomed any advance, whilst continuing to push for additional improvements in women's status. A further success came in 1928 when the Equal Franchise Act extended the vote to women on exactly the same terms as it was given to men. Women now formed over half of the parliamentary electorate, and parties continued to pursue their votes and aim propaganda specifically at women.

Internal party structures changed too. The Conservative and Liberal Parties had large women's organisations before the First World War which were auxiliary to the main party apparatus, while socialist women had equal membership and separate organisations. Now that women could vote, all parties sought to integrate them into membership, while party women had to decide how much separate organisation they wished to retain. There were also a number of small but significant new parties. The Communist Party of Great Britain, the British Union of Fascists, Plaid Cymru and the Scottish National Party formed at a time when women had political citizenship. They had no existing women's auxiliaries to integrate, and admitted women to full membership, but replicated the pre-war model by setting up separate women's groups as well. In common with the three mainstream parties Communists, Fascists and nationalists attempted to construct particular appeals to women voters, emphasizing their perspective on 'women's issues'.

Women Liberals, 1918–1928

The Women's Liberal Federation (WLF) pared down its activity during the First World War. This reduction combined with the arrival of limited suffrage has led many historians to conclude that the WLF was in disarray by 1918. According to Hirshfield, suffrage:

> came too late for the WFL which had been fatally fractured by years of internal strife and survived the war only to experience the ignominy of near-total irrelevance in the 1920s .... Women Liberals had indeed reached the 'promised land' only to find themselves tied to a dying faith.[5]

This interpretation is echoed by Martin Pugh. He concurs that there was a serious falling-off in WFL membership, and suggested that it did little to help shape the Liberal Party's appeal to women voters. Liberal feminists diverted 'much of their effort into non-party groups' at the expense of the WLF.[6] For women who remained loyal to the Party, the outlook was bleak. Brian Harrison has argued that they seriously diminished their chances of election to Parliament through working for 'the party with fewest safe seats at its disposal'.[7] Pat Thane has challenged this pessimistic picture to show that membership of the Women's National Liberal Federation (formed when the WLF and the Women's National Liberal Association (WNLA) amalgamated at the end of the war) reversed an immediate post-war decline to return to 100,000 by 1928. Thane suggested that women's commitment to liberalism surpassed their allegiance to the Liberal Party, and that the Federation continued to offer a supportive atmosphere as they endeavoured to devise the best means of utilising the citizenship they had secured.[8] Leading Liberal women like Margery Corbett Ashby combined Party activity with developing interests in new women's groups such as the Women's Citizens Associations and the National Union of Societies for Equal Citizenship. The Party's rapid decline did not prevent women from enjoying greater prominence within it in the inter-war years than in any other period. Only six women ever sat as Liberal MPs, and four of these (Margaret Wintringham, Lady Vera Terrinton, Hilda Runciman and Megan Lloyd George) were elected before 1929.

The WLF should have been in a strong position. Liberals never seriously questioned women's presence in politics, and although suffrage had strained relationships with the main Party, most Liberal men remained supportive of the WLF. The divisive legacy of suffrage evaporated when the WLF reunited with the smaller WNLA in 1918, leaving the reformed WNLF perfectly poised to take over the organisation of women within the Party. A small number of WLAs felt that there was no longer a need for a separate organisation, and merged with their local (male) Party branches, but most women Liberals still wanted to keep a distinct political space. Continuity was not unproblematic; the WLF's success up to this point discouraged the Liberal Party from developing appropriate structures to incorporate women as full Party members. While other political parties appointed women's officers or equivalent positions in the early 1920s, the Liberal Party did not take this step until late in 1927, when WNLF secretary Miss Harvey was given the additional title of secretary for women's organisation and an office at Liberal headquarters. Two positions on each of the Party's district federations were reserved for women, thus linking the WNLF more closely with the work of the Party.[9] Women were accepted as paid Party agents from the mid-1920s.

The WNLF now took on a dual role, campaigning for change that would benefit women while simultaneously attempting to recruit and retain more women Party members and to maximise their votes. Nationally it worked for issues such as equal votes and the retention and extension of the wartime women's police patrols. It attempted to incorporate welfare issues into the political mainstream. Mrs Scott Anderson from Cambridge WLA explained that the WNLF:

> put purity, temperance, housing, maternity and child welfare as high as the question of the state of Poland and the sooner those who stood for Parliament realized they had got to give more attention to these matters the better.[10]

Local WLAs shared these concerns and involved themselves where possible, for example by putting pressure on local authorities to adopt women police patrols in their areas. Most local work remained focused on political education, with canvassing critical now that women were called upon to attract women voters. WLAs provided canvassers' notes which dealt with major political issues such as peace and unemployment as well as those relating to women and children. Branches were encouraged to train and 'bring on' their own local speakers rather than rely on the Party's national stars.

Attracting women's votes

Liberalism couched its appeal to women as voters in a number of ways. It recognised their domestic role, presenting issues such as temperance as 'essentially a woman's question because the happiness of the home depends on it'.[11]

Women's power as consumers, a long-acknowledged dimension of their political potential, was emphasized. Shopping was used as a means of feminizing free trade. 'A Word to the Women', a leaflet issued in 1918 and 1920, addressed women voters as those with the responsibility of providing for families. They were advised to 'stick to Free Trade' to ensure that prices reduced as wages fell.[12] Liberal propaganda also acknowledged the economic independence of younger women, explaining that Conservative clothes taxes dictated that 'frocks and stockings and underclothes cost too much'.[13]

Unlike their colleagues in other parties, inter-war women Liberals had no problem with labelling themselves as 'feminist'. Their propaganda covered controversial issues such as divorce and the need to campaign against suggestions that the Contagious Diseases Acts might be reintroduced.[14] When birth control divided socialist women, the Federation discussed it and urged all women to study the question and make up their own minds. As feminists, they had confidence in women. and they expressed no fears over reducing the voting age to 21. Margery Corbett Ashby was dismissive of press scaremongering which involved 'pictures of "flappers" governing the country'. She explained that young married women could 'revolutionize our towns' if their votes were captured, while single women brought 'the point of view of the economically independent women'.[15] Party propaganda produced for the 1929 general election built on Ashby's nuanced view of younger women voters, and addressed distinctive constituencies such as business girls, factory workers and students, urging all of them to vote for the party that was 'looking forward to the future-not back to the past'.[16]

Conservative women

Relationships between the Conservative Party and its women's auxiliary organisations had been more ambivalent than amongst Liberals. On paper, Conservatives appeared to move quickly in accepting enfranchised women as active political subjects. Women were admitted to full party membership in April 1918, but ambivalence towards their presence remained in some quarters, and there was no consensus within the Party as to how this should be implemented. Most Conservatives preferred some form of separate organisation for women, but the Party had no equivalent to the WLF remaining. The Primrose League had declined. The Conservative and Unionist Women's Franchise Association (CUWFA) had offered Conservative women a platform during the war, but was disbanded in 1918.

The Party looked to the Women's Amalgamated Unionist Tariff Reform Association (WAUTRA) to underpin a new women's organisation, and gave its leaders places on the Executive Committee of the Party's National Union. A revision of Party rules allocated women at least one-third of places on the Party's representative bodies at constituency and national level, and further changes in 1927 ensured that at least a quarter of conference delegates would be women.[17] At Central Office a Women's Department was set up under the leadership of Marjorie Maxse, who oversaw its development and professionalisation. Her staff expanded annually, rising to almost 30 by 1928, with an annual budget of nearly £12,000, suggesting that their salaries approached those of the

Party's male workers.[18] A Central Women's Advisory Committee, established in 1919 to keep the Party informed on women's issues, was formally drawn into the Party's structures in 1928.[19] One immediate result of this rapid structural change was an increase in the numbers of women joining the Women's Unionist Organisations. By 1924 there were over 4,000 branches, making them the largest of any of the three major parties' women's sections.[20]

This dramatic increase in membership has encouraged historians to interpret Conservative reaction to the 1918 and 1928 Reform Acts as 'a straightforward success – another feather in the cap of popular Toryism', whereby the Party recognised what women wanted, learned how to present it to them and gained their votes in return.[21] Recent analysis has suggested a more complicated picture. Women were given space at the level of organisational leadership but there was much less agreement as to the best means of changing the majority of women from auxiliary supporters to Party members. Tensions arose in several areas, but were most evident around the question of how – and where – women should be organised, and how far they should be admitted into political work.

Organising women, 1918–28

Conservatives were uncertain where to put women within their current structures. Previous opponents of women's suffrage favoured inclusion as they feared that separation would lead to conflicts based around gendered interests. Robert Topping, the Party's principal agent from 1928, argued that mixed-sex organisations would encourage women's fuller participation at all levels as their abilities became evident to the men who they worked alongside.[22] Others took the opposite view. Topping's predecessor, Leigh Maclachlan, felt that separate organisations promoted a healthy spirit of rivalry between male and female groups to the overall benefit of constituencies.[23] Marjorie Maxse believed separate branches were the only way for women to gain political experience, and most Conservative women concurred, suggesting that their experiences of working in mixed organisations before the war may not have been overwhelmingly positive.[24] What finally emerged was a flexible solution. Central Office made it clear that a separate organisation was its preferred model but did not impose this, offering those constituencies that favoured integration the option of appointing a Women's Divisional Advisory Committee. Few took this up in England and Wales although in Scotland McCrillis found that the norm was for mixed associations with separate, financially autonomous women's committees.[25]

Most constituencies had paid party agents, but as the number of women's branches grew some appointed their own organisers, disconcerting male agents who feared 'that the feminine tide may sweep everything before it'.[26] Men's fears worsened in the late 1920s when women were admitted to the Agent's Examination, although this was welcomed in Scotland where agents were paid less than in England, which caused difficulties in recruitment.[27] Women agents found it impossible to secure the more prestigious posts. Men strongly guarded their membership of the National Society of Conservative Agents and refused to admit women, so women established the National Association of

Conservative and Unionist Women's Organisers. Relations between the two were hostile; a national conference dinner in 1922 saw women 'isolated on one table, as though they all had the measles'.[28] It was not until after the Second World War that the groups merged.

Attracting women's votes

Some Conservative men perceived women voters as a problem, wanting 'enthusing, educating and training' as one male agent put it.[29] Elections now represented:

> an entirely different proposition to what [they were] before ... two thirds of the electorate are politically entirely uneducated ... one must not lose sight of the fact that practically half of the electors are women, who are undoubtedly more strongly influenced by an appeal to their senses and are inclined to judge by appearances.[30]

Much of the Conservative Party's propaganda addressed women's perceived lack of political education. Women were reminded that 'the vote carries the gravest responsibility', and urged to learn how to use it 'by joining the women's branch of the Unionist Association'.[31] Discussion of women's 'natural' Conservatism was now joined by a contradictory concern, that naïve women voters could be drawn to socialism, which was engaged through leaflets such as 'What Bolshevism Means to Women'. By 1924 the Conservative Party manifesto had added a section on 'Women and children', which covered issues such as widow's pensions and the adoption and guardianship of children, and similar sections began to appear in Conservative candidates' election addresses.

From 1923 to 1930 the Party produced a magazine for women, *Home and Politics,* a sister paper to its main publication *Man in the Street.* Jarvis' analysis of its content revealed how this drew on earlier Conservative discourses concerning women's distinct political identity, while simultaneously revising these to suit the context of women as active political subjects. As equal enfranchisement approached it evolved an ideal Conservative woman, a mature 'bastion of common sense and homely wisdom', who would guide younger, inexperienced women voters.[32] This theme was repeated in broader propaganda. A series of leaflets from 1923 entitled 'Over the Garden Wall' featured the daily conversations between two neighbours. The older, wiser Mrs Brown warned Mrs Jones of the dangers of socialism, the Labour Party and free trade, and advised her that her best interests, as a woman, were served by the Conservative Party.[33]

Conservative Party literature from the inter-war period recognised that women had progressed from auxiliary members to voters, and addressed them as such. At the same time it retained earlier notions of where women's political interests lay. The home remained central. Activists were reminded of the need to appeal to 'the viewpoint of the homemaker as well as that of the breadwinner', while the Party's engagement with unemployment painted 'a lurid picture of the perils' facing families with unemployed fathers and working mothers.[34] There were reminders of the threat that socialism posed to marriage and the family.[35] The Conservative view of gendered domesticity extended to encompass the Empire; a series of articles exhorted housewives to support the broader imperial family through the purchase of Empire goods.

Labour Party women

At the end of the First World War, women came into the Labour Party in large numbers. The Party overhauled its constitution in 1917, moving from affiliate to individual membership. Women no longer had to channel their membership through unions or similar groups, which *Labour Woman* described as 'almost a revolution in itself', and over 150,000 joined the Labour Party in the next six years. At the same time, plans were laid for the absorption of the Women's Labour League. This was autocratically arranged by Marion Phillips, the League's secretary, who then became the Party's first woman officer, heading a Women's Department with eight organisers. League branches became women's sections, with representation on the Party's local executive committees, Women's Advisory Councils in each region and an annual Women's Conference. They were also guaranteed four representatives on the Party's National Executive Committee, but these were elected by the Party rather than the Women's Conference. Attempts by some Labour women to overturn this and give the Women's Conference greater power were unsuccessful, leading to criticism that women's own concerns were being marginalised. Women were also organised through the Standing Joint Committee (SJC), formed during the war as the Standing Joint Industrial Women's Committee. Yet, although opportunities for participation were there, Labour women faced particular problems when deciding whether to integrate or retain a level of separate organisation. Full integration, had they chosen to accept it, would have marginalised them within the Party because of the internal mechanisms which gave a privileged voice to the trade unions, particularly those from male trades. On the other hand, many Labour women remained committed to class-based politics and were cautious of being labelled 'feminist'. Collette has recently argued that the SJC's identification with working women showed 'a class prejudice that some feminists deplored'.[36] This weakened women's organisation as it worked against Labour women's ability to make connections with women's groups outside the Party.

Labour women were more active at local level. They often worked in areas which had been marked out as female territory before the war, such as welfare, improving the lives of their female constituents through initiatives such as increasing the numbers of public wash houses. Women continued to argue for a role for themselves on the grounds of their special expertise in areas such as infant welfare, maternity provision and household budget management, but presented this as part of a broader campaign to improve working-class lives rather than as a woman's issue. These initiatives did not go unnoticed at local level; the first Labour women lord mayors were elected in the inter-war period, demonstrating a level of recognition for their role in municipal socialist politics. In their work around welfare issues in the inter-war period, Labour Party women arguably helped to prepare the way for the introduction of the post-war welfare state.[37] The national picture was more complicated. A bitter battle was fought out over birth control, which showed how difficult it was for women to raise unpopular ideas. Many socialist women saw this question in class terms. They linked large families with poverty in working-class communities, and presented birth control as the means of improving living standards. Some working-class women resisted this, associating birth control with upper-class immorality rather than their own experiences of marital sex. Dora Russell tried to get the Party to commit to making birth control advice available against strong opposition from Marion Phillips. Many branches (and rank and file men) supported Russell, but Phillips and other leaders feared losing the working-class Irish vote, and kept the issue as a matter of conscience. Russell then worked outside the Party with her Workers' Birth Control Group, which succeeded in implementing change through local health authorities.

The importance of birth control and other controversies receded in the 1930s in the face of the economic crisis. This had local impact through the introduction of the means test in 1931. Men and women opposed the measure, but it seemed to have special relevance to women, as its insistence on household, not individual, income amounted to an attack on the working-class family rather than on the unemployed male. Women played a prominent part in demonstrations against the means test as individuals and through organizations such as the Women's Labour League (WLL).[38] At Merthyr, over a thousand women took part in a raid on the offices of the Unemployment Assistance Board, where they smashed windows and burned claimants' records.[39] Labour members of the Boards of Guardians often refused to administer the means test, although these protests were largely symbolic as they could be swiftly removed and replaced by non-elected commissioners.

Graves' study of women in the inter-war Labour Party concluded that the women's sections declined in size and strength in the 1930s. A report after Marion Phillips' death in 1932 suggested that the need for separate organisations was passing. Difficulties were reported in sustaining their branches in the period; some closed, while in others such as York the previously lively section was reduced to a handful of members. Many of the respondents in Graves' study found this a positive development, remembering the 1930s as a time of exhilaration. The economic crisis and the deteriorating international situation encouraged many women to prioritise class politics over the demands of gender. However, at the same time, Graves suggested that the struggle for separate-but-equal status was effectively lost. One effect of this, noted by Andrew Thorpe, was that more politically active women in the 1930s 'were deliberately bypassing the women's organization, realizing its impotence'.[40] It would be some decades before Party women would attempt to pursue more radical gender policies under the auspices of a separate party organisation.[41]

There were other sites of activity for socialist women in the inter-war period. The Independent Labour Party (ILP) remained strong in certain areas, although it was weakened by the decision to disaffiliate from the Labour Party in 1931. Many socialist women also involved themselves in the Women's Co-Operative Guild (WCG), which had formed in 1883 (1892 in Scotland) and maintained a network of local branches. The WCG had been an important site for working-class women's activity before the First World War, and continued to be influential in the inter-war period. It campaigned on a number of issues including maternity and infant welfare, although its members were often simultaneously involved in the Labour Party, making it difficult to disaggregate their work.

Women in the Communist Party

The Communist Party of Great Britain (CPGB) which formed in 1920 drew its membership from Marxist and left socialist groups. Many of its women members had prior political experience in such parties or as suffragettes. For socialist women who shared the CPBG's revolutionary commitment, the Party offered an opportunity to break with the gendered assumptions of past models of political organisation and devise new ways for enfranchised men and women to work together towards a socialist revolution. Yet, from the outset, there were other pressures shaping British communism. The disparate groups that fed into the CPGB had been part of the Second International. Members shared a sense of disillusionment at its failure to prevent war in 1914, and a commitment to spreading the advances of the Bolshevik revolution worldwide. This fuelled a drive for internationalism within the CPGB, which affiliated to the Third International (Comintern), the Second International's Russian-led successor. The Comintern was a less eclectic, more autocratic body, fiercely revolutionary and willing to expel parties or individuals who deviated from its principles of democratic centralism. This meant that from the outset the CPGB was less able to react to uniquely British contexts than other political parties.

The relationship with the Comintern had implications for how British women experienced communism, as much of their Party's ideology and organisational structures were determined at international level. The Comintern's founding congress recognised that its vision for international socialism needed 'the energetic participation of working women', but had less to say on how this might be achieved.[42] The Second International's suspicion of feminism as a movement primarily concerned with advancing the claims of bourgeois women continued into the Comintern. The main debate on women and socialism which took place at its Third Congress in 1921 stated that it was 'firmly opposed to any kind of separate women's associations', and refuted the notion that there were valid 'women's issues' beyond more general political questions.[43] Yet, in practice, the Comintern was prepared to support women's organisations. A Conference of Communist Women met annually with its approval from 1920, and an International Secretariat for work amongst women was represented on its Executive Committee. The 1921 resolution that refuted separate organisation concluded that there was a need for 'special methods of work among women', and charged national communist parties with organising this through women's departments or committees.[44] One result of this ambiguity was that there was little will amongst the Comintern's leadership to pursue this, and at the Fourth Congress it admitted that 'some sections ... have either failed to take measures to organize women Communists within the Party, or failed to set up the Party organizations vital for work among the masses of women'.[45] Britain was evidently amongst these, as at the same congress Clara Zetkin met with Minnie Birch, a CPGB member who was attending as a technical worker, and urged her to press her Party to move on this issue. A Women's National Committee was established with Birch in charge of propaganda, along with a press officer (Mary Moorhouse) and treasurer (Nellie Lansbury).

The Committee achieved little compared with the work that was now being done by women's sections of other political parties. In 1924 the Party's

Congress learned that four women's sections had been established in Dundee, Bradford, Motherwell and Newcastle, but that the remainder of the country remained untouched, while the following year it had 'not got any great results' to report.[46] In some areas such as Glasgow and Edinburgh, women's sections met with opposition from mixed branches.[47] A more serious attempt to redress this came the same year with the first National Conference of Communist Women. The event's timing – it ran concurrently with the Party Congress – forced women to chose between the two meetings, and only 27 attended.[48] The conference tightened up organisation, set up a Central Women's Department at the CPGB headquarters, and elected Beth Turner, a Yorkshire textile worker, as national women's organiser. Turner undertook national propaganda tours and oversaw the formation of local committees with some success. A paper, *The Working Woman*, was also launched, although the Party closed it after three years.

Bruley's study divided Communist Party women into 'cadres' and 'supporters', the latter being wives of Party activists. Recent biographical research by Gidon Cohen and Andrew Flinn suggested that the CPGB offered restricted political roles to its women members. Rose Kerrigan, one of the founders of the Glasgow Communist Party, explained how her activism involved keeping her communist husband free from 'the worries of the home' to pursue his political work.[49] Kerrigan's experience was shared by other women who had been very active before marrying; Molly Murphy, who had organized for the WSPU, did less in the Party than her husband, Jack. Such women may have benefited from women's sections, but Bruley found that those who viewed themselves as cadres were inclined to be dismissive of them. Women's sections became identified with less political roles such as organising social events and fundraising, or providing a space for communist wives to get together. One communist teacher from Newcastle explained that women's sections would be useful 'if we had ... a large number of women who were tied domestically', but that she 'never was a member', preferring to work in the mixed branch. With little pressure to develop women's sections from the top of the movement and little enthusiasm for them amongst the grass-roots membership, the initiative was unlikely to succeed. When the Comintern moved away from organising women in the 1930s, British women lost a key external ally, and the women's section was disbanded in 1932, passing the work over to the general Party.

The Communist Party and the woman worker

The CPGB's priority was industrial work, particularly in heavy, male-dominated industries, which impeded attempts to integrate women. Very few Communist women recognised women's political potential beyond the workplace. Beth Turner's report in 1925 exemplified this dilemma. Responding to criticisms that her department was doing too much work with housewives, she explained: 'We had practically no factory women in our Party. We had to take the women we had, and develop the work according to the circumstances'.[50] When the Party's women's organiser took the factory worker as the norm, it was difficult for women in other circumstances to make their way into Communist politics.

Some women were drawn into Party work through supporting their husbands at times of industrial unrest. Stuart McIntrye's pioneering investigation of grass-roots left activism in the Scottish and Welsh coalfields found several examples of wives demanding that their menfolk took part in strikes.[51] The General Strike proved equally politicising. Although the main unions called out by the TUC were male-dominated, some women went on strike, particularly in the printing trades. The unique circumstances of a general strike enhanced the importance of the supportive work attached to it, and women did much to sustain the strike. They set up feeding centres, typed strike bulletins and stood on picket lines. There were later examples of spontaneous activities by working women, notably in the Lancashire textile industry during the 1930s where Communist women were to the fore.[52] Yet these were exceptions, and, crucially, the Party failed to capitalise on them by converting newly politicised women into long-term recruits.

The economic depression of the 1930s offered Communist women other avenues of activity. Much grass-roots campaigning against the economic crisis was coordinated by the National Unemployed Workers Movement (NUWM), a Communist-dominated organisation whose membership exceeded the CPGB. The NUWM had its own Women's Department led by Maud Brown, which was embedded in the overall organisation, with representation on the national committee. It dealt with problems relating specifically to unemployed women, such as the Anomalies Act, a cost-saving measure passed in 1931 which made it almost impossible for married women to claim any unemployment benefit in their own right. There were also women's sections in a number of local areas which mirrored the work of the national campaign, coordinating women's sections of hunger marches or organising local demonstrations. The Women's Department pushed concerns which were more suggestive of the broader type of 'women's issue' that had not featured heavily in the Communist Party; some sections agitated for free school milk and meals, and the Sheffield and Manchester groups joined in larger campaigns aimed at reducing maternal mortality.

Bruley's study of women in the Communist Party noted a paradox between its theory and practice:

> On the one hand, there was staunch support for sexual equality ... together with the conviction within the party that men and women should have equal rights and duties .... On the other side was their implicit acceptance of the traditional role of women in gender-defined roles which effectively subordinated them to men.[53]

Communist women encountered attitudes to their work in the 1920s and 1930s which appeared more suited to the previous century. On one of her first tours of Scotland, Beth Turner described 'one collection of primitive males who have yet to be convinced that woman is any good in the world'.[54] There was an ambivalence towards women's participation at branch level too, where it was felt that 'many comrades discourage their wives, sisters and women friends from attending party meetings, or from taking any part whatever in our work'.[55] The CPGB's prioritisation of industrial work did not help this. Andrew Thorpe's careful analysis of CPGB membership up to 1945 has concluded that it was 'not only a man's party, but a young man's party', with women never exceeding 21 per cent of its membership.[56] Research into their work suggests that they failed to break the existing mould for women in political parties, and replicated many of the gendered positions established in earlier socialist parties. Although Communism attracted a number of women who had been active in politics before the First World War, Karen Hunt and Matthew Worley concluded that 'little was found for these politically experienced women to do in the new CPGB', and few women came to prominence in its ranks.[57]

Fascist parties

If the success of the Conservative Party in attracting women as voters and members questions presumptions that women involved in politics will gravitate towards liberal or leftward-leaning parties, then the relationship between women's political activism and fascism in the inter-war period ought finally to dispel them. The two main fascist organisations in Britain, the British Fascisti (BF) and the British Union of Fascists (BUF), recruited women at all levels, arguably with more success than the Communist Party. Although British fascism was not international in the same sense as British communism, it shared key features with other European fascist parties responding to post-war industrial unrest: fear of socialism; modernization and rapid change drawing 'from both the right and left, seeking to create a radical "Third Way" which was neither capitalist nor communist'.[58] British fascism was no less masculine or paramilitary than its German and Italian counterparts, but paradoxically 'made a special effort to recruit [women] and developed structures and policies in an attempt to make Fascism attractive to [them]' in common with other political parties.[59] Recent research into how it did this, and how women themselves engaged with the movement on their own terms, has challenged portrayals of Britain's fascist women as the unfortunate dupes of an ideology that ran counter to all their interests. It suggested a more complex picture, in terms of both the message fascism sent out to women and the way that women received it.[60]

Women in the British Fascisti

The fascist movement in Britain was founded by a woman, Rotha Lintorn-Orman, who set up the British Fascisti (BF) in 1923 to combat communism and resist industrial unrest. The BF was the most obviously fascist of several anti-left-wing groups initiated by women, including Flora Drummond's Women's Guild of Empire and Dorothy Walthall's Victory Corps. Each of these expected women to practice first aid and to be prepared to drive vehicles in the event of widespread strikes, which drew on many of their members' experiences during the First World War. The BF formed a series of women's units with organisers throughout Britain. Much of their work suggested that certain areas of politics were more feminine, or better suited to women's alleged abilities. Women's units took the lead in promoting the BF's work with children. BF leaders were concerned by the success of socialist Sunday schools, which they saw as leading to the 'Socialist corruption of the minds of the British children'.[61] Miss Blake, area commander for Edinburgh, drew up a scheme of children's clubs to combat this in 1925. Within a year over 40 were running, largely in inner-city areas, where children were offered a blend of patriotism and education aimed at instilling national pride alongside games with little or no political content.

The BF placed great emphasis on physical fitness, and prepared its women members for direct forms of political action more than other parties. Women's units ran classes in first aid and ju-jitsu, and organised regular sessions of drill and physical training. Many BF women became involved in its Special Patrol groups. These were mainly based in London and were open to any member aged between 18 and 40 who was over 5 ft tall and prepared to go on evening patrols dissuading women from prostitution. Women enjoyed the camaraderie of the patrols, which was enhanced through the training classes and by the initiative of an annual women's camp 'on service lines in order to accustom Women Fascists to discipline, camp routine, and the organisation of a community under canvas or in huts'.[62] Camps were often attacked by Communist opponents, leading to fierce fighting during which BF women were able to demonstrate their physical prowess.

The BF split during the General Strike when the government refused to allow it to participate in the work of the Organization for the Maintenance of Supplies (OMS) unless it first agreed to drop its separate organisation. Some members complied but others wished to retain a fascist identity. Julie Gottlieb has claimed that their resistance was partly due to prominent BF women who rejected the secondary role allocated to women in the OMS. Yet, as Martin Durham has shown, the women's units in Scotland were at the forefront of the drive to accept the conditions.[63] BF women's units did play a role in the General Strike as drivers, in canteens and distributing news sheets. After this point the BF declined in numbers, until it finally disbanded in 1935.

Women's role in the British Union of Fascists

The BUF which was formed in 1932 established a women's section almost immediately. There was little to distinguish much of its work, which was aimed at educating women voters, training women speakers and fundraising. One difference was the amount of attention paid to training women to cope with political unrest. Branches offered classes in first aid and self-defence. At larger meetings the BUF deployed women stewards to eject female protesters. This moved women beyond a supportive role, as they were often attacked. One woman remembered an incident at the Free Trade Hall in Manchester where her friend, who had been trained to deal with a certain amount of violence, had 'a pretty tough fight with a communist .... Fortunately she wore black underwear so managed to come out of it with dignity even when her shirt was ripped off.'[64]

Women's separate organisation in the BUF did not necessarily equate to their marginalisation. Stephen Cullen's research identified several instances in Scotland where women 'subvert[ed] the official structure of the movement', such as Maire Inglis in Edinburgh, who was acknowledged as one of the country's most effective fascist leaders.[65] Similarly, on Merseyside, Yolande Mott organised both women's and men's branches for a period of time.[66] Julie Gottlieb used the presence of women in fascism's local leadership throughout Britain to caution against assuming that organising men was the key role. She argued that this overlooks the importance of women's leadership over other women, which formed much of their work across the women's sections of all political parties in the 1930s, and offered women leading roles in fascism in many areas.[67]

BUF women took part in elections. The Party linked this to women's education, deemed necessary because 'without a sound knowledge of Fascism it is impossible for the women to undertake what is essentially their work for the movement: that of canvassing'.[68] The BF had been ambivalent about extending the vote to younger women; one of its activists, Nesta Webster, queried their political level, and worried that socialists would 'promise the mill and factory girls silk stockings and an easy life to get their votes'.[69] The BUF, formed after the event, put up women candidates in elections. Ten were selected as prospective parliamentary candidates in 1936, representing 10 per cent of the Party's total. Although the anticipated general election never occurred, some of the candidates fought local elections where they fared no worse than male fascist candidates.

British fascism's appeal to women

The BUF recognised gendered roles for men and women, but these could be malleable. Mosley's declaration that fascism wanted 'men who are men and women who are women' did not preclude more complex discussions of women's role in a future fascist society.[70] The BUF privileged motherhood over women's employment but did not dismiss women as workers. Mosley's 1934 pamphlet, *Blackshirt Policy*, suggested removing artificial barriers to women's employment and introducing equal pay; male fears that this might provoke a rise in unemployment were assuaged by assurances that the future corporate state would have 'enough jobs to go round'.[71] However, as Gottlieb has noted, women were not intended to be the main beneficiaries of equal pay.[72] The BUF's chief woman's organiser, Annie Brock Griggs, denied that it was a feminist issue, and more pragmatic BUF publications hinted at another benefit; that women would not be prevented from working, but by offering men 'a wage that is equitable and ample ... the need for women to go out to work would be removed'.[73] One BUF member, Agnes Booth, argued that as some women did want to go out to work, the benefit of raised wages lay in their potential to increase the number of domestic servants, thus offering women greater choice than the stark alternatives of employment or marriage.[74] Fascism's position on equal pay was ambiguous rather than wholly reactionary or emancipatory.

Concern with motherhood led the BUF to take an unexpected position on pacifism during the 1930s. As Durham has commented, this stands at odds with the 'customary view of the nature of Fascism ... as bellicose, a movement that despises pacifism and glorifies violence and war'.[75] Rather than portraying women as patriotic mothers producing sons to defend the country through war, the BUF used similar rhetoric to that of the feminist peace movement, emphasising their role as lifegivers. BUF propaganda invoked gendered hardships of war, and reminded women that it was 'their husbands, their brothers, their children' who would suffer.[76] The anti-war campaign intensified rather than diminished in 1939 when a Women's Peace Campaign was launched. This aimed to dissuade women from engaging in the war effort, which put it into territory traditionally occupied by the left. Yet there were distinctions. The broader women's peace movement opposed war *and* fascism, whilst BUF women couched their opposition to war in terms of support for the fascist cause across Europe. Women blackshirts showed this when they disrupted a meeting organised by the Women's League Against War and Fascism in January 1940.

The ambiguities towards women in British fascist thought attracted an unexpected amalgam of followers. Historians have made much of the presence of a some prominent suffragettes in the BUF's leadership, finding 'a certain logic in this progression', despite the fact that the majority of WSPU officials who remained in political life after the First World War located themselves on the left.[77] Mary Richardson and Nora Elam both used their militant past as part of their justification for fascism, arguing that the women's movement had failed to deliver much of what it had promised. It is possible to see what may have attracted militant women to fascism; much of what is often presented as the movement's 'new' role for them (the uniformed processions, drum bands and ju-jitsu training) featured in the work of the WSPU. On the other hand, Richardson at least became disillusioned with the movement, and claimed to have been expelled after she attempted to organise a protest against Mosley's exploitation of his women members.[78]

Women in post-war political parties

During the Second World War general elections were suspended and a coalition government was put in place, which had implications for women's party work. The Conservative women's organisation suspended its annual conference during the war. Labour women continued to meet but their discussions were dominated by immediate concerns regarding the war's impact on women as mothers.[79] At the same time, as we have seen, exceptional wartime conditions encouraged women to return to more collective modes of working, particularly in Parliament, although this did not continue after the war.

Women's role in political parties in the 1950s and 1960s has received less attention than the inter-war period to date. Much of what exists has concentrated on the experience of electoral candidates and the difficulty in selection, and more research is needed to assess how post-war ideologies shaped women's experiences of grass-roots political activity. The small amount of research into the structure of post-war women's party organisations suggests continuity with the inter-war period. The Labour, Conservative and Liberal Parties broadly retained the systems they established in response to the Representation of the People Act in 1918. In a survey of women in the Labour Party in the late 1980s, Sarah Perrigo discovered that little had changed since the 1930s. Women members had a parallel committee structure, with 'local and regional women's sections and councils, the National Conference of Labour Women and the National Labour Women's Committee'.[80] Jill Hills found that by the 1970s they were mainly found 'in the rural areas and the North of England' where they functioned 'as both a training ground for women and as a pressure group' pressing women's issues.[81] The Conservative Party was similarly unaltered, with a women's association in each constituency and the Women's National Advisory Committee (which replaced the earlier Central Women's Advisory Committee after the war) coordinating women's work nationally. Liberal Party women continued to benefit from the established presence of the WLF.[82] Women clearly valued these groups and continued to work within them, although their separate identity made it easier for them to be marginalised by the main Party.

Data on individual party membership is hard to procure for this period, complicating assessments of the strength or success of women's organisations. Hills found that women made up an estimated 40 per cent of the Labour Party's membership and 51 per cent of that of the Conservative Party by this stage. They were under-represented at the higher levels of each party, although slightly less so in the Conservative Party, which retained its practice of reserving a number of places for women at all levels of its organisation.[83] Women's Liberal Associations continued to elect delegates to their area federation, which in turn sent representatives to the main Party executive.[84] Martin Cole's investigation into the absence of Liberal women MPs between 1951 and 1986 found that the WLF became 'one of its strongest organisations', and often came to the aid of Party branches that were struggling.[85] This did not translate into equal representation, however, and Cole also found that as the Party floundered electorally it was less likely to run the perceived risk of a woman candidate.

It is unclear how these structures shaped women's broader experience of politics in the post-war period, as little research has been undertaken into their work at the level of grass-roots activism. Much of what exists has concentrated on the experiences of Labour Party women. Collette has suggested that the 1960s and 1970s were a period 'when goals were won by Labour women, when their achievements were possible because it was relatively easy to lobby'.[86] She believed that this was eased when the Party was in power, and cited legislation on equal pay and sex discrimination as examples of the Party responding to feminist pressure. Collette's conclusions, however, rest on her interpretation of the papers of Hilda Smith, a prominent member of the National Joint Committee of Working Women's Organisations, whose experiences may not replicate those of women in local branches. Beatrix Campbell has suggested that Conservative women were equally successful in shaping the agenda of the new right, although she also noted tension between those who took extremely hard lines on issues such as capital punishment and sexual permissiveness, and those who pursued more liberal equality agendas.[87] Less attention has been paid to the Liberal Party because of its continued decline. Celia Goodhart, who had been a member of the Social Democratic Party in the 1980s, described the WLF as 'antediluvian' at the time of the merger between the two parties, 'mired in … social, tea and bazaar activities'.[88] This sits at odds with Hollie Voyce's claim that the WLF continued to produce important policy documents and train women for a more active role in politics, although Voyce based her observations on organisational records rather than individual women's experience, and it is possible that the activities she describes did not reach all branches.

Women remained active in minority parties in the post-war period. Elizabeth Wilson has noted that while the post-war British Communist Party shared European communists' emphasis on woman's domestic role, 'individual women Party members were active in a whole range of community struggles, in the peace movement and in the trade unions'.[89] At the same time, post-war industrial change meant that the Party's focus on workers was more likely to include women, who dominated the assembly lines of the new consumer goods industries. Many large women's strikes received Communist Party support.[90] Andrew Thorpe's analysis of the gender of inter-war Communist Party membership has yet to be repeated for the post war period, but electoral statistics, which show over 20 Communist women PPCs between 1950 and 1970, suggest that women were rising to the top of the Party's structures at this time.[91]

Women in Wales and Scotland also participated in the post-war rise of nationalist parties, where Charlotte Aull Davies has argued that they were able to access a 'dual role' as 'political activists and nurturers of the nation'.[92] Plaid Cymru and the Scottish National Party (SNP) adhered to the dominant model for women in politics, and set up women's sections in 1925 and 1929 respectively. Laura McAllister has claimed that the women's section in Plaid Cymru moved from being a fundraising body to a 'far more political force' in the post-war era, although this did not translate into electoral success for women before 1979.[93] Women were also to the fore in Cymdeithas Yr Laith, taking direct action in support of the Welsh Language.[94] In Scotland, the high-profile electoral victories of Winifred Ewing, Margo MacDonald and Margaret Bain helped to link nationalism and women MPs in the public mind, increasing women's chances of securing an electoral nomination.[95] Women's participation in nationalist politics altered in the 1990s. The introduction of devolved government in the Scottish Parliament and the Welsh National Assembly (WA) showed how a radical strand within nationalist politics was prepared to experiment with different selection procedures to ensure more equal parliamentary representation, with the result that 37 per cent of MSPs and 40 per cent of WA members were women.[96] This dramatic change has focused attention on the period immediately prior to and after devolution. As a consequence we still know very little about the role of women in the rank and file of Plaid Cymru or the SNP up to this point, although the prominence of a small number of women in the leadership of both parties suggests that this would be an area for fruitful future research.

Party women remaind subject to pressure from external women's organisations. The growth of the Women's Liberation Movement (WLM) from the 1960s began to impact on the national structures of political parties by the 1970s. Whilst the early WLM groups placed themselves outside of existing models of political organisation, as we shall see, Elizabeth Meehan's research found that women who began their political work in the movement 'were able to use this as a base for fuller participation in other organisations' in later years.[97] Most moved into a variety of left-wing groups. Anna Coote and Beatrix Campbell noted how socialist feminism was a key feature of WLM politics from its early days, popularised amongst women who were simultaneously involved in the WLM and the Labour Party, Communist Party or International Socialists but predominantly by 'non-aligned feminists'.[98] As the WLM divided over emphasis and tactics, some socialist feminists returned to the Labour Party. Sheila Rowbotham described how some of them became 'profoundly disoriented' as a result, as the Party initially shunned 'aspects of women's liberation politics' which could not be 'codified into demands' that fitted its analysis of the state.[99] Labour Party feminists responded through initiatives such as the Women's Action Committee of the Campaign for Labour Party Democracy and local women's action groups, although it was not until the 1990s that their demands resulted in structural changes.

Many women found it easier to advance feminist demands in a party context at local level. Local government could meet women's immediate needs through comparatively small responses which had wider political implications. The WLM's concern with male violence, for example, led to the formation of a number of local Women's Aid groups in the 1970s which managed to secure funding for women's refuges and rape crisis centres in their areas. Some women lobbied local health authorities for improvements in the provision of contraceptive and abortion advice or for improved cervical and breast screening. Feminists' success in engaging in local politics paved the way for a number of authorities to establish separate women's committees in the 1980s. These groups, which were particularly associated with the larger metropolitan authorities abolished in 1985, promoted advanced policies on equal opportunities and did much to integrate feminist demands into mainstream politics. After Margaret Thatcher's election their progressive stance on gender and sexuality made them a key site for opposition to the agenda of the Conservative right.

Conclusion

Studies of women in British politics after the First World War which argue that the vote brought little change in practice have overlooked some significant points. Women's votes precipitated a change in the organisational structures of British political parties. The Liberal and Conservative parties now admitted women to membership, as did the newer parties which formed after the 1918 Representation of the People Act. There were also some attempts by each of the three major parties to guarantee women a level of representation in their management. While women broadly welcomed these changes, many who had been active in political parties before the First World War were loath to let go of their older organisations, with the result that these remained largely intact. The new parties that formed in the 1920s followed the same pattern of providing equal membership plus women's sections, which gave party women the chance to participate in the shadow structures of single-sex groups as well as in the body of the main parties themselves. The women's sections were clearly valued by their members, who found that they offered opportunities for learning essential political skills such as public speaking or the mechanisms of formal committee work. Yet at the same time, it was easy for the main body of a party to sidestep these organisations, which were usually seen as advisory bodies, so they were easily ignored.

The vote also precipitated changes in the presentation of party policy. Parliamentary propaganda had to take account of women's presence in constituencies. Existing political parties were not complacent over the failure of a women's party to materialise in 1918. Each one clearly believed that there was a collective 'woman's vote' to be captured, and that their electoral success could well depend on securing this. Party manifestos began to address themselves to women as a matter of course, and separate propaganda initiatives developed these messages. This tendency continued after the Second World War, when policies such as rationing brought the domestic arena to the political fore. Belief in a 'woman's vote' had direct implications for the opportunities of politically ambitious women within parties, as it was simultaneously felt that women were in the best position to address other women. Posts for women's organisers and officers and women agents were thus established, enabling some women to turn political activism into a paying career.

None of these important changes altered the fact that political power within parties remained overwhelmingly gendered as male at the national level. Most MPs and party leaders were men, as were the district and national officials who controlled party structures and organisations. Many women who felt that the pace of change was too slow within their parties believed that their marginalisation within party hierarchies was to blame, although it was difficult to alter this. No party made attempts to address this through strategies such as quotas, positive discrimination or all-woman short lists until the 1990s, beyond the scope of this study. Yet at local level, women managed to place quite radical demands on party agendas. Many local authorities were pressured by alliances between party women and independent women's groups to deliver feminist policies. Women's experience as grass-roots party activists after 1945 needs to be fully integrated into the narrative of women and party politics if the impact of the vote is to be assessed accurately.

9
Beyond Party Politics – the Reconfiguration of Feminist Organisations, 1920–79

Introduction

Suffrage dominated the women's movement for half a century, but most campaigners never saw their work as being limited to the vote alone. They hoped voting would enable women to overturn sexual inequalities themselves, and transform the gendered structures of the Edwardian state. After the 1918 Representation of the People Act, feminists followed different paths towards achieving their wider goals. For those whose feminism was shaped by conservative, liberal or socialist ideology, the possibility of equal membership convinced them to put their energies into the political parties which were attempting to integrate women into their structures. Others rejected mixed-sex organisations in an effort to retain the autonomy of the suffrage movement by working collectively with other women beyond the confines of party politics. The failure of the Woman's Party experiment in 1918 confounded hopes for a feminisation of politics via an autonomous sex-based party. This left the women's movement working on several demands across a number of different pressure groups, often with overlapping memberships, which lacked the coherence of the suffrage movement. Some of these were reconfigured versions of older suffrage organisations; others represented new developments responding to broader societal changes. Shifts continued after the Second World War, when the groups that formed in 1920s were confronted with an emerging generation of activists with no experience or memory of the Edwardian women's movement.

Until recently, historians argued that there was a lull in feminist politics in the inter-war period. The popularity of the wave metaphor has encouraged neglect of the events separating the Women's Liberation Movement from the Edwardian suffrage campaign. Recent work has revised this through investigating the activities of a number of women's organisations. Johanna Alberti and Cheryl Law have demonstrated that the suffrage campaign continued in some form until equal suffrage was awarded in 1928, while the organisations behind it transformed and diverged, complicating attempts to map their influence.[1] This pattern continued in later decades. For the 1940s and 1950s Catherine

Blackford found ten groups self-identifying as 'feminist': the Association for Moral and Social Hygiene, the London and National Society (later the Fawcett Society), the Married Women's Association, the Open Door Council (ODC), the St Joan's Social and Political Alliance, the Six Point Group (SPG), the Status of Women Committee, the Suffragette Fellowship, Women for Westminster and the Women's Freedom League.[2] Other groups including the National Union of Societies for Equal Citizenship (NUSEC) and the Women's Publicity and Planning Association could be added to this list. So although parliamentary politics remained dominated by party concerns, gender-based politics survived in a number of extra-parliamentary organisations.

New and equality feminism

All feminists sought further advancements for women following the limited suffrage measure, but there was no consensus as to what to prioritise. The most obvious divergence developed between proponents of what became known as 'new' or 'welfare' feminism and its opponents, variously categorised as 'equality' or 'old' feminists. Equality feminists sought full sex equality in all areas of life, and wished to use their new political citizenship to achieve this. New feminism, which became associated with Eleanor Rathbone, questioned whether full equality was possible given women's reproductive role. In 1925, during her sixth presidential address to NUSEC (the successor organisation to the National Union of Women's Suffrage Societies, NUWSS), Rathbone outlined the differences between 'the old and the new feminism' as she saw them, and argued that it was time for feminism to shift its priorities. 'Old' feminism's search for parity with men in all fields responded to a male agenda. It saw women's problems 'through men's eyes', and limited its demands to 'what men have got'. 'New' feminism recognised women as a separate group whose requirements were not identical to those of men. Rather than seeking to blur gender differences it emphasised them, demanding that women should be given 'what [they] need to fulfil the potential of their own natures'.

The 'newness' of new feminism remains a matter of some discussion. Harold Smith argued that much of its ideology 'did not originate in [the post-war] period' but had been articulated by feminists including Rathbone at the height of the suffrage campaign.[3] Johanna Alberti concurred that new feminism was underpinned by ideas about sexual difference which 'had been running parallel to those of "old" feminism for a generation'.[4] Other historians see new feminism as a post-war development that emerged from women's disagreements about how to use the vote to best effect. Brian Harrison attributed it to women's realisation that 'nominal equality was not enough'.[5] Jane Lewis also saw it as very different from 'the nineteenth-century tradition of equal-rights feminism', and believed that it 'had the potential to develop a radical analysis of women's position'.[6] A third interpretation, from Susan Kingsley Kent, suggested that new feminism is better understood as regressive rather than radical. For Kent, the continuity in new feminist ideology lay not with feminist thought but in the biologically based arguments of many who had sought to curb women's entry into politics in the nineteenth century. In the face of a collective desire to return to normality after the upheavals of war, many feminists were willing to accept 'scientific theories of sexual difference' rather than challenge them, as in previous decades.[7]

Many supporters of new feminism argued that old feminism had a restricted appeal. Susan Pedersen's biography of Eleanor Rathbone underlined how her knowledge of the real-life problems of Liverpool's working-class housewives shaped her politics. When equality-feminist Rose Macaulay remarked that 'a house unkept cannot be so distressing as a life unlived', Pedersen imagined Rathbone concluding that these 'fine words for a bohemian spinster' had nothing to say to the working-class mother of five.[8] Several of Rathbone's contemporaries agreed, pointing out what they saw as the irrelevance of equality feminism's demands to most women. The *Women's Leader* criticised approaches which put the right of women to enter the boxing ring on equal terms with men over analyses that elevated motherhood, while Katharine Courtney memorably dismissed equal rights feminism as being simply 'me too feminism'.[9] Critics had a point. Winifred Holtby, one of the generation who considered themselves the inheritors and successors of the suffrage campaign, confessed in her defence of old feminism that she had embraced it mainly because she wanted 'an end of the whole business, the demands for equality, the suggestion of sex warfare … I want to be about the work in which my real interests lie … the writing of novels and so forth.'[10] New feminism argued that most women lacked the luxury of such a choice.

Two main issues divided new and equality feminists. The first was family allowances. During the war, Rathbone mobilised feminist networks to alleviate poverty amongst the families of working-class soldiers who initially received no separation allowances from the state. This experience confirmed her hypothesis that economic independence would have profound psychological effects on women, increasing their self-confidence and enabling them to become active citizens. Rathbone also believed that married women's economic dependence impacted on all women through normalising a male family wage. She saw family allowances, paid to mothers, as the answer and formed a small group, the Family Endowment Committee (later Society) to lobby for this in government and amongst women's organisations. In 1925 family allowances were added to NUSEC's programme, to the concern of equality feminists who feared that they were losing ground in the organisation. Many equality feminists supported the principle of family allowances but preferred to prioritise equal pay. They argued that this undermined the model of a male breadwinner by directly attacking gender difference in the workforce, whereas family allowances perpetuated it through rewarding women who fulfilled a biological role.

New and equality feminists also divided over protective legislation. NUSEC started from the broadly equality-feminist position of rejecting legislation based on the sex of the worker rather than the type of work being done. It campaigned against the 1924 Factories Bill, which proposed shorter working hours for women and not for men, but in March 1927 Eleanor Rathbone moved an amendment at the Executive Committee approving protective legislation in certain circumstances. When it was passed by one vote, 11 EC members resigned and the National Union of Women Teachers disaffiliated in protest.

Differences between new/welfare and old/equality feminists spilled into the international arena through the International Women's Suffrage Alliance. The Alliance voted to exclude the National Women's Party, America's leading proponent of equality feminism, in response to pressure from welfare feminists in the League of Women Voters. Lady Rhondda withdrew her equality-feminist organisation the SPG from the Alliance in protest. The SPG remained committed to international work, but changed its focus to concentrate on the International Labour Organization (ILO) of the League of Nations. It sent annual delegations to Geneva to lobby ILO delegates with regard to the status of their women citizens, but as Shirley Eoff pointed out, without the legitimacy of an international body behind them, their effectiveness was decreased.[11]

There is some debate as to how polarised the women's movement actually was in the inter-war period, although the differences between new and equality feminists were broadly reflected within organisations. Equality feminism drove the agenda of two new bodies, the SPG and the ODC. It also underpinned the continuing work of the Women's Freedom League which campaigned for equal votes for women and lobbied for equal employment opportunities. New feminism was increasingly associated with NUSEC after the split of 1927. Many Women Citizens' Associations also pursued new feminist demands in their local campaigns. Johanna Alberti saw divisions between NUSEC and the SPG in particular as a continuation of the militant/constitutional divide over suffrage, but other interpretations have found more common ground between the two positions.[12] Equality feminists, Harold Smith reminded us, did not oppose protective legislation per se, but its unequal application on the grounds of sex.[13] They supported measures such as the 1922 Criminal Law Amendment Act, which raised the age of consent from 13 to 16, increasing young women's legal protection against uninvited sexual advances. New feminists continued to push for equality measures, if not to prioritise them, and the different organisations combined in several campaigns. Lady Rhondda's biographer summarised that for her, 'the central issue was not whether equality or social betterment was preferable but which one deserved primacy in the feminist struggle'.[14]

Equality feminism in practice: the Six Point Group and the Open Door Council

Two groups, the SPG and the ODC, emerged to champion equality feminism in the 1920s, and continued until the 1960s. The SPG, often described as 'the leader among British feminist groups' between the wars, was established by the ex-WSPU member Margaret Haig (now Lady Rhondda) in February 1921.[15] Rhondda founded and edited *Time and Tide*, an influential independent feminist journal. Although it never became the SPG's official organ, *Time and Tide* gave much space to its work, and its regular writers such as Rebecca West and Cicely Hamilton were strong SPG supporters.

The SPG responded to the concerns of ex-suffrage activists that the vote had failed to deliver as much as feminists had hoped because it was being used ineffectively. Rhondda wished to establish an organisation of women which would be a 'definite practical body ... doing all in its power' to achieve legislative reform which would enhance equality between women and men.[16] The group's name derived from the six key points it identified as the targets for its work. Originally these were: satisfactory legislation on child assault, satisfactory legislation for unmarried mothers and their children, satisfactory legislation for widowed mothers, equal guardianship rights for married parents, equal pay for men and women teachers, and equal opportunities for men and women in the civil service. As one point was achieved, it was replaced by another one. In the 1930s the six points covered broad areas of economic, legal, occupational, moral, social and political equality. By the 1970s they were equal pay, equal partnership in marriage, equal retirement age, equal basis for pensions, equal education and equal opportunity.[17] Most feminists in the 1920s would have agreed with all six points, but some thought there were more pressing issues. The SPG's initial restriction of its demands for equal pay to teachers and equal employment conditions to civil servants drew criticism from those on the left who had long suspected feminism as being a movement that was only concerned with the rights of middle-class women. Yet at the same time, the SPG was 'designated the Left Wing feminist group' by its opponents, and never denied this appellation, which raised suspicions amongst Conservative women as to the nature of its political agenda.[18]

The SPG's methods distinguished it from other women's organisations. Some historians feel that its 'more urgent style' derived from its connections with militant suffrage – its leading lights included ex-Women's Social and Political Union (WSPU) organisers Dorothy Evans and Helen Archdale.[19] While NUSEC emphasized the need for political education, the SPG saw itself as a group for action. 'Everyone has grown tired of talking', it declared, 'We all want to get something done'.[20] Rhondda felt that women should be prepared to be 'so unpleasant to the powers that be' in pursuit of their demands that they would force capitulation.[21] The SPG drew up a blacklist of MPs based on their performance against the six points, which it published in *Time and Tide* before elections in the 1920s. This achieved some success, particularly in 1922 when nine of the 21 blacklisted MPs who stood for re-election were defeated. Despite scepticism about the relationship between the blacklist and such defeats, Pugh admitted that many MPs 'suffered slightly from their reputation as anti-feminists'.[22] In an era when parties were striving to comprehend the implications of voting women, the blacklist alerted MPs to the need to take feminist demands seriously. Yet while the SPG positioned itself within the militant tradition, it recognised that enfranchised women had different avenues available to them. Rhondda explained to Vera Brittain that 'militancy is right after one has tried other methods. But to open with militancy is like a naughty child which howls before it has any cause.'[23] The SPG never advocated a return to pre-war militant methods.

By the 1930s the SPG had started to take up concerns associated with new feminism. Jessica Bronwyn Thurlow's study of its work noted a shift in focus to look more closely at women's domestic situation, including their 'needs as mothers and wives', which reduced divisions between new and equality feminism.[24] The SPG considered forming a 'Housewives Group' to consider these issues, and set up a subcommittee led by Dorothy Evans and Juanita

Frances. In 1938 this evolved into a separate group, the Married Women's Association, which expanded during the war to form several local branches. Its mixture of practical demands (such as improved analgesia in childbirth) and feminist analysis of women's economic dependence within marriage proved popular amongst a younger generation of women activists who carried no memory of the suffrage campaign into their politics.

The Open Door Council

A second equality feminist organisation, the ODC, was formed in 1926 by Elizabeth Abbott and Chrystal Macmillan. The ODC had a narrower focus than the SPG, leading to a significant overlap in membership between the two groups. Abbot and Macmillan formed the ODC after a meeting of the International Women's Suffrage Alliance, where they had held informal delegates' meetings to discuss the idea of national societies and an international organisation for 'obtaining complete economic liberty and responsibility for adult women'.[25] It had one aim, to campaign against protective legislation for women that did not apply to men, a practice which it thought reflected a belief in 'the delicacy of women' that was 'a heritage from the days when women ... were also non-citizens'.[26] The ODC's understanding of the infantilising potential of continuing political inequality led it to briefly adopt the secondary aim of equal suffrage until 1928, when it reverted to being a single-issue body.

The ODC was never a large group (its membership was 349 by 1929), but it attempted to build some branches. These only materialised in the North West, where ex-suffragettes Hannah Mitchell and Lillian Forrester provided much of the driving force. The branches were active throughout the 1930s but stopped meeting during the Second World War. During the depression the ODC campaigned to protect women workers from attacks. It resisted the suggestion of a parliamentary commissioned report on 'Industrial Conditions in Certain Depressed Areas' that limiting women's labour would be one way of solving male unemployment. It challenged negative representations of working women and suggestions that particular jobs might be gendered; when the BBC broadcast a careers programme which implied that engineering was not a suitable job for girls to consider, the ODC sent a strong protest supported by evidence about women's current work in that field. During the Second World War it monitored how the government deployed women's labour, noting wryly that James Maxton's opposition to female conscription suggested he 'had never before heard of women industrial workers'.[27]

The ODC could be at odds with other organisations. Not all feminist groups agreed with its opposition to protective legislation, although its affiliate members included the St Joan's Alliance and the National Union of Women Teachers, which had left NUSEC over this issue. Some labour women's groups who shared the ODC's view of protective legislation were suspicious of its feminism. A propaganda feud developed with the Standing Joint Council of Industrial Women's Organisations (SJCIWO), as both organisations vied to represent the interests of working-class women.[28] This was exacerbated by the ODC's industrial focus, which meant that it targeted groups such as the

Women's Labour League and Women's Co-Operative Guilds which the SJCIWO was also involved with. In 1928 when the ODC attempted to set up a meeting with Ramsay Macdonald, the Labour Party's woman officer Marion Phillips warned him off, saying that the Council comprised 'feminists who had no industrial knowledge' and that 'oblivion would suit it better than anything else.'[29]

The SPG and the ODC also worked through two international pressure groups, Equal Rights International and Open Door International. Equal Rights International aimed to get an equal rights treaty through the League of Nations, and sent Helen Archdale to Geneva to work for this. Open Door International grew from feminists' dissatisfaction with the ILO, which they felt offered little or no space for adequate representation of women. Its international work mirrored the ODC's domestic agenda, and involved agitating for the removal of legal inequalities that existed, as well as protesting against those which were being introduced. Open Door International was alert to the reactionary nature of fascist regimes from an early stage, and sent a resolution to Hitler in 1934 protesting against 'the general lowering of the status of women in Germany'.

Women Citizens' Associations

The SPG and the ODC functioned as committees or pressure groups and were less concerned with developing into mass organisations. Other women's groups formed networks of branches throughout Britain. Women Citizens' Associations (WCAs) flourished in the inter-war period. The first WCA was set up by Eleanor Rathbone in Liverpool in 1911, as a politically independent group which would demonstrate the relevance of suffrage to women's lives. Rathbone expanded the initiative via the NUWSS in 1913, but felt that WCAs came into their own in the First World War, allowing women who 'had discovered themselves to be citizens for the first time' through war work to have their 'newly aroused consciousness ... captured, fostered and directed ... [to] become a permanent source of strength to the feminist movement'.[30] With support from the NUWSS and the National Union of Women Workers, a National Women Citizens' Association was inaugurated in 1918 and a Scottish Women Citizens' Association in 1919. The two national bodies remained separate due to the legal and administrative differences between Scotland and England and Wales, but worked closely together and held joint council meetings from 1968. Local WCA branches were left free to determine their own programmes and, unusually, were not obliged to affiliate to the national association, which explains why some continued to meet after the national association closed down in the 1970s.

Rathbone originally intended that the WCAs should foster a sense of citizenship in women, encourage self-education in civic and political questions, increase the numbers of women in local government and achieve the parliamentary vote. The National WCA (NWCA) broadly followed this agenda, although its concern was now with using the vote rather than getting it. Local government was an important focus; it took over the work and much of the membership of the Women's Local Government Association, offered support and training for women candidates, and hosted an annual local government conference for women councillors from the late 1930s until after the Second World War.

WCAs continued a pre-war feminist commitment to party independence. In Scotland, Sue Innes found that branches were 'happy to describe themselves as political, just not party political', which was also the case in England and Wales.[31] This was not always welcome; *The Scotsman* criticised the Scottish WCA's support for women as women on the grounds that this represented nothing more than a women's party. Nor was it easy to maintain this independence against a party system; many branches assumed a political complexion despite trying not to do so, through the external affiliations of their membership. A confidential internal report into the health of associations in 1931 found that in Derby membership was depleted as 'the WCA is considered (quite unfairly) to be a Conservative ... or a Labour ... or a Liberal organisation because there may happen to be a preponderance of members from one party or another'.[32] At the same time, party politics pulled politically active women away from WCAs. The NWCA's jubilee pamphlet, published in 1968, identified the growth of party women's sections as one of the reasons for the decrease in local associations, and suggested that the non-party approach had failed, as without party support it was 'all but impossible to take an active part in national and local politics'.[33]

The freedom allocated to WCA branches encouraged the development of a diverse profile of activities. Some retained a small, discreet membership, but others such as Cambridge became an 'umbrella organisation' with 18 affiliated societies (including the local Women's Liberal Association, which cut across its apolitical stance).[34] The social composition of associations also varied, partly in response to other locally available organisations. In Liverpool, where Rathbone had hoped that WCAs might attract working-class women intimidated by the middle-class profile of the local NUWSS, they recruited some prominent labour women in the inter-war period; conversely in Nelson, where the NUWSS had been popular amongst trade union women, Selina Cooper found it almost impossible to bring them into the WCA.[35] A middle-class profile could be useful, however, as in Arbroath where Sarah Browne's research concluded that their presence 'helped to legitimise the cause' of the local WCA.[36] The eclecticism of its branches did not prevent the NWCA from collective national campaigning, with some success. Looking back in 1968 it noted that many of its campaigns had resulted in legislative change, including the right of married women to retain their nationality, the appointment of women police, cervical screening and extended hours for visiting children in hospital.[37]

Other women's organisations

Analyses of the effectiveness of inter-war feminist groups have shifted in recent years. Previously it was thought that winning the vote had taken away the focus of the women's movement and blunted its edge. Many contemporaries would have agreed with Lady Rhondda, who described herself as 'a little bored' with the legislative focus of inter-war campaigns, the 'heap of niggling little laws that need altering .... I want bigger game than that'.[38] Participants found inter-war organisations less consuming than their predecessors. Hazel Hunkins Hallinan, the last president of the SPG, believed that they lacked 'the unity, dedication and vigour of the past'.[39] More recently Helen Jones has suggested that diversity might be read as revealing a stronger movement than was hitherto recognised, and that 'the range of organisations in which women were involved ... was a sign of flourishing thought among women and a means of them trying to order priorities'.[40]

Recognising diversity in inter and post-war feminism has also encouraged study of a broader range of organisations. Not all non-party women's groups adopted the label of feminist. Some found this an unattractive identity, as Vera Brittain recognised when she described its stereotype, 'spectacled, embittered women, disappointed, childless, dowdy and generally unloved'.[41] Catriona Beaumont has argued that a concentration on the realignment of suffrage organisations missed the true extent of the inter-war women's movement, and ignored the importance of numerous groups that did not define themselves as feminist but recruited large numbers of women and fought for women's issues.[42] Beaumont used the term 'mainstream' to describe bodies such as the National Federation of Women's Institutes (WIs), which formed in 1915 and had 238,000 members by the 1930s, more than the ODC, SPG , NUSEC and the WFL combined. Although their constitution precluded WIs from taking direct involvement in political issues, their membership was not apolitical; Edith Rigby, an ex-WSPU arsonist, and Elizabeth Robins, who had been on the WSPU's Executive Committee, were amongst a number of better-known recruits who chose to continue their work for women in this way.[43] Such women recognised the political dimensions of the WIs' campaigns around issues such as improved water and sanitation in rural districts and for the extension of the women police force, which often brought WI members into joint activity with women from overtly feminist groups.

Margaret Andrews' study of the WI argued that its obsession with domesticity should not be read as inherently apolitical or anti-feminist. Through its emphasis on consumption, she found the WI 'offering women an area of authority' which helped to transform the home into a legitimate site for political struggle.[44] WI work in the countryside was replicated in an urban context by branches of the National Union of Townswomen's Guilds. The Guilds evolved from NUSEC in 1928 at the suggestion of Margery Corbett Ashby, who wanted a group to 'combine the feminism of the National Union with the social activities of the rural Women's Institutes'.[45] The Guilds tried to emulate the WI's success at drawing apolitical women into some form of activity through a programme which combined political education with social activities beyond the home. Beaumont's study of 'mainstream' women's organisations in the inter-war period also points to the importance of religious groups such as the Mother's Union, Young Women's Christian Association and the Catholic Women's League. She notes that while these groups rejected the label of feminist, they all fought to extend women's rights as newly enfranchised citizens. Their incorporation into investigations of the inter-war women's movement broadens its size and scope considerably.

Feminist organisations in the Second World War

The effect of the Second World War on women's political organisations and activities has received less attention than its impact on women's social role, yet women's organisations were better placed to articulate their demands in 1939 than they had been in 1914. The First World War cut across a high-point in women's political activity and ended the combative phase of the suffrage campaign. In 1939 the situation was very different. Martin Pugh has argued that the Second World War was more significant for the women's movement than the First, as women 'entered it as citizens of their country'.[46] Women's politics were more formalised, located within established political parties as well as across a range of other organisations. Yet while women's citizenship enabled the state to call on their resources, it did not necessarily do this on the terms that feminist organisations would have wished. Helen Jones has suggested that the government preferred to contain women's activity within voluntary bodies such as the Women's Voluntary Service, established by Lady Reading in 1938 at the request of the home secretary.[47] James Hinton's detailed study of women's voluntary work during the war supports this, revealing a mistrust of what were considered 'extreme' feminist organisations by some engaged in voluntary work.[48]

The small amount of research to date on women's politics during the Second World War concurs that the period precipitated a 'modest' growth in organised feminist activity.[49] This was encouraged by the wartime political truce, which paused electoral contests and reduced party conflict within Parliament. It was unfortunate for the women's movement that the election of 1935 had reduced the number of women MPs to nine (although this rose to 14 during the war as a result of various by-elections); nevertheless, Brookes' survey of women MPs up to the 1960s concluded that in war time 'as at no other ... the women members of Parliament came nearest to acting as a women's party, speaking with one voice on behalf of their sex', something she ascribed to the 'marked reluctance' of male politicians to use women's resources at the start of the war.[50] Pugh agreed that 'something like a women's party' emerged at this time.[51] Beyond the parliamentary arena, Alison Oram's research concurred that the war 'presented an opportunity for the women's movement to reconcile' divisions between new and equality feminism as well as to articulate feminist demands in a different arena.[52] Wartime conditions offered opportunities, as the government's desire to maximise women's participation in the Home Front gave them a platform.

The revival of interest in collective activity by women had organisational implications. Alongside the continuing work of older groups including the WFL, SPG and ODC, several new ones emerged around the time of the war. The Women's Publicity Planning Association (WPPA) was set up in December 1939 by women active in existing organisations, including Margery Corbett Ashby and Rebecca Sieff. It was intended to facilitate information exchange between a number of women's groups in Britain and abroad. Many of its leaders retained the long-held feminist belief that political education offered the best hope of attracting large numbers of women into politics, thus bringing about some of the changes the suffrage movement had sought. The WPPA was intended to function as an umbrella organisation, and attracted a large range of groups to its initial meeting, ranging from trade unions to feminist bodies. In 1940 it took over the *International Women's News*, the former journal of the International Alliance of Women, as a means of disseminating news and information. Its best-known campaign centred on the Personal Injuries (Emergency Provisions) Act of 1939, which detailed compensation available to civilians injured through the war. This campaign, summed up by the title of an article in the *International Women's News*, 'Bombs don't discriminate', involved sustained lobbying of ministers and a large demonstration in Trafalgar Square (the first significant public protest of the war). WPPA activists were keen to emphasise the injustice of a system which insisted on equality when mobilising women for the war effort but continued to predicate its compensation scales on outmoded notions of male breadwinning. The WPPA claimed success in 1943 when the government agreed to offer equal compensation rates. This marked the end of the campaign, but the WPPA continued to lobby on similar issues; the influential post-war Equal Pay Campaign Committee developed from its Equal Compensation Committee.[53]

Broader equality was more elusive, and the WPPA had less success with its second major campaign around the Equal Citizenship (Blanket) Bill. The bill was largely the work of Dorothy Evans, the WPPA's paid organiser, who was also a member of the SPG. Evans' research for the bill, published as a pamphlet by the WPPA, identified 30 key areas in which the law still discriminated against women. The Blanket Bill aimed to overturn these and to prohibit further sexual discrimination in future legislation. As Oram noted, the bill's equality stance did not preclude recognition of difference, and it considered specific issues relating to housewives as well as taking account of inequalities in employment and public life.[54] The WPPA realised it needed party support to progress the bill, but could not persuade any of the main parties to take it up. When Evans died unexpectedly in 1944 the idea disappeared.

Women MPs' priority in Parliament was to ensure that government was making the best use of women in support of the war effort. All 14 women MPs approached the Treasury in February 1940 to demand a greater role for women. When no satisfactory response was received, Lady Astor formed the cross-party Woman Power Committee which met fortnightly throughout the war, acting as a conduit between feminist groups and government. Meeting regularly together encouraged women MPs to coordinate their approach. Nearly every one spoke in the first woman power debate in March 1941. They become more proactive on behalf of other women in broader areas, objecting to attempts to belittle their sex through propaganda such as the security poster which urged readers to 'Be like Dad, keep Mum'. The combined efforts of the committee had some effect. In April 1942 the government overturned a decision to set up an all-male committee to look at welfare in branches of the women's services, and appointed five women and three men in its place.

The conviction that legislative change was the best way to enhance women's social status encouraged the WPPA to initiate another organisation, Women for Westminster (WFW), in 1943. This was essentially a single-issue group aimed at increasing the numbers of elected women in national and local government. The idea for a group of this kind came after Edith Summerskill reminded the WPPA's annual general meeting of the difficulty the relatively small number of women MPs faced in ensuring that there was someone speaking for women on each of the multitude of parliamentary committees whose decisions affected women's lives. Its founders knew that a similar initiative in the 1920s had failed, so they discussed plans with the veteran feminist Teresa Billington Grieg to see what lessons could be drawn. They decided to revive the experiment despite her 'discouraging' account (although pessimism did not prevent Billington Grieg from taking a leading role in the new organisation herself).

At first WFW proved popular. Branches were established from Bournemouth to Glasgow, and over 1500 members were recruited by 1944. Like other groups, WFW remained convinced of the importance of political education for women. There were other echoes of previous campaigns too. Its 'Road to Westminster' leaflet spoke of the potential of war to politicise women in terms which echoed those of Eleanor Rathbone at the inauguration of the NWCA during the First World War. WFW devised a series of educational programmes which combined speakers' classes with lectures on the workings of local and national government. These had appeal beyond the party political arena, with the *British Journal of Nursing* reporting that 'there is nothing in the programme in which an intelligent nurse should not be interested'. There was less success in achieving the organisation's main aim. WFW leadership was aware that it had to be cross-party to appeal to all women, so it asked constituency representatives from all political parties to adopt women candidates. It found the response disappointing, something which it partly attributed to the poor state of much party machinery because of the wartime political truce.[55] Jessica Bronwyn Thurlow's account of the group's activities also suggests that it was unpopular within the Conservative Party despite numbering Conservative women amongst its members.[56] The general election of 1945 returned a disappointing number of female candidates. The group struggled on for a few years but floundered as women's sections of political parties regrouped. In 1949 it was amalgamated into the NWCA.

Feminist organisations in the post-war era

Helen Jones' study of the work of feminist organisations during the Second World War cautioned that although wartime circumstances had revitalised the movement, 'there was a difference between implementing policy and actually making it'.[57] The lack of real power transferred to women's groups during the war may explain why peace saw a downturn in their activities. Many pre-existing feminist organisations attempted to reinvigorate themselves in the 1950s but with little success. The SPG appointed Sybil Morrison, an ex-suffragette now working for WFW, as paid organiser but could not sustain her salary, and when she stepped down in 1950 she was not replaced. The ODC urged members 'to revive the spirit which had carried the suffrage campaign' into its work for economic equality, but failed to attract significant numbers of new members.

Feminist organisations continued lobbying on a number of issues, often working collectively. All were involved in campaigns over equal pay, and represented on the Equal Pay Campaign Committee which Mavis Tate MP formed after the war. The SPG called for the removal of property qualifications to ensure more women jurors in the 1960s, and monitored the introduction of the Equal Pay Act in the 1970s. The ODC continued to produce valuable research in support of feminist campaigns. In 1950 it produced a list of occupations that remained closed to women when it transpired that the Ministry of Labour had no such information. It also surveyed local authorities' policies on maternity leave for teachers, and revealed some surprising anomalies with regard to the points at which different authorities expected women to declare their pregnancies and to stop work.[58] Although many feminists would now disagree with its demand that maternity leave would be better served through certificates of incapacity (thus equating it with sickness), this did acknowledge that not all pregnancies were identical. The WCAs took an active interest in representations of women in the media, and lobbied the BBC to demand better coverage of the women's movement.[59]

Divisions between old and new feminism continued to diminish. In 1949 the SPG announced that the time had come to move beyond 'straightforward equalitarian issues' and to 'recognise that women's needs and values are often different from those of men'.[60] In the post-war era much SPG analysis focused on the situation of working mothers who retained overall responsibility for domestic management, and it called for tax reform to recognise this. This struck a chord with some younger women such as Clare Campbell, a journalist who joined the group in the 1950s and explained how the lines between old and new feminism had become blurred for her generation. 'With the old school I want equality ... but with the new school I am not prepared to swallow whole a man-made society's definition of what humanness consists in.'[61] Women like Campbell who had no historical memory of earlier campaigns were happy to look at both sides of the debate and take approaches from each.

The convergence of ideology and a decline in numbers prompted attempts to amalgamate groups. This met with mixed responses. WFW amalgamated with the NWCA, but negotiations between other groups failed. Organisations were beset by internal divisions. Several executive committee members resigned from the SPG in the early 1950s in protest at the promotion of causes such as opposition to the Korean War, which they felt were 'NOT strictly feminist.'[62] For older feminists such as Teresa Billington Grieg, a key issue was the vote's seeming inability to effect the changes her generation had expected of it, something she put down to 'the failure to organise the voting power of women' which underpinned ongoing inequality at work and in the home.[63] Many feminists still believed that electing more women would change this, and continued to offer suggestions as to how to bring this about. SPG feminists attempted to initiate some imaginative campaigns in the 1950s, briefly promoting the idea of a 'coupled vote' making each constituency elect a male and a female representative, but this was not popular. Neither was its call for women trade unionists to consider symbolic strike action for feminist demands. Indeed SPG leaders were surprised by the 'timidity and fear' of a younger generation of women, who were unwilling to engage in direct action and appeared mild in contrast to themselves.[64]

Between the end of the Second World War and the arrival of the Women's Liberation Movement in Britain, falling membership became an acute problem for the older feminist societies. This began in the war, when economy measures forced several branches to close. By the 1950s most societies were reduced to small committees, which hampered their effectiveness to function in wider forums. The SPG tried to affiliate to the Women's National Commission which reported directly to the United Nations Commission, but was rejected as it lacked 'branches throughout the country'.[65] It started a small number of regional branches; Hampshire was established in 1965 and had recruited 100 members in its first year, and a North West Branch formed in 1972. There were attempts to draw regional members into activity through schemes such as monitoring the success of women on local bodies, but no other branches emerged. The NWCA fared slightly better as its purpose had always been to coordinate a network of branches, but it too reported finding it 'impossible to ... open new branches' by the 1970s. The oldest remaining society, the Women's Freedom League, was unrecognisable from the original organisation with its network of branches and paid organisers before the First World War. Its weekly newspaper, *The Vote*, was replaced by a monthly *Bulletin*. This reported events of interest, ranging from the introduction of women's suffrage in the Bahamas to profiles of women parliamentary candidates, but made no mention of any specific WFL campaigns. The contents of later *Bulletins* stand as a metaphor for the final years of the older suffrage societies: a preponderance of obituaries and heavy coverage of the activities of the Suffragette Fellowship, an organisation of ex-suffragettes concerned with arranging commemorative activities and safeguarding suffrage history. Read collectively, they portray an organisation passing into history whose membership was literally dying out.

Some of the earlier generation of feminists attempted to engage with the concerns of the Women's Liberation Movement (WLM) which emerged in the late 1960s. The SPG spoke out in defence of the 1967 Abortion Act, and held an 'open forum' to discuss what a cohabitation contract might look like in 1973. Its final president, Hazel Hunkins Hallinan, saw the WLM as 'a new group of militants to carry on the old battle for equality'.[66] Yet while a small number of young feminists like Dale Spender recognized women like Hallinan as their predecessors, most felt remote from the older generation, and did not seek them out.[67] At the SPG's 50th anniversary celebrations in 1979 Eva Figes explained that 'although she appreciated what the "Six Point Group generation" had done for women, many of the younger generation did not.'[68] When the SPG closed in 1980, the nonagenarian Hallinan expressed her disappointment at the lack of an active programme which she felt would attract members; another committee member, V. Gilbert, made the more salient point that in her opinion the younger generation of feminists emerging in the 1970s were more interested in single-issue campaigns than in organisations that fought on a broad equality programme.[69]

The Status of Women Committee, which had operated as a coordinating body for around 20 feminist organisations in monitoring legislation that had equality implications, folded at around the same time. This group had also failed to recruit a younger membership, although in a more positive vein it noted that 'most of its original aims had been achieved'.[70] It also observed an increase in women's organisations, many of which were fighting for similar aims to the group, echoing the SPG's remarks on the greater appeal of single-issue campaigns. Other groups had already gone. The ODC continued its calls for equal pay throughout the 1950s but declined throughout the 1960s, issuing its final report in 1967. The NWCA disbanded in 1974, declaring that it had 'proved impossible to recruit large numbers of new members and to open new branches – largely because of present day society', although individual branches kept going in some districts.[71] The NWCA recognised that the new generation of feminists had more knowledge of politics but less free time than their predecessors, and were much more likely to be in full-time work; nevertheless it continued to hold its meetings in the afternoons, which suited its long-standing membership but made it more difficult to attract new generations. The longest-standing of all the inter-war groups, the WFL, closed in November 1961. In the final issue of the *Bulletin* its founder Teresa Billington Grieg acknowledged the difficulties in establishing a trans-generational feminist movement: 'There are still things to be done but our generation has had its day. The new generation has its own problems to solve and must find its own way to do so'.[72]

The Women's Liberation Movement

The new generation Billington Grieg referred to organised itself in the Women's Liberation Movement, which emerged in Britain in the late 1960s. Its origins were varied; some participants came from the New Left, from Marxist or socialist parties or from the peace movement via the Campaign for Nuclear Disarmament or smaller anti-Vietnam war groups. Others were women new to politics who reacted to the energy of the new movement, which encouraged them 'to talk to each other in a way they had not done before'.[73] Further impetus came from autonomous movements of working-class women in the later 1960s, which Vicky Randall felt distinguished the British movement from its American counterpart.[74] Lil Bilocca, a fisherman's wife from Hull, led other women on a series of protests demanding better conditions for their seafaring husbands, and women workers at the Ford Motor Company's plant in Dagenham fought for equal pay. Socialist feminists in the WLM supported these efforts in an attempt to bridge the politics of sex and class and forge alliances with working-class militants. A small group tried to unionise women working as night cleaners in London in 1971. With the help of cleaner May Hobbs they succeeded in gaining recognition for a cleaners' branch of the Civil Service Union and a pay rise for women working in Whitehall. Other attempts to unionise cleaners took place in Oxford and Durham. Sheila Rowbotham, one of the original organisers, credited the campaign with contributing to a shift in attitudes to low-paid women workers among the male-dominated trade union movement.[75]

At the same time, the growth of the WLM revealed some of the difficulties in building an inter-generational feminist movement. Some younger activists felt that it was important to safeguard the history of earlier feminist campaigns. Elizabeth Wilson's early account of the growth of WLM situated its origins in part in the 'ferment of political activity' in women's peace groups as they marked the fiftieth anniversary of the vote in 1968.[76] Many leading WLM activists were also historians, such as Sheila Rowbotham and Sally Alexander. Groups including the Birmingham Feminist History Group and magazines such as *Spare Rib* made some connections with older activists and recorded their stories.[77] At the same time, Joni Lovenduski has observed that 'generational differences became a leitmotif' for young women in the WLM who sought to emphasise the differences between their campaigns and those of previous emancipatory movements.[78] In the freer climate of the 1960s, the WLM placed greater emphasis on personal matters than on general equality issues, giving personal consciousness raising as much weight as legislative change. This compounded a sense of difference between the WLM and older feminists. Sandra Grey and Marian Sawer explained how the new generation of women were:

> distancing themselves from the 'polite' methods of their mothers' generation when they adopted and adapted the repertoire of the anti-war and student movement. Consciousness raising and radical collectivism seemed to belong to a different world to the club rooms and deputations of the previous generation of feminist advocates.[79]

There were also marked differences in the forms of organisation pioneered by the WLM. It eschewed formal structures in favour of a system of national conferences and regional issue-based events.[80] Local branches proliferated, driven, according to a report in the *Sunday Times*, by 'the principle ... that a group should reproduce ... the moment numbers begin to make meetings less personal'.[81] This gave the movement different characteristics depending on its regional and national context. Beddoe found that in Wales the importance of language was emphasised by many women during campaigns for nursery provision. In Scotland activists participated in some British campaigns but mainly organised on a Scottish scale, which Fiona Mackay ascribed to a resurgence of Scottish nationalism coupled with dissatisfaction with reforms which were 'seen as disproportionately impacting upon Scotland and Scottish women in particular'.[82] The first National Women's Liberation Movement Conference was held at Ruskin College, Oxford in February 1970 and attracted 600 delegates, twice the expected number.[83] The conference became an annual event, growing to 3000 delegates in 1977, until its final meeting in 1978. A national coordinating committee was attempted but this dissolved after a year amidst accusations that it was dominated by one political faction. It was the conference that determined WLM demands and provided the movement with a degree of coherence, albeit broad. These began as equal pay, equal education and job opportunities, free contraception and abortion on demand, and free access to 24-hour nurseries. In 1975 demands for financial and legal independence and for an end to discrimination against lesbians and the right for women to define their own sexuality were added, and a final demand, for an end to violence against women and to laws perpetuating male dominance and aggression, was adopted in 1978. From 1975 a fortnightly newsletter, *Wires*, communicated news of the movement between different groups.

By the late 1970s the WLM was increasingly fragmented, something Randall ascribed in part to its failure to develop any mechanism for national coordination.[84] Different tendencies emerged with different priorities. Radical or revolutionary feminists were influenced by the ideas of the American theorists such as Shulamith Firestone and Susan Brownmiller. They emphasised male violence and developed a critique of heterosexuality which led some of them to call for all feminists to adopt the position of political lesbianism. Socialist feminists were concerned with building connections with working-class women but also sought to develop a theoretical perspective which amalgamated Marxism and feminism.[85] The Annual Conference of 1978 broke up amidst disagreements between socialist and radical feminists, and no further annual conferences were held, although this did not mark the end of WLM as a movement. It is also important to note that, as with welfare and equality feminism in the 1920s and 1930s, radical and socialist feminists did not divide predictably on all questions but 'campaigned together on a number of specific issues' throughout the 1970s.[86]

A final important strand in British feminist politics emerged at the end of the 1970 amongst women of Afro-Caribbean and Asian backgrounds. The Organization of Women of African and Asian Descent was launched in 1978 and organised the first Black women's conference in 1979, which discussed issues such as health, immigration and access to education.[87] Black feminism developed a critique of certain aspects of the WLM, which it saw as marginalising their own concerns. Valerie Amos and Pratibba Parmar described 'the ways in which a particular tradition, Western and Eurocentric, has sought to establish itself as the only legitimate feminism', and challenged feminism to take more account of racism and imperialism.[88] Black feminism became established on the editorial board of *Spare Rib* from the early 1980s, as well as in the National Abortion Campaign, where a spin-off 'Women's Reproductive Rights Campaign' emerged taking more account of the economic and cultural settings in which 'choice' occurred.[89] Randall saw the emergence of a distinctive Black feminism as the 'real challenge' to radical feminism, rather than socialist feminism which was beginning to look to other political groups beyond the autonomous WLM.[90]

Studies of the WLM agree that fragmentation did not necessarily diminish the effect of feminism at all levels. Randall presented an optimistic picture of its 'diversification' by the early 1980s which drew 'older ... younger ... disabled ... anarchist women and so forth' into a number of campaigns.[91] Sheila Rowbotham suggested that the numerous competing claims from 'women of differing classes, colours, cultures, sexual preferences' had emerged as 'feminism became stronger'.[92] The 1970s saw women's groups throughout Britain campaigning on a number of different issues, often with success. Radical feminist critiques of male sexuality led to a focus on rape and violence against women. This came to centre on domestic violence, and led to the opening of the first safe house for battered women in Chiswick in 1972. By 1980 the Women's Aid Federation had a network of over 200 refuges, many partly supported through local government grants. There were campaigns around women's health, most obviously defending the 1967 Abortion Act and demanding better access to contraception, but also raising awareness of issues such as breast cancer (an early issue of the feminist magazine *Spare Rib* became the subject of an obscenity prosecution in Ireland for carrying an article instructing women how to examine their breasts for potentially lethal lumps). In the field of education many women graduates who had become involved in WLM as students carried their politics into their work as academics. Women's history, feminist literary criticism and feminist sociology were just some of the disciplinary shifts which precipitated the establishment of the first women's studies courses in the 1980s. At the same time, as in previous eras many women found the local arena more receptive to feminist politics. Several councils set up women's committees in the late 1970s and early 1980s, and funded women's centres. Thus although the national peak of second-wave feminism may be said to have ended by the middle of the decade, feminist organisation continued on a number of levels far beyond this date.

Conclusion

This chapter has shown the variety of non-party settings for women's politics after the First World War. The suggestion that there was no discernible feminist activity between the suffrage movement and the WLM was challenged in the early 1980s by Dale Spender, when the veteran campaigner Mary Stott reminded her that 'there's always been a women's movement this century'.[93] Research into the form that this movement took has shown that inter-war feminism remained an important presence in British politics as women sought to develop the potential of their political citizenship in different ways.

It is true that the inter-war movement lacked the coherence of its Edwardian predecessor, as it campaigned on a number of different issues rather than concentrating on one demand. This diversity, combined with its pursuit of more constitutional methods, possibly made it less newsworthy, and its activities are less familiar than those of the suffragettes. Nevertheless, it is clear that many women remained committed to developing a distinctive form of feminist politics after the Women's Party collapsed in 1918. While some sought to do this from within political parties, a number still worked in autonomous women's groups such as NUSEC, the SPG and WCAs. Others were attracted by the examples of the Townswomen's Guilds or Women's Institutes, which suggested a community-based model of politics which was feminised if not feminist.

Non-party women's political organisations entered the Second World War in a more confident position than they did the First, as their memberships comprised voters with a recognised relationship to the British state. The war also reduced party-political conflict, allowing women MPs to work collectively, which in turn encouraged coherence within the broader feminist movement. Yet while its leadership gained prominence through collective work, wartime conditions had a detrimental impact on grass-roots women's organisations. Many branches were forced to curtail their regular activities. When party affiliations reasserted themselves in the post-war era, the organised feminist movement found itself badly placed to counter these.

In the late 1960s the public profile of British feminism was revitalised with the growth of the WLM. Although this owed much to developments in America, it developed national distinctiveness in Britain through its emphasis on connecting with working-class activists. The WLM attracted younger women who felt a generational separation from older campaigners. There was little formal contact between new groups and older organisations, although many younger women sought to preserve the history of an earlier feminist movement as part of their activism. The WLM undertook high-profile campaigns which returned feminism to the public eye, but lacked the structural unity of previous groups, partly through its own commitment to non-hierarchical, independent models of organisation. It was composed of numerous small, autonomous groups which mobilised around the movement's demands in different ways.

Attempts to coordinate the WLM through a national conference were short-lived, with the final national conference in 1978 disintegrating into acrimonious disputes between supporters of radical and socialist feminism. The ending of national conferences did not mean that feminist activity ceased, however. Just as in the inter-war period, women continued to press political aims in a number of arenas in the 1970s, including local government, where many of the demands of the WLM were translated into policy initiatives. Many women moved from the WLM into party politics, particularly on the left, where they began to demand greater representation within existing political structures. These demands would eventually translate into a number of measures which collectively increased women's presence at all levels of party organisation, although these would not take place until the 1980s.

Conclusion

On 4 May 1979, Margaret Thatcher paused on the steps of number 10 Downing Street to talk to journalists before starting work as Britain's first woman Prime Minister. One journalist asked her if she had 'any thoughts at this moment about Mrs Pankhurst', a question which Thatcher chose to ignore.[1] Women's groups were similarly ambivalent about her appointment: while some welcomed the symbolic potential of a woman Prime Minister, others demonstrated with placards demanding 'women's rights, not a right-wing woman'.

In some ways 1979 is not the best place to end an overview of women in British politics. The arrival of the first woman prime minister at Westminster did little to improve the lives of the majority of British women per se. The sex of the prime minister is not the same as the sex of Parliament, and Parliament did not change under a woman prime minister. Although Thatcher spoke to the 300 Group (an organisation set up in 1980 which aimed to get 300 women into Parliament) about the benefits of women in public life and her wish to see more of these, she did nothing to try to bring this about. There were fewer women MPs in 1979 than there had been in previous years, and none were promoted to cabinet office. Outside Parliament too there was less evidence of political activity by women than there had been in the earlier part of the decade. The Women's Liberation Movement had fragmented amidst sectional infighting. And while there were still numerous feminist groups thriving at local level, many of these would soon find their funding cut as Thatcher's restructuring of local government abolished the Greater London Council and metropolitan county councils in the West Midlands, Merseyside, South Yorkshire and elsewhere in 1985.

It was not until 1997 that a significant number of women MPs were returned as a result of radical new selection procedures in all parties. When Tony Blair was photographed on the terrace of the House of Commons surrounded by 101 women MPs, the visual difference from images of Susan Lawrence, Margaret Bondfield and a handful of other women in the 1920s was marked. Nevertheless, women still remained in a minority in Parliament and were subject to the same criticisms which had surrounded the first intake of women MPs after the First World War. The resignation of Caroline Flint from the cabinet in the summer of 2009, when she accused the Prime Minister of using women MPs for 'female window dressing' attracted a barrage of headlines which had as much to say about her appearance as her politics.

On the other hand, as the study of women in political parties has shown, political women are not automatically feminist, nor should feminist history concern itself only with the history of feminism. The tendency to conflate the history of women in politics with the history of the women's movement has neglected those women who did not necessarily work with other women to advance the interests of their sex. When placed in the broader context of women's political activity across a wider political spectrum, the failure of even quite high numbers of women in Parliament to challenge the gendering of British politics appears less surprising given that for many of them this was never part of their agenda. Mary Astell, the National League for Opposing Women's Suffrage and several twentieth-century conservative women's organisations were all keen to see women's influence in public life, but wished this to occur without a shift in broader gender relations or advances in full sexual equality across society.

There are remarkable continuities in the rhetoric and actions of women in British politics over the three centuries covered by this book. The tensions between equality and difference, for example, predated debates between old and new feminists and continue to shape the thinking of political parties at the present time as they attempt to capture a 'woman's vote' in the face of empirical evidence (in the form of women MPs on all sides) that women do not vote on gendered lines. Available voting data suggests that it is true that more women have voted Conservative in the inter-war years, but not that all women have done so. Ongoing discussions about women's role in politics are simply not paralleled by debates about political men, which suggests that despite over 70 years of equal voting, the political still tends to be thought of as male and is normalised in this way. There are also continuities of absences or moments when women's involvement lessens following a period of backlash, such as was found after the Restoration, or in the early nineteenth century. Yet there are also differences, and despite my earlier cautioning about the over-use of the heroic voice in studies of women's politics, some of these may be considered improvements. Nobody now questions women's right to vote, for example, and although measures such as positive discrimination and the all-woman shortlist have attracted much criticism, opposition to the idea of a woman MP is much less evident than it was in Nancy Astor's day.

There is, however, a more pessimistic reading of these changes. Ultimately politics is about the exercise of power, wherever this is located. In her provocative defence of feminist history, *History Matters*, Judith Bennett suggested that a longer-term perspective on women's history might blunt some of the events that are seen as victories in shorter-term chronologies. She takes the metaphor of a ballroom dance to explain how 'many different sorts of women and men – move across the room, alter their steps, movement and rhythms, even change partners or groups, but always the men are leading.'[2] I would argue that this metaphor is equally applicable to the study of women and politics, particularly in the case of Parliament, where women have begun to make an impact, in terms of numbers at least, at precisely the point at which parliamentary politics is decreasing in relevance. In an age of globalisation the number of women prime ministers has increased across the world, but their power is limited compared with the power their male equivalents exercised in the nineteenth century. The most striking continuity in the history of women and politics remains their absence from the real centres of power, wherever they may be located.

Notes

Introduction

1. Amanda Vickery, 'Introduction', in Amanda Vickery (ed.), *Women, Privilege and Power: British Politics, 1750 to the Present* (Stanford, Calif., 2001).
2. Bertha Mason, *The Story of the Women's Suffrage Movement* (London, 1912), p. 93.
3. Verta Taylor and Leila Rupp, 'Preface', in Sandra Grey and Marian Sawer (eds), *Women's Movements: Flourishing or in Abeyance?* (London, 2008), pp. xii–xvi.
4. Dale Spender, *There's Always Been a Women's Movement This Century* (London, 1983).
5. Johanna Alberti, *Beyond Suffrage: Feminists in War and Peace* (Basingstoke, 1989); Cheryl Law, *Suffrage and Power* (London, 1997); Jessica Thurlow, 'Continuity and change in British feminism c.1940–1960', PhD thesis, University of Michigan (2006); Samantha Clements, 'Feminism, citizenship and social activity: the role and importance of local women's organisations, Nottingham, 1918–1969'. PhD thesis, University of Nottingham (2008).
6. Spender (1983), p. 7.
7. Hilda Smith (ed.), *Women Writers and the Early Modern British Political Tradition* (Cambridge, 1998), p. 4.
8. Kim D. Reynolds, *Aristocratic Women and Political Society* (Oxford, 1998), p. 1.
9. Government Equalities Office Factsheet: Women's Representation in the UK. HMSO, September 2008.
10. Catriona Beaumont, 'Citizens not feminists: the boundary negotiated between citizenship and feminism by mainstream women's organisations in England, 1928–39', *Women's History Review* 9, 2 (2000), pp. 411–29.
11. Bernard Capp, *When Gossips Meet: Women, Family and Neighbourhood in Early Modern England* (Oxford, 2003), p. 268.
12. Kirsti Bohata, 'For Wales see England? Suffrage and the New Woman in Wales', *Women's History Review* 11, 4 (2002), pp. 643–56.
13. Angela John (ed.), *Our Mother's Land: Studies in Welsh Women's History 1890–1939* (Cardiff, 1991); Jane Aaron, Teresa Rees, Sandra Betts and Moira Vincentelli (eds), *Our Sisters' Land: The Changing Identities of Women in Wales* (Cardiff, 1994); Deidre Beddoe, *Out of the Shadows* (Cardiff, 2001).
14. Lynn Abrams, 'Introduction' in Lynn Abrams, Eleanor Gordon, Deborah Simonton and Eileen Yeo (eds), *Gender in Scottish History Since 1700* (Edinburgh, 2006).

15. For example, Paul Chaney, Fiona Mackay and Laura McAllister (eds), *Women, Politics and Constitutional Change* (Cardiff, 2007); Esther Breitenbach and Pat Thane (eds), *Women and Citizenship in Britain and Ireland* (Leicester, 2009).

1 From Glorious Revolution to Enlightenment

1. For example H. N. Brailsford, *The Levellers in the English Revolution* (London, 1961).
2. Keith Wrightson, 'The politics of the parish in early modern England', in Paul Griffiths, Adam Fox and Steve Hindle (eds), *The Experience of Authority in Early Modern England* (Basingstoke, 1996).
3. Ralph Houlbrooke, 'Women's social life and common action in England from the fifteenth century to the eve of the Civil War', *Continuity and Change* 1 (1986), pp. 339–52; Jacqueline Eales, *Women in Early Modern England 1500–1700* (London, 1998); Sara Mendelson and Patricia Crawford, *Women in Early Modern England 1550–1720* (Oxford, 1998); Hilda Smith (ed.), *Women Writers and the Early Modern British Political Tradition* (Cambridge, 1998); Patricia Crawford and Laura Gowing (eds), *Women's Worlds in Seventeenth Century England: A Sourcebook* (London, 2000); James Daybell (ed.), *Women and Politics in Early Modern England 1450–1700* (Aldershot, 2004); Joseph Ward (ed.), *Violence, Politics and Gender in Early Modern England* (Basingstoke, 2008).
4. Mendelson and Crawford, *Women in Early Modern England*, p. 382.
5. Crawford and Gowing, *Women's Worlds*, p. 245.
6. L. Stewart, 'Jenny Geddes', in Elizabeth Ewen, Sue Innes, Sian Reynolds and Rose Pipes (eds), *The Biographical Dictionary of Scottish Women* (Edinburgh, 2007), pp. 133–4.
7. Keith Brown, 'Reformation to union', in R. A. Houston and W. W. J. Knox (eds), *The New Penguin History of Scotland* (London, 2001), pp. 182–275, p. 257.
8. Mendelson and Crawford, *Women in Early Modern England*, p. 419. For the religious content of women's pamphlets, see Lois Schwoerer, 'Women and the Glorious Revolution', *Albion* 18 (1986), pp. 195–218.
9. Frank O'Gorman, *The Long Eighteenth Century: British Political and Social History 1688–1832* (London, 1997), pp. 29–61, p. 54.
10. Ibid.
11. Mendelson and Crawford, p. 358.
12. Schwoerer, 'Women and the Glorious Revolution'.
13. Helen Payne, 'The Cecil Women at Court', in Pauline Croft (ed.), *Patronage, Culture and Power: The Early Cecils* (London, 2002), pp. 265–82; Helen Payne, 'Aristocratic women, power, patronage and family networks at the Jacobean court, 1603–1625', in Daybell (ed.), *Women and Politics*, pp. 164–81.
14. O'Gorman, *The Long Eighteenth Century*, p. 49.
15. Lois Schwoerer 'Women's public political voice in England, 1640–1740', in Smith (ed.), *Women Writers*, pp. 56–74.

16. Crawford and Gowing, *Women's Worlds*, p. 245.
17. Jane Rendall, 'Women and the Enlightenment in Britain c. 1690–1800', in Hannah Baker and Elaine Chalus (eds), *Women's History in Britain, 1700–1850* (London, 2005), p. 9.
18. Karen O'Brien, W*omen and Enlightenment in Eighteenth Century Britain* (Cambridge, 2009) pp. 4–5.
19. Barbara Caine, *English Feminism, 1780–1980* (Oxford, 1997), p. 11.
20. E. P. Thompson, *Customs in Common* (London, 1991), p. 324.
21. John Walter, 'Grain riots and popular attitudes to the law: Maldon and the crisis of 1629', in John Styles and John Brewer (eds), *An Ungovernable People* (London, 1980).
22. Quoted in Walter, 'Grain riots', p. 54.
23. See Andy Wood, *The Politics of Social Conflict: The Peak Country, 1520–1770* (Cambridge, 1999), pp. 255–7; Bernard Capp, *When Gossips Meet: Women, Family and Neighbourhood in Early Modern England* (Oxford, 2003), p. 316; Roger B. Manning, *Village Revolts: Social Protest and Popular Disturbances in England, 1509–1640* (Oxford, 1998), pp. 96–8.
24. T. M. Devine, *The Scottish Nation 1700–2000* (London, 1999), p. 426; R. A. Houston, 'Women in the economy and society of Scotland, 1500–1800', in R. A. Houston and I. White (eds), *Scottish Society, 1500–1800* (Cambridge, 1989), pp. 118–47, p. 138.
25. John Beattie, 'Crime and inequality in eighteenth century London', in J. Hagan and R. Peterson (eds), *Crime and Inequality* (Stanford, Calif., 1995), p. 124.
26. Rosalind Carr, 'Gender, national identity and political agency in eighteenth century Scotland', PhD thesis, University of Glasgow, 2008, pp. 124, 125.
27. Tim Harris, *London Crowds in the Reign of Charles II: Propaganda and Politics from the Restoration until the Exclusion Crisis* (Cambridge, 1987), p. 196.
28. Mendelson and Crawford, *Women in Early Modern England*, p. 427; R. B. Shoemaker, *Gender in English Society 1650–1850: The Emergence of Separate Spheres* (London, 1998), p. 235.
29. Capp, *When Gossips Meet*, p. 292.
30. Nicholas Rogers, *Crowds, Culture and Politics in Georgian Britain* (Oxford, 1998), p. 223.
31. Capp, *When Gossips Meet*, p. 288.
32. 'Some memoirs concerning the family of the Priestleys', in *Yorkshire Diaries and Autobiographies*, II, Surtees Society, 77 (1886), p. 26.
33. Patricia Higgins, 'The reactions of women with special reference to women petitioners', in Brian Manning (ed.), *Politics, Religion and the English Civil War* (London, 1973), pp. 179–222, p. 192.
34. Higgins, 'Women petitioners', pp. 199, 198.
35. Quoted in Mendelson and Crawford, *Women in Early Modern England*, p. 406.
36. Ann Hughes, 'Gender and politics in Leveller literature', in Susan D. Amussen and Mark A. Kishlansky (eds), *Political Cultures and Cultural Politics in Early Modern England* (Manchester, 1995), pp. 162–88, p. 181, p. 175.

37. Higgins, 'Reactions of women'.
38. Schwoerer, 'Women and the Glorious Revolution'.
39. Judith Richards, 'Mary Tudor as "Sole Quene"? Gendering Tudor monarchy', *Historical Journal* 40, 4 (1997), pp. 895–924.
40. Rachel Weil, *Political Passions: Gender, the Family and Political Argument in England 1680–1714* (Manchester, 1999), p. 236.
41. Clarissa Campbell Orr, 'Introduction', in Clarissa Campbell Orr (ed.), *Queenship in Britain 1660–1837* (Manchester, 2000), pp. 1–52, p.1.
42. Charles Beem, *The Lioness Roared: The Problems of Female Rule in English History* (Basingstoke, 2006), pp. 3, 2.
43. Campbell Orr, 'Introduction', pp. 3–4.
44. For an overview of such titles see Lois Schwoerer, 'Images of Queen Mary II, 1689–95', *Renaissance Quarterly* 42 (1989), pp. 717–48, pp. 723–5.
45. Constance Jordan, 'Women's rule in sixteenth-century British political thought', *Renaissance Quarterly* 40 (1987), pp. 421–51.
46. Schwoerer, 'Women and the Glorious Revolution', p. 197: Robert Bucholz, 'Queen Anne: victim of her virtues?' in Campbell Orr (ed.), *Queenship in Britain*, pp. 94–129, p. 111.
47. See Edward Gregg, *Queen Anne* (London, 2001), p. 11.
48. Lois Schwoerer, 'The queen as regent and patron', in Robert Maccubbin and Martha Hamilton-Phillips (eds), *The Age of William III and Mary II* (Williamsburg, 1989), pp. 217–24, p. 218; Schwoerer, 'Images of Queen Mary', p. 729.
49. Schwoerer, 'Images of Queen Mary', pp. 743–6.
50. Cited in Agnes Strickland, *Lives of the Queens of England* (London, 1846), vol. XI, p. 77.
51. Schwoerer, 'The queen as regent and patron', p. 221.
52. Clarissa Campbell Orr, 'Court studies, gender and women's history', in Campbell Orr (ed.), *Queenship in Britain*, pp. 1–52, p. 46 fn. 31; Robert Bucholz, *The Augustan Court: Queen Anne and the Decline of Court Culture* (Stanford, Calif., 1993), p. 31.
53. Martin Routh (ed.), *Bishop Burnet's History of the Reign of King James the Second* (Oxford, 1852), pp. 4, 211; William Speck, 'Queen Mary', *New Dictionary of National Biography*.
54. Alexander Dalrymple, *Memoirs of Great Britain and Ireland* (London, 1771), pp. 12–16; Routh (ed.), *Bishop Burnett's History*, pp. 4, 181–2.
55. William Speck, 'William – and Mary?' in Lois Schwoerer (ed.), *The Revolution of 1688–1689: Changing Perspectives* (Cambridge, 1992), pp. 131–47, p. 132.
56. Richard Doebner, *Memoirs of Mary Queen of England 1689–1693 Together with her Letters and those of Kings James II and William III to the Electress, Sophia of Hanover* (Leipzig, 1886), p. 29.
57. Dalrymple, *Memoirs*, p. 28; Hester Chapman, *Mary II Queen of England* (Bath, 1972), p. 185; Speck, 'William – and Mary?' p. 134.
58. Schwoerer, 'Images of Queen Mary', p. 737. See also Speck, 'William – and Mary?'
59. Bucholz, 'Victim of her virtues?' p. 94.

60. Beem, *The Lioness Roared*, p. 10.
61. Schwoerer, 'Images of Queen Mary', p. 728.
62. Gregg, *Queen Anne*, p. 15.
63. Isaiah 49: 23; Craig Rose, *England in the 1690s: Revolution, Religion and War* (Oxford, 1999), p. 41.
64. Bucholz, 'Victim of her virtues?' p. 101.
65. Gregg, *Queen Anne*, p. 136.
66. Bucholz, 'Victim of her virtues?' p. 101.
67. Ibid., p. 103.
68. Natalie Zemon Davis, 'Women in politics', in Georges Duby and Michelle Perot (eds), *A History of Women in the West*, Vol. III (Cambridge, Mass., 1993), pp. 167–84, p. 173.
69. Gregg, *Queen Anne*, p. 136.
70. Norbert Elias (trans.), *The Court Society* (Oxford, 1983).
71. Bucholz, *The Augustan Court*, p. 35.
72. Mendelson and Crawford, *Women in Early Modern England*, pp. 366–7.
73. Schwoerer, 'The queen as regnent and patron', p. 219.
74. James Falkner, 'Sarah Churchill', *New Dictionary of National Biography*.
75. Bucholz, *The Augustan Court*, p. 103.
76. Geoffrey Holmes, *British Politics in the Age of Anne* (London, 1967), p. 210.
77. Bucholz, *The Augustan Court*, p. 149.
78. Antonia Fraser, *The Weaker Vessel: Women's Lot in Seventeenth Century England* (London, 1984), p. 313.
79. Weil, *Political Passions*, p. 100.
80. Ibid., p. 165.
81. Karl von den Steinen, 'The daughters of Anne, duchess of Hamilton', in Elizabeth Ewan and Maureen Meikle (eds), *Women in Scotland, 1100–1750* (East Linton, 1999), pp. 112–22.
82. Charles Petrie, *The Jacobite Movement: The First Phase, 1688–1716* (London, 1948), pp. 204–11.
83. Murray Pittock, *Inventing and Resisting Britain: Cultural Identities in Britain and Ireland, 1685–1789* (Basingstoke, 1987), p. 87.
84. Maggie Craig, 'The fair sex turns ugly: female involvement in the Jacobite rising of 1745', in Yvonne Brown and Rona Ferguson (eds), *Twisted Sisters: Women, Crime and Deviance in Scotland since 1400* (East Linton, 2002), pp. 84–100, p. 87.
85. Paul Monad, 'The politics of matrimony: Jacobitism and marriage in eighteen-century England', in Eveline Cruickshanks and Jeremy Black (eds), *The Jacobite Challenge* (Edinburgh, 1988), pp. 24–41, p. 34.
86. Craig, 'The fair sex turns ugly', p. 96.
87. Ibid., p. 98.
88. Anna Clarke and Sarah Richardson, 'Introduction', in *A History of Suffrage 1760–1867* (London, 2000), p. xv.
89. James A. Sharpe, *Early Modern England: A Social History* (London, 1997) p. 352; Frank O'Gorman, *Voters, Patrons and Parties: The Unformed Electoral System of Hanoverian England 1734–1832* (Oxford, 1989), pp. 107–12.

90. Karl von den Steinien, 'The discovery of women in eighteenth-century English political life', in Barbara Kanner (ed.), *The Women of England from Anglo-Saxon Times to the Present* (Hamden, Conn., 1989), p. 247.
91. Daybell, *Women and Politics*, p. 3.
92. Ingrid Tague, *Women of Quality: Accepting and Contesting Ideals of Femininity in England, 1690–1760* (Woodbridge, 2002); Elaine Chalus, '"Ladies are often very good scaffoldings": women and politics in the age of Anne', *Parliamentary History* (2009), pp. 150–65.
93. Patricia Crawford, 'Public duty, conscience and women in early modern England', in John Morrill, Paul Slack and Daniel Woolf (eds), *Public Duty and Private Conscience in Seventeenth Century England* (Oxford, 1993), pp. 57–76, p. 65.
94. R. Fieldhouse, 'Parliamentary representation in the borough of Richmond', *Yorkshire Archaeological and Topographical Journal* 44 (1972), p. 208.
95. Schwoerer, 'Women and the Glorious Revolution', p. 217.
96. Rose Graham, 'The civic position of women at common law before 1800', *Journal of the Society of Comparative Legislation* 17, 1/2 (1917), pp. 178–93, p. 193.
97. See Hilda Smith, *All Men and Both Sexes: Gender, Politics and the False Universal in England, 1640–1832* (London, 2002), pp. 138–40.
98. Susan Staves, 'Investment, votes and "bribes"; women as shareholders in the chartered national companies', in Smith (ed.), *Women Writers*, pp. 259–78.
99. Chalus, 'Women and politics'.
100. Paul Langford, *Public Life and the Propertied Englishman 1689–1798* (Oxford, 1991), p. 120.
101. Elaine Chalus, 'My Minerva at my elbow', in Stephen Taylor, Richard Connors and Clive Jones (eds), *Hanoverian Britain and Empire* (Woodbridge, 1998).
102. Chalus, 'My Minerva', pp. 213, 221.
103. O'Gorman, *Voters*; J. A. Phillips, *Electoral Behaviour in Unreformed England* (Oxford, 1992).
104. Tague, *Women of Quality*, p. 210.
105. O'Gorman, *Voters*, p. 93.
106. Cited in Mark Knights, *Representation and Misrepresentation in Later Stuart Britain: Partisanship and Political Culture* (Oxford, 2005), p. 106.
107. *Commons Journals*, pp. xv, 38.
108. *Commons Journals*, pp. xv, 38.
109. Harris, *A Passion for Government*, p. 117; Speck, *Whigs and Tories*, p. 58.
110. Amanda Foreman, *Georgiana, Duchess of Devonshire* (London, 1998), pp. 136–59.
111. Foreman, *Georgiana*, p. 144.
112. Paula McDowell, *The Women of Grub Street: Press, Politics and Gender in the London Literary Marketplace 1678–1730* (Oxford, 1998), p. 4.
113. O'Gorman, *The Long Eighteenth Century*, p. 128.
114. Schwoerer, 'Women's public political voice', p. 57.

115. McDowell, *Women of Grub Street*, p. 31.
116. Cited in Schwoerer, 'Women's public political voice', p. 67.
117. See, for example, Valerie Bryson, *Feminist Political Theory: An Introduction* (Basingstoke, 1992), pp. 11–17.
118. E. J. Clery, *The Feminization Debate* (Basingstoke, 2004), p. 29.
119. Jane Rendall, 'Clio, Mars and Minerva: the Scottish Enlightenment and the writing of women's history', in T. M. Devine and J. R. Young (eds), *Eighteenth Century Scotland: New Perspectives* (East Linton, 1999), pp. 134–52, p. 147.
120. T. C. Smout, 'Born again at Cambuslang: new evidence on popular religion and literacy in eighteenth century Scotland', *Past and Present* 97 (1992), pp. 114–27.
121. Elaine Chalus, 'The Rag Plot: the politics of influence in Oxford, 1754', in Rosemary Sweet and Penelope Lane (eds), *Women and Urban Life in Eighteenth-Century England* (Aldershot, 2003), pp. 43–61.
122. Lawrence Klein, 'Coffeehouse civility, 1660–1714: an aspect of post-courtly culture in England', *Huntington Library Quarterly* 59, 1 (1996), pp. 30–51, p. 31.
123. James Van Horn Melton, *The Rise of the Public in Enlightenment Europe* (Cambridge, 2001), p. 243.
124. Klein, 'Coffeehouse civility', p. 40.
125. Carr, 'Gender', p. 220.
126. Steven Pincus, '"Coffee politicians does create": coffeehouses and Restoration political culture', *Journal of Modern History* 67, 4 (1995), pp. 807–34; Markman Ellis, 'Coffee-women, *The Spectator* and the public sphere in the early eighteenth century', in Elizabeth Eger, Charlotte Grant, Clíona Ó Gallchoir and Penny Warburton (eds), *Women, Writing and the Public Sphere, 1700–1830* (Cambridge, 2001), pp. 27–52, p. 31.
127. Brian Cowan, 'What was masculine about the public sphere? Gender and the coffeehouse milieu in post-Restoration England', *History Workshop Journal* 51 (2001), pp. 127–58, pp. 128, 141.
128. Margaret Jacob (ed.), *The Enlightenment: A Brief History with Documents* (Boston Mass., 2001), p. 22.
129. Donna Andrew, 'Popular culture and public debate: London, 1780', *Historical Journal* 39, 2 (1996), pp. 405–23; Donna Andrew, *London Debating Societies* (London Records Society, 1994); Mary Thale, 'Women in London debating societies in 1780', *Gender and History* 7, 1 (1995), pp. 5–24.
130. Carr, 'Gender', p. 288.
131. Andrew; *London Debating Societies*, pp. 76–113.
132. Anna Clark, 'Women in eighteenth-century British politics', in Sarah Knott and Barbara Taylor (eds), *Women, Gender and Enlightenment* (Basingstoke, 2005), p. 573.
133. Joan Scott, *Only Paradoxes to Offer: French Feminists and the Rights of Man* (London, 1996), p. 9.
134. Karen Offen, *European Feminisms 1700–1950* (Stanford, Calif., 2000), p. 68.

135. Pam Hirsch, 'Wollstonecraft's problematic legacy', in Clarissa Campbell Orr (ed.), *Wollstonecraft's Daughters* (Manchester, 1996), pp. 43–60, p. 44.
136. Jane Rendall, *Origins of Modern Feminism* (Basingstoke, 1985), p. 62.
137. Quoted in Taylor, *Mary Wollstonecraft and the Feminist Imagination*, p. 216.
138. Dorinda Outram, *The Enlightenment World* (Cambridge, 1995), p. 82.
139. Barbara Taylor, *Wollstonecraft and the Feminist Imagination* (Cambridge, 1993), p. 55.
140. Taylor, *Wollstonecraft*; Karen O'Brien, *Women and Enlightenment in Eighteenth Century Britain* (Cambridge, 2009).
141. See, for example, Adriana Craciun, *A London Literary Sourcebook on Mary Wollstonecraft's The Vindication of the Rights of Women* (London, 2002), p. 9; O'Brien, *Women and the Enlightenment*, p. 174; Karen O'Brien, 'The feminist critique of the Enlightenment', in Martin Fitzpatrick, Peter Jones, Christa Knellwolf and Iain McCalman (eds), *The Enlightenment World* (London, 2004), pp. 621–34, p. 622.
142. Jane Rendall, 'Feminizing the Enlightenment: the problem of sensibility', in Fitzpatrick et al., *The Enlightenment World*, pp. 253–71, p. 266.
143. Taylor, *Wollstonecraft*, p. 182.
144. Linda Colley, B*ritons: Forging the Nation*, 2nd edn (London, 2005), pp. 251–2.
145. Hannah Barker and Elaine Chalus, 'Introduction', in Hannah Barker and Elaine Chalus (eds), *Gender in Eighteenth Century England: Roles, Representations and Responsibilitie*s (London, 1997), pp. 16–21.
146. Jürgen Habermas, *The Structural Transformation of the Bourgeois Public Sphere* (trans.) (Cambridge, 1989).
147. Renate Bridenthal and Claudia Koonz, 'Introduction to "Angels in the devil's workshop: leisured and charitable women in nineteenth-century England and France"' in Renate Bridenthal and Claudia Koonz (eds), *Becoming Visible* (London, 1977), p. 296.
148. Leonore Davidoff and Catherine Hall, *Family Fortunes: Men and Women of the English Middle Class 1780–1850* (London, 1987).
149. Vickery, 'From golden age to separate spheres'; Colley, *Britons*.
150. Simon Morgan, *A Victorian Woman's Place: Public Culture in the Nineteenth Century* (London, 2007), p. 4.
151. Kathryn Gleadle, 'Our several spheres: middle-class women and the feminisms of early Victorian radical politics', in Kathryn Gleadle and Sarah Richardson (eds), *Women in British Politics, 1780–1860: The Power of the Petticoat* (Basingstoke, 2000).
152. Rendall, 'Women and the Enlightenment', p. 25.
153. Taylor, *Wollstonecraft and the Feminist Imagination*, p. 182.
154. Anne Stott, *Hannah More: The First Victorian* (Oxford, 2005), p. x.
155. Ray Strachey, *The Cause: A Short History of the Women's Movement in Great Britain* (London, 1978 repr.), p. 13.
156. Harriet Guest, 'Hannah More and conservative feminism', in Jennie Batchelor and Cora Kaplan (eds), *British Women's Writing in the Long*

Eighteenth Century: Authorship, Politics and History (Basingstoke, 2005).

157. Maggie Craig, *Damn Rebel Bitches: The Women of the '45* (Edinburgh, 1997).

2 Organised Politics before Suffrage

1. Strachey, *The Cause* (London, 1978 repr.), p. 3.
2. James Vernon, *Politics and the People: A Study in English Political Culture* (Cambridge, 1993), p. 336.
3. John Garrard, *Democratisation in Britain: Elites, Civil Society and Reform Since 1800* (Basingstoke, 2002), p. 28.
4. Miles Taylor, *The Decline of British Radicalism, 1847–1860* (Oxford, 1995), p. 7.
5. Philippa Levine, *Feminist Lives in Victorian England: Private Roles and Public Commitment* (Oxford, 1990).
6. Barbara Taylor, *Eve and the New Jerusalem* (London, 1983), p. 1.
7. Jane Rendall, *The Origins of Modern Feminism* (Basingstoke, 1985), p. 220.
8. Taylor, *Eve and the New Jerusalem*, ch. 8.
9. Rendall, *Origins*, p. 306.
10. Clare Midgley, *Women Against Slavery: The British Campaigns 1780–1870* (London, 1992), p. 23.
11. Vron Ware, *Beyond the Pale: White Women, Racism and History* (London, 1981), pp. 72–3.
12. Clare Midgley, *Feminism and Empire: Women Activists in Imperial Britain, 1790–1865* (London, 2007), p. 55.
13. Louis Billington and Rosamund Billington, '"A burning zeal for righteousness": women in the British anti-slavery movement, 1820–1860', in Jane Rendall (ed.), *Equal or Different: Women's Politics, 1800–1914* (Oxford, 1987), pp. 82–111, p. 85.
14. Midgley, *Women Against Slavery*, p. 44.
15. Ware, *Beyond the Pale*, p. 73.
16. Midgley, *Women Against Slavery*, p. 117.
17. Alison Twells, 'Missionary domesticity, global reform and "woman's sphere" in early nineteenth-century England', *Gender and History* 18, 2 (2006), pp. 266–84, p. 266.
18. Midgley, *Women Against Slavery*, p. 151.
19. Julia Bush, *Edwardian Ladies and Imperial Power* (Leicester, 2000), p. 3.
20. Antoinette Burton, *Burdens of History: British Feminists, Indian Women and Imperial Culture* (London, 1994) p. 207; Bush, *Edwardian Ladies*.
21. See for example Pat Grimshaw, 'Writing the history of Australian women', in Karen Offen, Jane Rendall and Ruth Roach Pierson (eds), *Writing Women's History: International Perspectives* (Basingstoke, 1991).
22. Catherine Hall, *Civilising Subjects; Metropole and Colony in the English Imagination 1830–1867* (Oxford, 2002); Alison Twells, *The Civilising Mission and the English Middle Class, 1792–1850: The 'Heathen' at Home and Overseas* (Basingstoke, 2009).

23. Midgley, *Feminism and Empire*, p. 9.
24. Vernon, *Politics and the People*, p. 39.
25. *Women's Suffrage Journal*, 1 February 1884.
26. Kathryn Gleadle, *Borderline Citizens: Women, Gender and Political Culture in Britain 1815–1867* (Oxford, 2009), pp. 190, 160–1.
27. Joan Allen and Owen Ashton, 'Introduction', in Joan Allen and Owen Ashton (eds), *Papers for the People: A Study of the Chartist Press* (Monmouth, 2005), pp. xi–xii.
28. Robert Hall, *Voices of the People: Democracy and Chartist Political Identity 1830–1870* (Monmouth, 2007), p. 48.
29. Anna Clark, 'Franchise reform in England 1832–1928', in James Vernon (ed.), *Rereading the Constitution: New Narratives in the Political History of England's Long Nineteenth Century* (Cambridge, 2006), pp. 239–53, p. 235.
30. Ruth and Edmund Frow (eds), *Political Women 1800–1850* (London, 1989), p. 183.
31. Malcolm Chase, *Chartism, A New History* (Manchester, 2007), p. 267.
32. Dorothy Thompson 'Women and nineteenth century radicalism', in Juliet Mitchell and Ann Oakley (eds), *The Rights and Wrongs of Women* (Harmondsworth, 1986), pp. 112–38, p. 123.
33. Chase, *Chartism*, p. 43.
34. David Jones, 'Women and Chartism', *History* 68, 222 (1983), pp. 1–21, pp. 10–13.
35. Chase, *Chartism*, p. 48.
36. Malcolm Thomis and Jennifer Grimmett, *Women in Protest* (London, 1982), pp. 111–12.
37. Jutta Schwarzkopf, *Women in the Chartist Movement* (Basingstoke, 1991), pp. 209–17.
38. Helen Rogers, *Women and the People* (Aldershot, 2000), p. 87.
39. Anna Clark, *Struggle for the Breeches: Gender and the Making of the British Working Class* (London, 1997), p. 229–30.
40. Clark, *Struggle for the Breeches*, p. 227; Schwarzkopf, *Women in the Chartist Movement*, p. 183.
41. Clark, *Struggle for the Breeches*, p. 227; Dorothy Thompson, *The Chartists* (Hounslow, 1984), p. 141.
42. Schwarzkopf, *Women in the Chartist Movement*, p. 183.
43. Ibid.
44. Thompson, *The Chartists*, p. 137.
45. Chase, *Chartism*, p. 144.
46. Thomis and Grimmett, *Women in Protest*, p. 117.
47. Schwarzkopf, *Women in the Chartist Movement*, p. 195; Thomis and Grimmett, *Women in Protest*, p. 117.
48. Thompson, *The Chartists*, p. 148.
49. Schwarzkopf, *Women in Chartism*, p. 125.
50. Ibid., p. 285.
51. Ibid., p. 4.
52. Thomis and Grimmett, *Women in Protest*, pp. 136–7.

53. Michelle De Larrabeiti, 'Conspicuous before the world: the political rhetoric of Chartist women', in Eileen Yeo (ed.), *Radical Femininity* (Manchester, 1998).
54. Helen Blackburn, *Women's Suffrage Record* (London, 1902), p. 1; E. Sylvia Pankhurst, *The Suffragette Movement* (London, 1977 repr.), p. 53.
55. Paul Pickering and Alex Tyrrell (2000) *The People's Bread: A History of the Anti-Corn Law League* (London, 2000), p. 119.
56. Archibald Prentice, *History of the Anti-Corn-Law League,* vol. 1 (London, 1853), p. 170.
57. Rendall, *Origins,* p. 244.
58. Morgan, *A Victorian Woman's Place,* p. 139.
59. Rendall, *Origins,* p. 244.
60. Morgan, *Woman's Place,* p. 141.
61. Ibid., pp. 140–1.
62. Alex Tyrrell, 'Woman's mission and pressure group politics 1825–1860', *Bulletin of the John Rylands Library* 63, (1980), pp. 194–230.
63. Simon Morgan, 'Women in the Anti-Corn Law League', in Kathryn Gleadle and Sarah Richardson (eds), *The Power of the Petticoat* (Basingstoke, 2000).
64. Rendall, *Origins,* p. 307.
65. Lee Holcombe, *Wives and Property* (Toronto, 1983), p. 123.
66. Pam Hirsch, *Barbara Leigh Smith Bodichon* (London, 1998), p. 194.
67. W. Gareth Evans, *Education and Female Emancipation: The Welsh Experience* (Cardiff, 1990).
68. Ann Dingsdale, 'Kensington Society (act. 1856–1868)', *New Dictionary of National Biography.*
69. Jane Rendall, 'Langham Place Group' (act. 1857–1866) *New Dictionary of National Biography.*
70. Millicent Fawcett, *What I Remember* (Unwin, 1924), p. 62.
71. Holcombe, *Married Women's Property,* p. 4.
72. See, for example, Marybeth Combs, '"A measure of legal independence": the 1870 Married Women's Property Act and the portfolio allocations of British wives', *Journal of Economic History* 65, 4 (2005), pp. 1028–57.
73. Lucy Bland, *Banishing the Beast: English Feminism and Sexual Morality 1885–1914* (Harmondsworth, 1995).
74. Judith Walkowitz, *Prostitution and Victorian Society* (Cambridge, 1980), p. 188.
75. Ibid., p. 175.
76. Ibid., p. 108.
77. Ibid., p. 109.
78. Ibid., p. 132.
79. Barbara Caine, *English Feminism 1780–1980* (Oxford, 1997), p. 109; Walkowitz, *Prostitution,* p. 130.
80. Susie Steinbach, *Women in England 1760–1914* (Basingstoke, 2004), p. 274.
81. Sandra Holton, *Suffrage Days: Stories from the Women's Suffrage Movement* (London, 1996), p. 33.
82. Walkowitz, *Prostitution,* p. 131.

83. Ibid., p. 180.
84. Caine, *English Feminism*, p. 111.
85. Walkowitz, *Prostitution*, p. 176.
86. Ibid., p. 142.
87. Holton, *Suffrage Days*, p. 37.
88. Sheila Jeffreys, 'Women and sexuality', in June Purvis (ed.), *Women's History: Britain 1850–1945* (London, 2000), pp. 193–216, p. 197.
89. Lucy Bland, 'Purifying the public world; feminist vigilantes in late Victorian England', *Women's History Review* 1, 3 (1992), pp. 397–412.
90. Patricia Hollis, 'Women in council', in Rendall, *Equal or Different*, p. 210.
91. Frank Prochaska, *Women and Philanthropy in Nineteenth Century England* (Oxford, 1980), p. 140.
92. Mary Clare Martin, 'Women and philanthropy in Walthamstow and Leyton 1740–1870', *London Journal* 19–20 (1994), pp. 119–50, p. 135.
93. Gleadle, *Borderline Citizens*, pp. 53–5.
94. Ibid., p. 49.
95. Ibid., p. 141.
96. Morgan, *Woman's Place*, p. 106.
97. June Hannam, 'Women and politics', in Purvis, *Women's History*, pp. 217–46.
98. Mica Nava, 'Modernity's disavowal: women, the city and the department store', in Mica Nava and Alan O'Shea (eds), *Modern Times: Reflections on a Century of English Modernity* (London, 1996), p. 44.
99. Ann Summers, 'A home from home: women's philanthropic work in the nineteenth century', in Sandra Burman (ed.), *Fit Work for Women* (London, 1979), p. 42.
100. Midgley, *Women Against Slavery*, p. 75.
101. *Englishwoman's Review*, 15 June 1881.
102. Robert D Anderson, *Education and the Scottish People 1750–1918* (Oxford, 1985), p. 171.
103. Steinbach, *Women in England*, pp. 73, 74.
104. Patricia Hollis, *Ladies Elect* (Oxford, 1987), pp. 210–11.
105. 'Are more women guardians needed', *Englishwoman's Review*, 15 March 1889; 'The approaching Poor Law Guardians election', *Englishwoman's Review*, 13 March 1883.
106. *Society for the Return of Women as Poor Law Guardians*, undated campaign leaflet.
107. David Rubinstein, *Before the Suffragettes: Women's Emancipation in the 1890s* (Brighton, 1986), p. 167.
108. 'Are more women guardians needed', *Englishwoman's Review*, 20 March 1889.
109. Hollis, *Ladies Elect*, chs 2–3.
110. Ibid., p. 251.
111. Ibid., p. 168.
112. Jane Martin, *Women and the Politics of Schooling in Victorian and Edwardian England* (Leicester, 1999), p. 146, also chs 6, 7, 8.

113. Jane Bedford, 'Margaret Ashton: Manchester's first lady', *Manchester Region History Review* 12 (1998), pp. 3–17.
114. Pat Thane, 'Women in the British Labour Party and the construction of state welfare, 1906–39', in Seth Koven and Sonya Michel (eds), *Mothers of a New World: Maternalist Politics and the Origins of Welfare States* (London, 1993), pp. 343–77, pp. 350–1.
115. Hollis, *Ladies Elect*, p. 463.
116. Martin Pugh, *The March of the Women: A Revisionist History of the Campaign for Women's Suffrage* (Oxford, 2000), p. 73.
117. Levine, *Feminist Lives*, p. 120.

3 The Campaign for Women's Suffrage

1. Strachey, *The Cause*, p. 101.
2. Jane Rendall, 'Who was Lily Maxwell: women's suffrage and Manchester politics 1866–1867', in J. Purvis and S. Holton (eds), *Votes for Women* (London, 2000), p. 58.
3. Rendall, 'Lily Maxwell', p. 59.
4. Holton, *Suffrage Days*.
5. Bertha Mason, *The Story of the Women's Suffrage Movement* (London, 1912), p. 51.
6. *Englishwoman's Review*, January 1868.
7. Lydia Becker to Mary Smith, 20 May 1868, M50/1/3, ff. 138–139, Manchester Central Library.
8. Laura Nym Mayhall, *The Militant Suffrage Movement: Citizenship and Resistance in Britain 1860–1930* (Oxford, 2003), p.64.
9. Leah Leneman, *A Guid Cause, The Women's Suffrage Movement in Scotland* (Aberdeen, 1991), p. 14.
10. Rendall, 'Lily Maxwell', p. 77.
11. Holton, *Suffrage Days*, p. 20.
12. Rosamund Billington, 'Women, politics and local liberalism: from female suffrage to votes for women', *Journal of Local and Regional Studies* 5 (1985), pp. 5–6.
13. Sandra Stanley Holton, 'Now you see it, now you don't: the Women's Franchise League and its place in contending narratives of the suffrage movement', in June Purvis and Maroula Joannou (eds), *The Women's Suffrage Movement* (Manchester, 1998).
14. Antonia Raeburn, *The Militant Suffragettes* (London, 1973), p. 4.
15. Sophia Van Wingerden, *The Women's Suffrage Movement in Britain, 1866–1928* (Basingstoke, 1999), p. 69.
16. Harold Smith, *The British Women's Suffrage Campaign*, 2nd edn (Harlow, 2007), p. 24; Jo Vellacott, *Pacifists, Patriots and the Vote: the Erosion of Democratic Suffragism in Britain During the First World War* (Basingstoke, 2007), p. 3.
17. Jill Liddington and Jill Norris, *One Hand Tied Behind Us: The Rise of the Women's Suffrage Campaign* (London, 1978).
18. Gifford Lewis, *Eva Gore Booth and Esther Roper* (London, 1988), p. 57.

19. Harold Smith, *The British Women's Suffrage Campaign*, 2nd edn (Harlow, 2007), p. 39.
20. Ibid., p. 19.
21. Holton, *Suffrage Days*, p. 24.
22. Ibid., pp. 40–1.
23. Ursula Masson, 'Political conditions in Wales are quite different ... party politics and votes for women in Wales, 1912–15', *Women's History Review* 9, 2 (2000), pp. 369–88.
24. For example Krista Cowman, *Mrs Brown is a Man and a Brother: Women in Merseyside's Political Organisations 1890–1920* (Liverpool, 2004); Jill Liddington, *Rebel Girls: Their Fight for the Vote* (London, 2006).
25. Leneman, *A Guid Cause*, p. 72; Krista Cowman, *Women of the Right Spirit: Paid Organisers in the Women's Social and Political Union* (Manchester, 2007), p. 149.
26. Kay Cook and Neil Evans, 'The petty antics of the bell-ringing band? The women's suffrage movement in Wales, 1890–1918', in Angela John (ed.), *Our Mother's Land: Chapters in Welsh Women's History 1830–1939* (Cardiff, 1991), pp.159–88.
27. Joyce Marlow, *The Virago Book of Suffragettes* (London, 2001), pp. 79–80.
28. Margaret Haig, *This Was My World* (London, 1933), p. 133.
29. Ann Morley with Liz Stanley, *The Life and Death of Emily Wilding Davison* (London, 1988), p. 153.
30. *The Suffragette*, 13 December 1912.
31. Krista Cowman, *The Militant Suffrage Movement in York* (York, 2008).
32. June Purvis, *Emmeline Pankhurst* (London, 2002), pp. 201–2.
33. Andrew Rosen, *Rise Up Women: The Militant Campaign of the Women's Social and Political Union 1903–14* (London, 1974); Strachey, *The Cause*, pp. 302, 303.
34. Martin Pugh, *The March of the Women: A Revisionist Account of the Campaign for Women's Suffrage 1866–1914* (Oxford, 2000), p. 210; Brian Harrison, 'The act of militancy: violence and the suffragettes,' in Brian Harrison, *Peaceable Kingdom* (Oxford, 1992), pp. 27, 26.
35. Pugh, *March of the Women*, p. 212.
36. Elizabeth Sarah, 'Christabel Pankhurst; reclaiming her power', in Dale Spender (ed.), *Women of Ideas and What Men Have Done to Them* (London, 1983), pp. 256–84, p. 280.
37. Barbara Green, *Spectacular Confessions: Autobiography, Performative Activism and the Sites of Suffrage 1905–38* (London, 1999).
38. Wendy Parkes, *Fashioning the Body Politic* (New York, 2002), p. 102.
39. Mary Richardson, *Laugh a Defiance* (London, 1953), p. 80.
40. Mayhall, *The Militant Suffrage Movement*, pp. 72–4.
41. Krista Cowman, 'The United Suffragists', in June Purvis and Mary Joannou (eds), *The Women's Suffrage Movement* (Manchester, 1998), p. 79.
42. See Rosemary Taylor, *In Letters of Gold: The Story of Sylvia Pankhurst and the ELFS in Bow* (London, 1993).
43. See Barbara Winslow, *Sylvia Pankhurst: Sexual Politics and Political Activism* (London, 1996).

44. Brian Heeney, *The Women's Movement in the Church of England* (Oxford, 1988), p 105.
45. Frances Mason, 'The newer Eve: the Catholic Women's Suffrage Society in England 1922–1923', *Catholic Historical Review* 72 (1986), pp. 620–38.
46. Elizabeth Crawford, *The Women's Suffrage Movement* (London, 1999), p. 233.
47. AJR (ed.), *The Suffrage Annual and Women's Who's Who* (London, 1913).
48. See Lisa Tickner, *The Spectacle of Women: Imagery of the Suffrage Campaign, 1907–14* (Chicago, 1988).
49. See Julie Hollege, *Innocent Flowers: Women in the Edwardian Theatre* (London, 1981).
50. David Mitchell, *Women on the Warpath: The Story of the Women of the First World War* (London, 1966), p. 49.
51. Angela Smith, *Suffrage Discourse in the First World War* (Aldershot, 2005).
52. Krisztina Roberts, 'Gender, class and patriotism; women's paramilitary units in First World War Britain', *International History Review* 19, 1 (1997), pp. 52–65; Janet Watson, 'Khaki girls, VADs and Tommy's sisters: gender and class in First World War Britain', *International History Review* 19, 1 (1997), pp. 32–51.
53. Quoted in Liddington and Norris, *One Hand Tied Behind Us,* p. 81.
54. Vellacott, *Pacifists, Patriots and the Vote*, p. 17.
55. Philippa Levine, 'Walking the streets in a way no decent woman should: women police in World War 1', *Journal of Modern History* 66 (1994), pp. 34–78.
56. Sandra Holton, *Feminism and Democracy: Women's Suffrage and Reform Politics in Britain* (Cambridge, 1987), p. 133.
57. Arthur Marwick, *Women at War, 1914–18* (London, 1977).
58. Nicoletta Gullace, *The Blood of our Sons: Men, Women and the Renegotiation of British Citizenship During the Great War* (Basingstoke, 2002), pp. 171–4.
59. Duncan Tanner, *Political Change and the Labour Party* (Cambridge, 1990).

4   Women and the Liberal Party

1. Juliet Mitchell, 'Women and equality', in Ann Phillips (ed.), *Feminism and Equality* (Oxford, 1987), p. 37.
2. Holton, *Suffrage Days*, pp. 57–8.
3. Ursula Masson, *'Women's Rights and Womanly Duties': The Aberdare Women's Liberal Association, 1891–1910* (Cardiff, 2005), pp. 15–16.
4. 'The Women's Liberal Federation', *Hearth and Home*, 28 April 1892.
5. Hollis, *Women in Public*, p. 317.
6. Millicent Fawcett, *Women's Suffrage: A Short History of a Great Movement* (London, 1912), p. 30.
7. Eliza Orme, *Lady Fry of Darlington* (London, 1898), p. 112.

8. Ibid., pp. 122–3.
9. Linda Walker, 'Party political women: Liberal women and the Primrose League' in Rendall, *Equal or Different*, p. 168; Cowman, *Mrs Brown is a Man and a Brother*, pp. 45–6.
10. Masson, *Women's Rights*, p. 58.
11. Fawcett, *Women's Suffrage*, p. 31.
12. Blackburn, *Women's Suffrage*, p. 171.
13. WLF *Annual Report* 1888.
14. Linda Walker, 'Gender, suffrage and party: Liberal women's organisations', in Myriam Boussahba-Bravard (ed.), *Suffrage Outside Suffragism* (Basingstoke, 2007), pp. 77–102, pp. 83–4.
15. *Women's Penny Paper*, 16 November 1889.
16. Masson, *Women's Rights*, minutes of Abadere Women's Liberal Association meeting, 4 February 1892.
17. *Women's Penny Paper*, 9 November 1889.
18. Hollis, *Ladies Elect*, pp. 58–9.
19. *The Liver*, April 1893.
20. Hollis, *Ladies Elect*, p. 151.
21. *Liverpool Review of Politics*, 9 April 1898.
22. Patricia Hollis, 'Women in council', in Rendall, *Equal or Different*, p. 211.
23. Bedford, 'Margaret Ashton'.
24. Hollis, *Ladies Elect*, p. 62.
25. Barbara Caine, *Destined to be Wives* (Oxford, 1986), p. 165.
26. Walker, 'Liberal women's organisations', p. 84.
27. Ibid.
28. Walker, 'Party political women', p. 187.
29. Margaret Barrow, 'Teetotal feminists: temperance leadership and the campaign for women's suffrage', in Claire Eustance, Joan Ryan and Laura Ugolini (eds), *A Suffrage Reader: Charting Directions in British Suffrage History* (Leicester, 2000), p. 80.
30. Hollis, *Ladies Elect*, p. 64.
31. Pugh, *March of the Women*.
32. Claire Hirshfield, 'Fractured faith: Liberal Party women and the suffrage issue in Britain', *Gender and History* 2 (1990), pp. 173–97, p. 186.
33. Ibid. pp. 180–1.
34. Leneman, *A Guid Cause*, pp. 44–5; Cowman, *Mrs Brown*, pp. 124–7.
35. Leslie Parker Hume, *The National Union of Women's Suffrage Societies* (New York, 1982); Constance Rover, *Women's Suffrage and Party Politics in Britain, 1866–1914* (London, 1967), pp. 129–43.
36. *Women's Liberal Federation News*, November 1910.
37. Hirshfield, 'Fractured faith', pp. 184–5.
38. Walker, 'Liberal women's organisations', p. 96.
39. Pat Thane, 'Women, Liberalism and citizenship', in Eugenio Biagini (ed.), *Citizenship and Community: Liberals and Collective Identities in the British Isles, 1865–1931* (Cambridge, 1996), pp. 66–92, p. 81.
40. Jo Vellacott, *From Liberal to Labour with Women's Suffrage: The Story of Catherine Marshall* (Montreal, 1993).

5 Women and the Conservative Party

1. Joni Lovenduski, Pippa Norris and Catriona Burness, 'The party and women', in Anthony Seldon and Stuart Ball (eds), *Conservative Century: The Conservative Party since 1900* (Oxford, 1994), pp. 611–35.

2. For example Murray Goot and Elizabeth Reid, 'Women: if not apolitical then Conservative', in Janet Siltanen and Michelle Stanworth (eds), *Women and the Public Sphere: A Critique of Sociology and Politics* (London, 1984), pp. 122–36.

3. Olive Banks, *Becoming a Feminist: The Social Origins of First Wave Feminism* (Brighton, 1986), p. 22; Caine, *Victorian Feminists*, p. 57.

4. Beatrix Campbell, *The Iron Ladies: Why Do Women Vote Tory?* (London, 1987).

5. Joan Kinnaird, 'Mary Astell and the conservative contribution to English feminism', *Journal of British Studies* 19 (1979), pp. 53–79; G. E. Maguire, *Conservative Women: A History of Women and the Conservative Party* (Basingstoke, 1998), p. 2.

6. Caine, *Victorian Feminists*.

7. For example Pugh, *The March of the Women*, pp. 102–6; David Jarvis, 'The Conservative Party and the politics of gender, 1900–1939', in Martin Francis and Ina Zweiniger-Bargielowska (eds), *The Conservatives and British Society, 1880–1990* (Cardiff, 1996), pp. 172–93.

8. Janet Robb, *The Primrose League* (New York, 1942), p. 136.

9. Maguire, *Conservative Women*; Jarvis, 'The Conservative Party and the politics of gender', p. 173.

10. Norris et al., 'The party and women', p. 612.

11. Caine, *Victorian Feminists*, p. 86.

12. Walker, 'Party political women', p. 190.

13. Martin Pugh, *The Tories and the People* (Oxford, 1986), p. 12.

14. Lord Ronaldshay, *The Life of Lord Curzon*, vol. 1 (London, 1928), p. 100.

15. Pugh, *Tories and the People*, p. 19.

16. Robb, *Primrose League*, pp. 52–3.

17. Deidre Beddoe, *Out of the Shadows: Women in Twentieth Century Wales* (Cardiff, 2000), pp. 40–1.

18. Walker, 'Liberal women', pp. 171–2.

19. Pugh, *Tories and the People*, p. 49.

20. Ibid., p. 50.

21. *Hearth and Home*, 18 September 1895.

22. Pugh, *Tories and the People*, p. 47; Robb, *Primrose League*, p. 134.

23. Campbell, *Iron Ladies*, p. 10.

24. *Aberdeen Journal*, 7 October 1886.

25. Campbell, *Iron Ladies*, p. 11.

26. Pugh, *Tories and the People*, p. 52.

27. *Myra's Journal of Dress and Fashion*, 1 December 1887.

28. Campbell, *Iron Ladies*, pp. 12–13.

29. Maguire, *Conservative women*, p. 37.

30. *Aberdeen Weekly Journal*, 10 December 1897.

31. Robb, *Primrose League*, p. 121.
32. Walker, 'Liberal women', p. 180.
33. Pugh, *Tories and the People*, p. 53.
34. Robb, *Primrose League*, p. 136.
35. 'Chats with celebrities', *Hearth and Home*, 21 January 1892; P. J. Waller, *Democracy and Sectarianism* (Liverpool, 1982), p. 64.
36. Pugh, *Tories and the People*, p. 55.
37. *Primrose League Gazette*, 24 December 1887; 15 October 1887.
38. Campbell, *Iron Ladies*, p. 28.
39. 'Chats with celebrities', *Hearth and Home*, 21 January 1892; Mitzi Auchterlonie, *Conservative Suffragists: The Women's Vote and the Tory Party* (London, 2007), p. 40.
40. Auchterlonie, p. 40.
41. See Eliza Reidi, 'Women, gender and the promotion of empire: the Victoria League, 1901–14', *Historical Journal* 45 (2002), pp. 569–99.
42. Pugh, *Tories and the People*, p. 172.
43. *Primrose League Gazette*, March 1904.
44. Pugh, *Tories and the People*, p. 172.
45. Auchterlonie, *Conservative Suffragists*, pp. 86–8.
46. Ibid., p. 88.
47. L. Maguire, 'The Conservative Party and women's suffrage', in Boussahba-Bravard, *Suffrage Outside Suffragism*, p. 54; Pugh, *March of the Women*, p. 116; Auchterlonie, *Conservative Suffragists*, p. 91.
48. Julia Bush, *Women Against the Vote: Female Anti-Suffragism in Britain* (Oxford, 2007), p. 175.
49. Maguire, 'The Conservative Party', p. 55.
50. Pugh, *March of the Women*, pp. 115–17.
51. Auchterlonie, *Conservative Suffragists*, p. 93.
52. *The Times*, 9 November 1908.
53. Philippe Vervaecke, 'The Primrose League and women's suffrage', in Boussahba-Bravard, *Suffrage Outside Suffragism*, pp. 180–202, pp. 188–9.
54. Auchterlonie, *Conservative Suffragists*, ch. 5.
55. Bush, *Women Against the Vote*.

6   Women and Socialism

1. Eleanor Gordon, *Women and the Labour Movement in Scotland* (Oxford, 1991), pp. 270–3.
2. Karen Hunt, *Equivocal Feminists: The SDF and the Woman Question* (Cambridge, 1996).
3. Hunt, *Equivocal Feminists*, pp. 28–9.
4. June Hannam and Karen Hunt, 'Propagandising as socialist women: the case of women's columns in British socialist newspapers', in Bertrand Taithe and Tim Thornton (eds), *Propaganda, Political Rhetoric and Identity* (Stroud, 1999).
5. *The Clarion*, 12 March 1898.

6. Ibid., 23 March 1895.

7. Isabella Ford, 'Women and the Labour Movement', *Labour Prophet*, December 1894.

8. Keir Hardie, 'After twenty years all about the ILP', ILP pamphlet (1913), p. 13.

9. Banks, *Faces of Feminism*, p. 123; Liddington and Norris, *One Hand Tied Behind Us*, p. 125.

10. 'To the Women of the ILP', ILP pamphlet, 1894.

11. Hannah Mitchell, *The Hard Way Up* (London, 1977), p. 130.

12. June Hannam and Karen Hunt, *Socialist Women* (London, 2002), p. 82.

13. Krista Cowman, 'Reading between the lines: letters to Eleanor Keeling Edwards', in Caroline Bland and Máire Cross (eds), *Gender and Politics in the Age of Letter Writing* (Aldershot, 2004), pp. 173–84, p. 178.

14. Gordon, *Women and the Labour Movement*, p. 274.

15. Karen Hunt, 'Fractured universality: the language of British socialism before the First World War', in John Belchem and Neville Kirk (eds), *Languages of Labour* (Aldershot, 1997), pp. 65–80.

16. Liddington and Norris, *One Hand Tied Behind Us*, pp. 128–9.

17. David Clarke, *Colne Valley: Radicalism to Socialism* (London, 1981), p. 48.

18. Hannam and Hunt, *Socialist Women*, p. 81.

19. Gordon, *Women and the Labour Movement*, pp. 258–9.

20. Henry Pelling, *Origins of the Labour Party* (Oxford, 1965), p. 155.

21. Hannam and Hunt, *Socialist Women*, p. 22.

22. Ibid., pp. 90–92.

23. Hunt, *Equivocal Feminists*, p. 227.

24. Ibid., pp. 227–8.

25. Pankhurst, *The Suffragette Movement*, p. 244.

26. Christine Collette, *For Labour or for Women* (Manchester, 1989), p. 183.

27. Ibid.

28. Caroline Rowan, 'Mothers, vote Labour! The state, the labour movement and working-class mothers, 1900–1918', in Rosalind Brunt and Caroline Rowan (eds), *Feminist Culture and Politics* (London, 1982), pp. 59–85.

29. John Bruce Glasier, 'Keir Hardie: the man and his message', ILP pamphlet (1913).

30. Liddington and Norris, *One Hand*.

31. Mitchell, *The Hard Way Up*, p. 99.

32. Laurence Thompson, *The Enthusiasts* (London, 1971), p. 136.

33. *The Clarion*, 30 October 1903.

34. Hannam and Hunt, *Socialist Women*, pp. 108–9.

35. Liddington and Norris, *One Hand*, p. 181.

36. Quoted in Hunt, *Equivocal Feminists*, p. 167.

37. Hunt, *Equivocal Feminists*, p. 173.

38. Ibid., p. 176.

39. Liddington and Norris, *One Hand*, p. 232.

40. Hunt, *Equivocal Feminists*, p. 179.

41. Hannam and Hunt, *Socialist Women*, p. 123.

42. Liddington and Norris, *One Hand*, pp. 232–5.
43. Hannam, 'Politics', in Purvis, *Women's History*, p. 227.

7   Women Members of Parliament

1. Eleanor Rathbone, 'Changes in political life', in Ray Strachey (ed.), *Our Freedom and its Results* (London, 1936), p. 28.
2. *Hansard*, HC Deb 23 October 1918, vol. 110 cc, 785–857.
3. Elizabeth Vallance, *Women in the House: A Study of Women MPs* (London, 1979), p. 24.
4. Purvis, *Emmeline Pankhurst*, p. 302.
5. Rosen, *Rise Up Women*, p. 267.
6. Martin Pugh, *The Pankhursts* (London, 2001), pp. 346–8.
7. Cheryl Law, *Suffrage and Power: The Women's Movement 1918–1928* (London, 1997), p. 117.
8. Margaret Cole, *Women of Today* (London, 1938), p. 125.
9. Johanna Alberti, *Beyond Suffrage: Feminists in War and Peace* (Basingstoke, 1989), p. 96.
10. Ibid., p. 97.
11. Law, *Suffrage and Power*, p. 125.
12. Brian Harrison, 'Women in a men's House', *Historical Journal* 29 (1986), pp. 623–54, p. 625.
13. Vallance, *Women in the House*, p. 27.
14. Beverley Stobaugh, *Women and Parliament 1918–1970* (New York, 1978), p. 54.
15. Pugh, *Women and the Women's Movement*, p. 162.
16. Colin Rallings and Michael Thrasher, *British Electoral Facts 1832–1999* (Aldershot, 2000).
17. Donley T. Studlar, 'Women and Westminster', in Marian Sawer, Manon Tremblay and Linda Trimble (eds), *Representing Women in Parliament: A Comparative Study* (London, 2006), p. 87.
18. Brookes, *Women at Westminster*, p. 244.
19. Stobaugh, *Women and Parliament*, p. 93.
20. Vallance, *Women in the House*, p. 45.
21. Joni Lovenduski and Pippa Norris, *Gender and Party Politics in Britain* (London, 1993), p. 40.
22. Vallance, *Women in the House*, pp. 32–3.
23. Catriona Burness, 'Count up to twenty one: Scottish women in formal politics, 1918–1990'. in Esther Breitenbach and Pat Thane (eds), *Women and Citizenship in Britain and Ireland in the 20th Century: What Difference Did the Vote Make* (Leicester, 2010).
24. Brookes, *Women at Westminster,* p. 126.
25. Pat Hornsby Smith, 'Women in public life', in Hazel Hunkins Hallinan (ed.), *In Her Own Right* (London, 1968) p. 134.
26. Law, *Suffrage and Power*, p. 150.
27. Harold Smith, 'British feminism in the 1920s' in Harold Smith (ed.), *British Feminism in the Twentieth Century* (Aldershot, 1990) p. 51.

28. Brookes, *Women at Westminster,* p. 146; Martin Pugh, 'Domesticity and the decline of feminism', in Smith (ed.), *British Feminism,* p. 281.
29. Pugh, 'Domesticity and the decline of feminism', p. 160.
30. Lovenduski and Norris, *Gender and Party Politics,* p. 35.
31. Stobaugh, *Women and Parliament.*
32. Harrison, 'Women in a men's House', p. 629.
33. Vallance, *Women in the House,* p. 110–11.
34. Brookes, *Women at Westminster,* p. 43.
35. Ibid., p. 100; Vallance, *Women in the House,* p. 50.
36. Vallance, *Women in the House,* p. 39.
37. Thelma Cazalet-Keir, *From the Wings* (London, 1967), p. 141.
38. Brookes, *Women at Westminster,* p. 51.
39. Brian Harrison, *Prudent Revolutionaries: Portraits of British Feminists Between the Wars* (Oxford, 1987), p. 80; Hornsby Smith, 'Women in public life', p. 138; Vallance, *Women in the House,* p. 74.
40. Mary Agnes Hamilton, *Remembering My Good Friends* (London, 1944), p. 180.
41. Vallance, *Women in the House,* p. 40.
42. Brookes, *Women at Westminster,* pp. 62–3.
43. HC Deb. 29 February 1924, vol. 170, cc. 859–944.
44. Brookes, *Women at Westminster,* p. 177.
45. Harrison, 'Women in a men's House', p. 637.
46. Brookes, *Women at Westminster,* p. 130.
47. Harold Smith, 'British feminism and the equal pay issue in the 1930s', *Women's History Review* 5, 1 (1996), pp. 97–110.
48. Pugh, *Women and the Women's Movements,* pp. 300–1; Helen Jones, *Women in British Public Life, 1914–1950* (Harlow, 2000), pp. 224–5.
49. April Carter, *The Politics of Women's Rights* (London, 1988), p. 58.
50. Vallance, *Women in the House,* p. 93; Sheila Rowbotham, *The Past is Before Us* (London, 1999), p. 152.
51. Anna Coote and Beatrix Campbell, *Sweet Freedom: The Struggle for Women's Liberation* (London, 1982), p. 136.
52. Vallance, *Women in the House,* p. 180.
53. Harold Smith, 'The women's movement, politics and citizenship, 1960s–2000', in Ina Zweiniger-Bargoelowska (ed.), *Women in Twentieth Century Britain* (Harlow, 2001), pp. 278–91, p. 285.
54. Pat Thane, 'What difference did the vote make', in Amanda Vickery (ed.), *Women, Privilege and Power: British Politics 1750 to the Present* (Stanford, Calif., 2001).
55. See Sarah Childs (2008) *Women in British Party Politics: Descriptive, Substantive and Symbolic Representation* (London, 2008), p. xxi.

8 Women in Political Parties, 1918–1945

1. Strachey, *The Cause,* p. 367.
2. Vicky Randall, *Women and Politics* (Basingstoke, 1998), p. 220; Smith, 'British feminism in the 1920s', pp. 52–3.

3. Millicent Fawcett, *The Women's Victory and After – Personal Reminiscences, 1911–18* (London, 1920), p. 165.

4. Pat Thane, 'What difference did the vote make? Women in public and private life in Britain since 1918', *Historical Research* 76, 192 (2003), pp. 268–85.

5. Hirshfield, 'Fractured faith', pp. 188–9.

6. Pugh, *Women and the Women's Movement*, pp. 139–41.

7. Harrison, *Prudent Revolutionaries*, p. 203.

8. Pat Thane, 'Women, liberalism and citizenship', p. 68.

9. *Women's Liberal Magazine*, September 1927.

10. Thane, 'Women, Liberalism and citizenship', p. 83.

11. *Liberal Party Pamphlets and Leaflets 1918/27*, Harvester.

12. *Liberal Party Pamphlets and Leaflets 1918/29; 1920/9*, Harvester.

13. *Liberal Party Leaflets and Pamphlets 1928/19*, Harvester.

14. *Liberal Party Pamphlets and Leaflets 1918/27*, Harvester.

15. *Women's Liberal Magazine*, November 1927.

16. *Liberal Party Pamphlets and Leaflets 1927/19*, Harvester.

17. Pugh, *Tories and the People*, p. 178.

18. Neal McCrillis, *The British Conservative Party in the Age of Universal Suffrage: Popular Conservatism 1918–28* (Columbus, Ohio, 1998), p. 49.

19. Lovenduski et al. 'The party and women', p. 620.

20. McCrillis, *British Conservative Party*, p. 48.

21. Jarvis, 'The Conservative Party and the politics of gender', p. 174.

22. Robert Topping, 'Women's organisation: a plea for joint organisations', *Conservative Agents Journal*, August 1920.

23. Leigh Maclachlan, 'Women's organisation', *Conservative Agent's Journal*, June 1920.

24. Marjorie Maxse, 'Women's organisation', *Conservative Agent's Journal*, June 1924.

25. McCrillis, *British Conservative Party*, p. 52.

26. *Conservative Agents Journal*, 1926, cited in Jarvis, 'The Conservative Party and the politics of gender', p. 176.

27. Maguire, *Conservative Women*, pp. 99–100.

28. *Conservative Agents Journal*, October 1922, cited in Lovenduski et. al., 'The Party and women'.

29. *Conservative Agents Journal*, August 1919.

30. Ibid., February 1923.

31. *Archives of the British Conservative Party Series 1, Pamphlets and Leaflets, 1919/18, 1919/17*, Harvester.

32. David Jarvis, 'Mrs Maggs and Betty: the Conservative appeal to women voters', *Twentieth Century British History* 5 (2) (1994), pp. 129–52, p. 133.

33. *Archives of the British Conservative Party Series 1, Pamphlets and Leaflets, 1923/167; 1923/174; 1923/179*, Harvester.

34. Pugh, *Women and the Women's Movement*, p. 129; 1923 leaflet cited in Lovenduski et al., 'The Party and women', p. 632.

35. Campbell, *Iron Ladies*, p. 56.
36. Christine Collette, *The Newer Eve: Women, Feminists and the Labour Party* (Basingstoke, 2009), p. 70.
37. Pat Thane, 'Women in the British Labour Party and the construction of state welfare, 1906–39', in Seth Koven and Sonya Michel (eds), *Mothers of a New World: Maternalist Politics and the Origins of Welfare States* (London, 1993), pp. 343–77.
38. Stephanie Ward, 'The means test and the unemployed in South Wales and the north-east of England, 1931–1939', *Labour History Review 73*, 1 (2008), pp. 113–32.
39. Beddoe, *Out of the Shadows*, pp. 92–3.
40. Andrew Thorpe, *A History of the British Labour Party* (Basingstoke, 1997), p. 175.
41. Pamela M. Graves, *Labour Women: Women in British Working-Class Politics 1918–1939* (Cambridge, 1994), pp. 218–19.
42. Alan Alder (ed.), *Theses, Resolutions and Manifestos of the First Four Congresses of the Third International* (London, 1980), p. 47.
43. Ibid., p. 217.
44. Ibid., p. 218.
45. Ibid., p. 325.
46. Sue Bruley, *Leninism, Stalinism and the Women's Movement in Britain, 1920–1939* (New York, 1986), p. 102; Karen Hunt and Matthew Worley, 'Rethinking British Communist Party women in the 1920s', *Twentieth Century British History* 15, 1 (2004), pp. 1–27, p. 8.
47. Bruley, *Leninism*, p. 71.
48. Ibid., p. 103.
49. Gidon Cohen and Andrew Flinn, 'In search of the typical British Communist', in Kevin Morgan, Gidon Cohen and Andrew Flinn (eds), *Agents of the Revolution* (London, 2005), p. 41.
50. *CPGB Congress Report*, 1925, pp. 119–20.
51. Stuart McIntyre, *Little Moscows* (London, 1980), p. 146.
52. Sue Bruley, 'Women and communism: a case study of the Lancashire weavers in the Depression', in Geoff Andrews, Nina Fishman and Kevin Morgan (eds), *Opening the Books: Essays on the Social and Cultural History of the British Communist Party* (London, 1995), pp. 64–82.
53. Bruley, *Leninism*, p. 90.
54. *Workers Weekly*, 1 August 1924.
55. Hunt and Worley, 'Rethinking Communist women', p. 10.
56. Andrew Thorpe, 'The membership of the Communist Party of Great Britain, 1920–1945', *Historical Journal* 43, 3 (2000), pp. 777–800, p. 783.
57. Hunt and Worley, 'Rethinking Communist women', p. 6.
58. Roger Eatwell, *Fascism: A History* (London, 1995), p. i.
59. Martin Durham, 'Women and the British Union of Fascists', in Tony Kushner and Kenneth Lunn (eds), *The Politics of Marginality: Race, the Radical Right and Minorities in 20th Century Britain* (London, 1990), pp. 3–18, p. 4.

60. See for example Martin Durham, *Women and Fascism* (London, 1998); Julie Gottlieb, *Feminine Fascism: Women in Britain's Fascist Movements* (London, 2003).

61. Martin Durham, 'Britain', in Kevin Passmore (ed.), *Women, Gender and Fascism in Europe 1919–1945* (Manchester, 2003), p. 216.

62. Durham, 'Britain', p. 218.

63. Gottlieb, *Feminine Fascism*, p. 22; Durham, 'Britain', p. 218.

64. Stephen Cullen, 'Four women for Mosley: women in the British Union of Fascists, 1932–1940', *Oral History* 24 (1996), pp. 49–59, p. 55.

65. Stephen Cullen, 'The fasces and the saltire: the failure of the BUF in Scotland 1922–40', *Scottish Historical Review* 87 (2008), pp. 306–31, p. 315.

66. Cullen, 'Four women for Mosley', p. 56.

67. Gottlieb, *Feminine Fascism*, p. 44.

68. Quoted in Martin Durham, 'Women in the British Union of Fascists', in Sybil Oldfield (ed.), *This Working Day World: Women's Lives and Cultures in Britain 1914–1944* (London, 1994), p. 104.

69. Durham, 'Britain', p. 219.

70. Durham, 'Women and the BUF', p. 11.

71. Durham, 'Britain', p. 225.

72. Gottlieb, *Feminine Fascism*, p. 124.

73. Durham, 'Women and the BUF', p. 7.

74. Durham, 'Britain', p. 228.

75. Durham, 'Women and the BUF', p. 9.

76. Ibid., p. 10.

77. Gottlieb, *Feminine Fascism*, p. 171; Cowman, *Women of the Right Spirit*, p. 201.

78. Durham, 'Britain', p. 230.

79. Pugh, *Women and the Women's Movement*, p. 280; Pugh, 'Domesticity and the decline of feminism', pp. 158–9.

80. Joni Lovenduski and Vicky Randall, *Contemporary Feminist Politics* (Oxford, 1993), p. 139.

81. Jill Hills, 'Britain', in Joni Lovenduski and Jill Hills (eds.), *The Politics of the Second Electorate: Women and Public Participation* (London, 1981), pp. 8–33, p. 18.

82. Lovenduski et al., 'The party and women'; Martin Cole, 'The yellow glass ceiling: the mystery of the disappearing Liberal MPs', *Journal of Liberal History* 62 (2009), pp. 26–35.

83. Hills, 'Britain'.

84. Hollie Voyce, 'From WLF to WLD: Liberal women's grassroots campaigning', *Journal of Liberal History* 62 (2009), pp. 41–6.

85. Cole, 'The yellow glass ceiling'.

86. Collette, *The Newer Eve*, p. 117.

87. Campbell, *Iron Ladies*, ch. 3.

88. Celia Goodhard, 'Women in alliance politics: a personal view', *Journal of Liberal History* 62 (2009), pp. 56–60.

89. Elizabeth Wilson, *Only Halfway to Paradise* (London, 1980), p. 75.

90. Miriam Glucksman, *Women Assemble* (London, 1990), p. 191.
91. C. Rallings and M. Thrasher, *British Electoral Facts 1832–1999* (Aldershot, 2000), p. 133.
92. Charlotte Aull Davies, 'Women nationalism and feminism', in Jane Aaron, Teresa Rees, Sandra Betts and Moira Cincentelli (eds), *Our Sisters' Land* (Cardiff, 1994), p. 242.
93. Laura McAllister, 'Gender, nation and party: An uneasy alliance for Welsh nationalism', *Women's History Review* 10, 1 (2001), pp. 51–70.
94. Beddoe, *Out of the Shadows*, p. 157.
95. Catriona Burness, 'Drunk women don't look at thistles: women and the SNP 1934–1994', *Scotlands* 2 (1994), pp. 131–54.
96. Sue Innes and Jane Rendall, 'Women, gender and politics', in Lynn Abrams, Eleanor Gordon, Deborah Simonton and Eileen Janes Yeo (eds), *Gender in Scottish History since 1700* (Edinburgh, 2006), pp. 43–83.
97. Elizabeth Meehan, 'British feminism from the 1960s to the 1980s', in Smith (ed.), *British Feminism*, pp. 189–204, p. 194.
98. Coote and Campbell, *Sweet Freedom*, p. 31.
99. Sheila Rowbotham, *The Past is Before Us* (London, 1989), p. 161.

9 Beyond Party Politics

1. Law, *Suffrage and Power*; Alberti, *Beyond Suffrage*.
2. Catherine Blackford, 'Wives and citizens and watchdogs of equality: postwar British feminists', in Jim Fyrth (ed.), *Labour's Promised Land? Culture and Society in Labour Britain 1945–51* (London, 1995), p. 71 n. 8.
3. Harold Smith, 'British feminism in the 1920s', in Smith (ed.), *British Feminism*, p. 48.
4. Alberti, *Beyond Suffrage*, p. 164.
5. Harrison, *Prudent Revolutionaries*, p. 315.
6. Jane Lewis, 'Feminism and welfare', in Juliet Mitchell and Ann Oakley (eds), *What Is Feminism* (Oxford, 1986), pp. 85–100, p. 94.
7. Susan Kingsley Kent, 'Gender reconstruction after the First World War', in Smith (ed.), *British Feminism in the Twentieth Century*, pp. 66–83.
8. Susan Pedersen, *Eleanor Rathbone and the Politics of Conscience* (London, 2004), p. 191.
9. *Women's Leader*, 12 March 1926.
10. Dale Spender, *Women of Ideas and What Men Have Done to Them* (London, 1983), p. 626.
11. Shirley Eoff, *Viscountess Rhondda, Equalitarian Feminist* (Columbus, Ohio, 1991), p. 91.
12. Alberti, *Beyond Suffrage*, pp. 136–7.
13. Smith, *British Feminism*, p. 59.
14. Eoff, *Viscountess Rhondda*, p. 76.
15. Deborah Gorham, 'Vera Brittain and inter-war feminism' in Smith (ed.), *British Feminism in the 20th Century*, p. 94.
16. 'The New Group', *Time and Tide*, 25 February 1921.

17. See *Six Point Group* leaflet n.d. c. 1974, Six Point Group Papers, Women's Library 5/SPG/E/12.
18. Six Point Group *Annual Report* 1933–4.
19. Law, *Suffrage and Power*, p. 193.
20. 'The New Group', *Time and Tide*, 25 February 1921.
21. Quoted in Law, *Suffrage and Power*, p. 193.
22. Pugh, *Women and the Women's Movement*, p. 143.
23. Quoted in Eoff, *Viscountess Rhondda*, p. 95.
24. Jessica Thurlow, 'Continuity and change in British feminism c.1940–1960', unpublished PhD thesis, University of Michigan (2006), p. 40.
25. Open Door Council, *12th Annual Report*.
26. Open Door Council, *1st Annual Report*.
27. Open Door Council, *15th Annual Report*.
28. Law, *Suffrage and Power*, p. 195.
29. Harrison, *Prudent Revolutionaries*, p. 148.
30. Eleanor Rathbone, 'Women citizens' associations', *Common Cause*, 30 June 1916.
31. Sue Innes, 'Constructing women's citizenship in the interwar period: the Edinburgh WCA', *Women's History Review* 13, 4 (2004), p. 627.
32. Confidential Report on Visits Paid to Associations, 23 February 1931. 5/NWC/E8/1, Women's Library.
33. NWCA, *National Women Citizens Association 1918–1968,* 5/NWC/13/1, Women's Library.
34. Pugh, *Women and the Women's Movement,* p. 60.
35. Jill Liddington, *Life and Times of a Respectable Rebel* (London, 1986).
36. Sarah Browne, *Making the Vote Count: The Arbroath Women Citizen's Association 1931–45* (Dundee, 2007), p. 26.
37. NWCA, *National Women Citizens Association 1918–1968,* 5/NWC/13/1, Women's Library.
38. Haig, *This Was My World,* pp. 298–9.
39. Hazel Hunkins Hallinan, 'Forward', in Hunkins Hallinan (ed.), *In Her Own Right,* p. 13.
40. Jones, *Women in British Pubic Life.*
41. Catriona Beaumont, 'Citizens not feminists: the boundary negotiated between citizenship and feminism by mainstream women's organisations in England, 1928–39', *Women's History Review* 9, 2 (2000), pp. 411–29, p. 412.
42. Beaumont, 'Citizens not feminists'.
43. Maggie Andrews, *The Acceptable Face of Feminism: The Women's Institute as a Social Movement* (London, 1997), pp. ix–x.
44. Andrews, *Acceptable Face,* p. 153.
45. Beaumont, 'Citizens not feminists', p. 418.
46. Pugh, *Women and the Women's Movement* , pp. 264–5.
47. Jones, *Women in British Public Life,* p. 186.
48. James Hinton, *Women, Social Leadership and the Second World War* (Oxford, 2002), p. 195.
49. Ibid., p. 179.

50. Brookes, *Women at Westminster*, p. 130.
51. Pugh, *Women and the Women's Movement*, p. 276.
52. Alison Oram, 'Bombs don't discriminate! Women's political activism in the Second World War', in Christine Gledhill and Gillian Swanson (eds), *Nationalising Femininity: Culture, Sexuality and British Cinema in the Second World War* (Manchester, 1996), p. 54.
53. 'Equal Pay Campaign Committee, Summary of its Origins', EPCC 263. Women's Library.
54. Oram, 'Bombs don't discriminate', p. 61.
55. Mss notes 'Origins of Women for Westminster Movement', 5SPG/B/14, Women's Library.
56. Thurlow, 'Continuity and change', p. 113.
57. Jones, *Women in British Public Life*, p. 215.
58. Open Door Council, *24th Annual Report*.
59. Circular Letter 17, April 1947, 5/NWC/E8/1, Women's Library.
60. *Six Point Group Newsletter*, January 1949.
61. Six Point Group Leaflet, 'Why I support the women's movement' n.d. c. 1950.
62. *Six Point Group Newsletter*, 1951. For the Korean War issue see Sybil Morrison, interview with HHH, 26 Oct 1971 [5/SPG/m//10], Women's Library.
63. *Six Point Group Newsletter*, February 1956.
64. Ibid., March 1954.
65. Ibid., 1971.
66. Ibid., June 1969.
67. Dale Spender, *There's Always Been a Women's Movement This Century* (London, 1983).
68. *Six Point Group Newsletter*, April 1979.
69. Six Point Group EC minutes, 2 October 1979, SPG/A/311–333, Women's Library.
70. Status of Women Committee Liaison Sub Committee Minutes, 30 June 1980, SPF/5/SWC/A, Women's Library.
71. NWCA membership circular, 4 Feb 1974, 5/NWC/1/K/14, Women's Library.
72. *WFL Bulletin*, 17 November 1961.
73. Coote and Campbell, *Sweet Freedom*, p. 14.
74. Vicky Randall, *Women and Politics: An International Perspective* (Basingstoke, 1987), p. 230.
75. Sheila Rowbotham, 'Cleaners organizing in Britain: a personal account', *Antipode* 38, 3 (2006), p. 618.
76. Wilson, *Only Halfway to Paradise*, p. 180.
77. Birmingham Feminist History Group, 'Feminism as femininity in the 1950s', *Feminist Review* 3 (1979), pp. 48–65.
78. Joni Lovenduski, *Feminizing Politics* (Cambridge, 2004), p. 41.
79. Sandra Grey and Marian Sawer, 'Introduction', in *Women's Movements; Flourishing or in Abeyance?* (London, 2008), p. 1.

80. Joyce Gelb, 'Feminism in Britain: politics without power', in Drude Dahlerup (ed.), *The New Women's Movement: Feminism and Political Power in Europe and the USA* (London, 1986), p. 108.

81. *Sunday Times* n.d. (?1971) cutting in 'Women's Liberation UK' scrapbook vol. 1 10/52/1, Women's Library.

82. Beddoe, *Out of the Shadows*, pp. 160–3; Fiona Mackay, 'The state of women's movements in Britain', in Grey and Sawyer (eds), *Women's Movements*, p. 25.

83. Coote and Campbell, *Sweet Freedom*, p. 20.

84. Randall, *Women and Politics*, p. 231.

85. A short overview of the two positions can be found in Coote and Campbell, *Sweet Freedom*, pp. 26–33.

86. Ibid., p. 33.

87. Brixton Black Women's Group, 'Black women organizing autonomously', *Feminist Review* 17 (1984), pp. 84–99.

88. Valerie Amos and Pratibha Parmar, 'Challenging imperial feminism', *Feminist Review* 17 (1984), pp. 3–19.

89. Randall, *Women and Politics*, p. 234.

90. Randall, *Women and Politics*, p. 233.

91. Randall, *Women and Politics*, p. 234.

92. Rowbotham, *The Past is Before Us*, p. 19.

93. Spender, *There's Always Been a Women's Movement*.

Conclusion

1. Margaret Thatcher Foundation, 'Remarks on becoming Prime Minister,' speeches and remarks file 1608.

2. Judith Bennett, *History Matters: Patriarchy and the Challenge of Feminism* (Manchester, 2006).

Select Bibliography

A. J. R. (ed.), *The Suffrage Annual and Women's Who's Who* (London, 1913).

Lynn Abrams, Eleanor Gordon, Deborah Simonton and Eileen Yeo (eds), *Gender in Scottish History Since 1700* (Edinburgh, 2006).

Johanna Alberti, *Beyond Suffrage: Feminists in War and Peace* (London, 1989).

Valerie Amos and Pratibha Parmar, 'Challenging imperial feminism', *Feminist Review* 17 (1984), pp. 3–19.

Donna Andrew, *London Debating Societies* (London, 1994).

Maggie Andrews, *The Acceptable Face of Feminism: The Women's Institute as a Social Movement* (London, 1997).

Mitzi Auchterlonie, *Conservative Suffragists: The Women's Vote and the Tory Party* (London, 2007).

Olive Banks, *Becoming a Feminist: The Social Origins of First Wave Feminism* (Brighton, 1986).

Hannah Barker and Elaine Chalus (eds), *Gender in Eighteenth Century England: Roles, Representations and Responsibilities* (London, 1997).

Hannah Barker and Elaine Chalus (eds), *Women's History 1700–1850* (London, 2005).

Catriona Beaumont, 'Citizens not feminists: the boundary negotiated between citizenship and feminism by mainstream women's organisations in England, 1928–39', *Women's History Review* 9, 2 (2000), pp. 411–29.

Deidre Beddoe, *Out of the Shadows: A History of Women in Twentieth Century Wales* (Cardiff, 2000).

J. Bedford, 'Margaret Ashton: Manchester's first lady', *Manchester Region History Review* 12 (1998), pp. 3–17.

Charles Beem, *The Lioness Roared: The Problems of Female Rule in English History* (Basingstoke, 2006).

Helen Blackburn, *Women's Suffrage* (London, 1902).

Catherine Blackford, 'Wives and citizens and watchdogs of equality: post-war British feminists', in Jim Fyrth (ed.), *Labour's Promised Land? Culture and Society in Labour Britain 1945–51* (London, 1995).

Myriam Boussahba-Bravard (ed.), *Suffrage Outside Suffragism* (Basingstoke, 2007).

Renate Bridenthal and Claudia Koonz (eds), *Becoming Visible* (London, 1977).

Esther Brietenbach and Eleanor Gordon (eds), *Out of Bounds: Women in Scottish Society 1800–1945* (Edinburgh, 1992).

Esther Brietenbach and Pat Thane (eds), *Women and Citizenship in Britain and Ireland in the Twentieth Century: What Difference did the Vote Make?* (Leicester, 2010).

Pamela Brookes, *Women at Westminster* (London, 1967).

Yvonne Brown and Rona Ferguson (eds), *Twisted Sisters: Women, Crime and Deviance in Scotland since 1400* (East Linton, 2002).

Sue Bruley, *Leninism, Stalinism and the Women's Movement in Britain 1920–1939* (New York, 1986).

Valerie Bryson, *Feminist Political Theory: An Introduction* (Basingstoke, 1992).

Robert Buchloz, *The Augustan Court: Queen Anne and the Decline of Court Culture* (Stanford, Calif., 1993).

Julia Bush, *Edwardian Ladies and Imperial Power* (Leicester, 2000).

Julia Bush, *Women Against the Vote: Female Anti-Suffragism in Britain* (Oxford, 2007).

Barbara Caine, *Victorian Feminists* (Oxford, 1992).

Barbara Caine, *English Feminism 1780–1980* (Oxford, 1997).

Beatrix Campbell, *The Iron Ladies: Why Do Women Vote Tory?* (London, 1987).

Clarissa Campbell Orr (ed.), *Queenship in Britain 1660–1837* (Manchester, 2000).

Bernard Capp, *When Gossips Meet: Women, Family and Neighbourhood in Early Modern England* (Oxford, 2003).

Rosalind Carr, 'Gender, national identity and political agency in eighteenth century Scotland', PhD thesis, University of Glasgow, 2008.

Elaine Chalus, '"Ladies are often very good scaffoldings:" women and politics in the age of Anne', *Parliamentary History* (2009), pp. 150–65.

Elaine Chalus, 'My Minerva at my elbow', in Stephen Taylor, Richard Connors and Clive Jones (eds), *Hannoverian Britain and Empire* (Woodbridge, 1998).

Elaine Chalus, 'The Rag Plot: the politics of influence in Oxford, 1754', in Rosemary Sweet and Penelope Lane (eds), *Women and Urban Life in Eighteenth-Century England* (Aldershot, 2003), pp. 43–61.

Malcolm Chase, *Chartism, A New History* (Manchester, 2007).

Sarah Childs, *Women in British Party Politics: Descriptive, Substantive and Symbolic Representation* (London, 2008).

Anna Clark, *The Struggle for the Breeches: Gender and the Making of the British Working Class* (London, 1997).

Martin Cole, 'The yellow glass ceiling: the mystery of the disappearing Liberal MPs', *Journal of Liberal History* 62 (2009), pp. 26–35.

Christine Collette, *For Labour or for Women* (Manchester, 1989).

Christine Collette, *The Newer Eve* (Basingstoke, 2009).

Linda Colley, *Britons: Forging the Nation*, 2nd edn (London, 2005).

Anna Coote and Beatrix Campbell, *Sweet Freedom: The Struggle for Women's Liberation* (London, 1982).

Krista Cowman, *Mrs Brown is a Man and a Brother: Women in Merseyside's Political Organisations 1890–1920* (Liverpool, 2004).

Krista Cowman, *Women of the Right Spirit: Paid Organisers in the Women's Social and Political Union* (Manchester, 2007).

Elizabeth Crawford, *The Women's Suffrage Movement* (London, 1999).

James Daybell (ed.), *Women and Politics in Early Modern England 1450–1700* (Aldershot, 2004).

Jackie Eales, *Women in Early Modern England* (London, 1998).

Shirley Eoff, *Viscountess Rhondda, Equalitarian Feminist* (Columbus, Ohio, 1991).

Claire Eustance, Joan Ryan and Laura Ugolini (eds), *A Suffrage Reader: Charting Directions in British Suffrage History* (Leicester, 2000).

Elizabeth Ewan and Maureen Meikle (eds), *Women in Scotland, 1100–1750* (East Linton, 1999).

Millicent Fawcett, *Women's Suffrage: A Short History of a Great Movement* (London, 1912).

Millicent Fawcett, *What I Remember* (London, 1924).

Martin Fitzpatrick, Peter Jones, Christa Knellwolf and Iain McCalman (eds), *The Enlightenment World* (London, 2004).

Ruth and Edmund Frow (eds), *Political Women 1800–1850* (London, 1989).

Joyce Gelb, 'Feminism in Britain: politics without power' in D. Dahlerup (ed.), *The New Women's Movement; Feminism and Political Power in Europe and the USA* (London, 1986).

Kathryn Gleadle, *Borderline Citizens: Women, Gender and Political Culture in Britain 1815–1867* (Oxford, 2009).

Kathryn Gleadle and Sarah Richardson (eds), *The Power of the Petticoat* (Basingstoke, 2000).

Miriam Glucksman, *Women Assemble* (London, 1990).

Eleanor Gordon, *Women and the Labour Movement in Scotland* (Oxford, 1991).

Julie Gottlieb, *Feminine Fascism: Women in Britain's Fascist Movements* (London, 2003).

Sandra Grey and Marian Sawer (eds), *Women's Movements: Flourishing or in Abeyance?* (London, 2008).

June Hannam and Karen Hunt, *Socialist Women: Britain, 1890s–1920s* (London, 2002).

Brian Harrison, *Prudent Revolutionaries: Portraits of British Feminists Between the Wars* (Oxford, 1987).

Brian Harrison, 'Women in a men's house', *Historical Journal* 29 (1986), pp. 623–54.

Patricia Higgins, 'The reactions of women with special reference to women petitioners', in Brian Manning (ed.), *Politics, Religion and the English Civil War* (London, 1973), pp. 179–222.

Jill Hills, 'Britain', in Joni Lovenduski and Jill Hills (eds), *The Politics of the Second Electorate: Women and Public Participation* (London, 1981), pp. 8–33.

Pam Hirsch, *Barbara Leigh Smith Bodichon* (London, 1998).

Clare Hirshfield, 'Fractured faith: the Liberal Party and the suffrage issue in Britain', *Gender and History* 2, pp. 173–9.

Lee Holcombe, *Wives and Property* (Toronto, 1983).

Patricia Hollis, *Ladies Elect* (Oxford, 1987).

Sandra Holton, *Feminism and Democracy: Women's Suffrage and Reform Politics in Britain* (Cambridge, 1987).

Sandra Holton, *Suffrage Days: Stories from the Women's Suffrage Movement* (London, 1996).

Pat Hornsby Smith, 'Women in public life', in Hazel Hunkins Hallinan (ed.), *In Her Own Right* (London, 1968).

Ann Hughes, 'Gender and politics in Leveller literature', in S. D. Amussen and M. A. Kishlansky (eds), *Political Cultures and Cultural Politics in Early Modern England* (Manchester, 1995).

Leslie Hume, *The National Union of Women's Suffrage Societies* (New York, 1982).

Karen Hunt, *Equivocal Feminists: The SDF and the Woman Question* (Cambridge, 1996).

David Jarvis, 'The Conservative Party and the politics of gender, 1900–1939', in Martin Francis and Ina Zweiniger-Bargielowska (eds), *The Conservatives and British Society, 1880–1990* (Cardiff, 1996).

Angela John (ed.), *Our Mother's Land: Chapter in Welsh Women's History 1830–1939* (Cardiff, 1991).

David Jones, 'Women and Chartism', *History* 68 (1983), pp. 10–13.

Helen Jones, *Women in British Public Life* (Harlow, 2000).

Sara Knott and Barbara Taylor (eds), *Women, Gender and Enlightenment* (Basingstoke, 2007).

Cheryl Law, *Suffrage and Power* (London, 1997).

Leah Leneman, *A Guid Cause, The Women's Suffrage Movement in Scotland* (Aberdeen, 1991).

Philippa Levine, *Feminist Lives in Victorian England: Private Roles and Public Commitment* (Oxford, 1990).

Jill Liddington, *Rebel Girls: Their Fight for the Vote* (London, 2006).

Jill Liddington and Jill Norris, *One Hand Tied Behind Us: The Rise of the Women's Suffrage Campaign* (London. 1978).

Joni Lovenduski, *Femimizing Politics* (Cambridge, 2004).

Joni Lovenduski and Pippa Norris, *Gender and Party Politics in Britain* (London, 1993).

Joni Lovenduski, Pippa Norris, and Catriona Burness, 'The Party and women', in Anthony Seldon and Stuart Ball (eds), *Conservative Century: The Conservative Party since 1900* (Oxford, 1994), pp. 611–35.

Joni Lovenduski and Vicky Randall, *Contemporary Feminist Politics* (Oxford, 1993).

G. E. Maguire, *Conservative Women: A History of Women and the Conservative Party* (Basingstoke, 1998).

Bertha Mason, *The Story of the Women's Suffrage Movement* (London, 1912).

Ursula Masson, *'Women's Rights and Womanly Duties': The Aberdare Women's Liberal Association, 1891–1910* (Cardiff, 2005).

Laura Nym Mayhall, *The Militant Suffrage Movement: Citizenship and Resistance in Britain 1860–1930* (Oxford, 2003).

Neal McCrillis, *The British Conservative Party* (Columbus, Ohio, 1998).

Sarah Mendelson and Patricia Crawford, *Women in Early Modern England* (Oxford, 1998).

Claire Midgley, *Women Against Slavery: The British Campaigns 1780–1870* (London, 1992).

Simon Morgan, *A Victorian Woman's Place: Public Culture in the Nineteenth Century* (London, 2007).

Karen O'Brien, *Women and Enlightenment in Eighteenth Century Britain* (Cambridge, 2009).

Frank O'Gorman, *The Long Eighteenth Century: British Political and Social History 1688–1832* (London, 1997).

Frank O'Gorman, *Voters, Patrons and Parties: The Unformed Electoral System of Hanoverian England 1734–1832* (Oxford, 1987).

Karen Offen, *European Feminisms 1700–1950* (Stanford, Calif., 2000.).

Estelle Sylvia Pankhurst, *The Suffragette Movement* (London, 1977).

John A. Phillips, *Electoral Behaviour in Unreformed England* (Princeton, N.J./ London, 1982).

Paul Pickering and Alex Tyrrell, *The People's Bread: A History of the Anti-Corn Law League* (Leicester, 2000).

Frank Prochaska, *Women and Philanthropy in Nineteenth Century England* (Oxford, 1980).

Martin Pugh, *The Tories and the People* (Oxford, 1986).

Martin Pugh, *The March of the Women: A Revisionist History of the Campaign for Women's Suffrage* (Oxford, 2000).

Martin Pugh, *The Pankhursts* (London, 2001).

Martin Pugh, *Women and the Women's Movement in Britain* (Basingstoke, 1992).

June Purvis (ed.), *Women's History in Britain* (London, 2000).

June Purvis, *Emmeline Pankhurst* (London, 2002).

June Purvis and Sandra Holton (eds), *Votes for Women* (London, 2000).

June Purvis and Maroula Joaanou (eds), *The Women's Suffrage Movement* (Manchester, 1998).

Antonia Raeburn, *The Militant Suffragettes* (London, 1973).

Vicky Randall, *Women and Politics: An International Perspective* (Basingstoke, 1987).

Eleanor Rathbone, 'Changes in political life', in R. Strachey (ed.), *Our Freedom and its Results* (London, 1936).

Jane Rendall, *The Origins of Modern Feminism* (Basingstoke, 1985).

Jane Rendall (ed.), *Equal or Different: Women's Politics 1800–1914* (Oxford, 1987).

Janet Robb, *The Primrose League* (New York, 1942).

Andrew Rosen, *Rise Up Women: The Militant Campaign of the Women's Social and Political Union 1903–14* (London, 1974).

Constance Rover, *Women's Suffrage and Party Politics in Britain, 1866–1914* (London, 1967).

Sheila Rowbotham, *The Past is Before Us* (London, 1989).

David Rubinstein, *Before the Suffragettes: Women's Emancipation in the 1890s* (Brighton, 1986).

Jutta Schwarzkopf, *Women in the Chartist Movement* (Basingstoke, 1991).

Lois Schwoerer, 'Women and the Glorious Revolution', *Albion* 18 (1986), pp. 195–218.

Robert B. Shoemaker, *Gender in English Society 1650–1850: The Emergence of Separate Spheres* (London, 1998).

Harold Smith (ed.), *British Feminism in the Twentieth Century* (Aldershot, 1990).

Harold Smith, *The British Women's Suffrage Campaign*, 2nd edn (Harlow, 2007).

Hilda Smith (ed.), *Women Writers and the Early Modern British Political Tradition* (Cambridge, 1998).

Hilda Smith, *All Men and Both Sexes: Gender, Politics and the False Universal in England, 1640–1832* (London, 2002).

Dale Spender, *There's Always Been a Women's Movement This Century* (London, 1983).

Susie Steinbach, *Women in England 1760–1914* (Basingstoke, 2004).

Beverly Stobaugh, *Women and Parliament 1918–1970* (New York, 1978).

Ray Strachey, *The Cause: A Short History of the Women's Movement in Great Britain* (London, 1978).

Ingrid Tague, *Women of Quality: Accepting and Contesting Ideals of Femininity in England, 1690–1760* (Woodbridge, 2002).

Barbara Taylor, *Mary Wollstonecraft and the Feminist Imagination* (Cambridge, 2003).

Barbara Taylor, *Eve and the New Jerusalem* (London, 1983).

Pat Thane, 'Women in public life in Britain since 1918', *Historical Research* 76, 192 (2003), pp. 268–85.

Pat Thane, 'Women, Liberalism and citizenship', in Eugenio Biagini (ed.), *Citizenship and Community: Liberals and Collective Identities in the British Isles, 1865–1931* (Cambridge, 1996), pp. 66–92.

Malcolm Thomis and Jennifer Grimmett, *Women in Protest* (London, 1982).

Dorothy Thompson, *The Chartists* (Hounslow, 1984).

Jessica Thurlow, 'Continuity and change in British feminism c.1940–1960', PhD thesis, University of Michigan, 2006.

Alex Tyrrell, 'Woman's mission and pressure group politics 1825–1860', *Bulletin of the John Rylands Library* 63 (1980), pp. 194–230.

Elizabeth Vallance, *Women in the House: A Study of Women MPs* (London, 1979).

Sophia Van Wingerden, *The Women's Suffrage Movement in Britain, 1866–1928* (Basingstoke, 1999).

Jo Vellacott, *Pacifists, Patriots and the Vote: The Erosion of Democratic Suffragism in Britain During the First World War* (Basingstoke, 2007).

James Vernon, *Politics and the People: A Study in English Political Culture* (Cambridge, 1993).

Amanda Vickery, *Women Privilege and Power: British Politics 1750 to the Present* (Stanford, Calif., 2001).

Hollie Voyce, 'From WLF to WLD: Liberal women's grassroots campaigning', *Journal of Liberal History* 62 (2009), pp. 46–41.

Judith Walkowitz, *Prostitution and Victorian Society* (Cambridge, 1982).

Vron Ware, *Beyond the Pale: White Women, Racism and History* (London, 1981).

Rachel Weil, *Political Passions: Gender, the Family and Political Argument in England 1680–1714* (Manchester, 1999).

Elizabeth Wilson, *Only Halfway to Paradise* (London, 1980).

Ina Zweiniger-Bargoelowska (ed.), *Women in Twentieth Century Britain* (Harlow, 2001).

Index

Aaron, Jane, 5, 171, 195
Abbot, Fanny, 105
Aberdare, 81, 82
Aberdeen, 66
Abrams, Lynn, 6, 171, 195
Actresses' Franchise League, 72
Adult Suffrage Society, 109, 110
Alberti, Johanna, 3, 150, 151, 153, 171, 190, 195
Alexander, Sally, 165
Allen, Joan, 189
Allen, Mary, 66
Amos, Valerie, 166, 198
Amussen, Susan D, 173
Anderson, Robert D, 182
Anderson, Mrs Scott, 133
Andrew, Donna, 177
Andrews, Margaret, 158, 196
Anne, Queen, 10, 14, 17–19
    conception of queenship, 16, 17
    education, 14
    health, 18
    relationship with courtiers, 16, 18
Anti-Corn Law League, 39–41, 47
    class composition of, 39
    'Great Bazaar', 40;
    spread, 39
    women's membership, 39–40
Anti-Slavery movement, 33–4, 47
Archdale, Helen, 154
Archer, Hannah, 49
aristocratic women, 4, 10
    Conservative Party and, 90
    at Court, 17–19
Artists' Suffrage League, 72
Ashby, Margery Corbett, 132, 134, 158, 159
Ashton, Margaret, 53, 83
Ashton, Owen, 180
Ashwell, Lena. 72
Asquith, Herbert, 86, 117
Association for Moral and Social Hygiene, 151

Association for Promoting the Education of Girls in Wales, 42
Astell, Mary, 13, 23, 89, 179
Astor, Nancy, 119, 120, 121, 123, 124, 124, 124, 160
Athenian Mercury, 23
Atholl, Katherine, Duchess of, 19
Atholl, Duchess of (MP), 124, 125
Auchterlonie, Mitzi, 96, 99, 188
Aveling, Edward, 102
Ayles, Bertha, 111

Bacon, Alice, 125
Bain, Margaret, 147
Balfour, Lady Frances, 64
Banks, Olive, 89, 103, 187, 189
Barker, Hannah, 173, 178
Barmby, Catherine, 33
Barrett, Rachel, 66
Barrow, Margaret, 186
Batchelor, Jennie, 178
Beattie, John, 173
Beaumont, Catriona, 5, 158, 171, 196
Bebel, August, 102
Becker, Lydia, 44, 60, 61
Beddoe, Deidre, 5, 165, 171, 187, 193, 195, 198
Bedford, Jane, 183, 186
Beem, Charles, 14, 16, 173, 175
Belchem, John, 189
Bennett, Judith, 169, 198
Betts, Sandra, 171, 195
Biagini, Eugenio, 186
Biddle, Hester, 23
Billington, Louis, 179
Billington, Rosamund, 179
Bilocca, Lil, 164
Birch, Minnie, 129
Birmingham, 53, 67, 79, 93
Birmingham Female Political Union, 36
birth control, 137–8
'Black Friday', 67
Black, Jeremy, 175

Blackburn, Helen, 40, 81, 180
Blackford, Catherine, 151, 195
Bland, Caroline, 189
Bland, Lucy, 181, 182
Bodichon, Barbara, 41, 42, 43, 60
Bohata, Kirsti, 5, 171
Bondfield, Margaret, 109, 110, 125, 169
Booth, Agnes, 144
Booth, Eva Gore, 63
Boucherett, Jessie, 41, 42, 44, 93
Boussahba-Bravard, Myriam, 186, 188
Boyle, Nina, 116
Bradford, 53, 81
Brailsford, Henry, 87, 172
Breitenbach, Esther, 172, 190, 191
Brewer, John, 173
Bridenthal, Renate, 178
*Brief Summary of the Laws in England
    Concerning Women* (Bodichon), 43
Bright, Jacob, 51, 60, 61, 64
Bright, Ursula, 44
Bristol, 53, 61
Bristol and West of England National
    Society for Women's Suffrage, 52
Britannia, 73
British Fascisti, 142
    Women's Units of, 143
British Socialist Party, 106
British Union of Fascists, 122, 132
    organisation of women by, 144–5
    women candidates and, 122
British Women's Temperance Association,
    85
Brittain, Vera, 154
Brookes, Pamela, 121, 122, 125, 159,
    190, 191, 197
Brown, Agnes, 106
Brown, Keith, 172
Brown, Maud, 141
Brown, Yvonne, 174
Brown v Ingram, 62
Browne, Sarah, 196
Browning, Elizabeth Barrett, 44
Bruley, Sue, 140, 141, 193
Brunt, Caroline, 189
Bryson, Valerie, 177
Bucholz, Robert, 17, 18, 174, 175
Burman, Sandra, 182
Burness, Catriona, 90, 122, 187, 190,
    195
Burton, Antoinette, 35, 179

Bush, Julia, 34, 99, 179, 188
Butler, Josephine, 43, 44, 45, 46, 62,
Byles, Mrs, 81

Caine, Barbara, 46, 89, 90, 173, 182,
    186, 187
Cameron, Jenny, 19
Cambridge, 157
Campbell, Beatrix, 90, 93, 128, 146, 147,
    187, 188, 191, 193, 195, 197, 198
Campbell, Clare, 162
Capp, Bernard, 5, 12, 171, 173,
Cappe, Catharine, 48–9
Carr, Rosalind, 24, 173, 177
Carter, April, 128, 191
Castle, Barbara, 128
Catholic Women's League, 158
Catholic Women's Suffrage Society, 71
Cavendish, Margaret, 13
Cazalet, Thelma, 124, 191
Central Committee of the National
    Society for Women's Suffrage, 61, 62
Central Committee for Women's
    Employment, 74, 115
Central National Society for Women's
    Suffrage, 62
Chalus, Elaine, 20, 21, 23, 173, 176,
    177, 178
Chaney, Paul, 172
Chapman, Hester, 174
Charity Organisation Society, 49
Chartist movement, 31, 33, 35–9, 47, 54
Chartist women, 35–9
    class background, 35
    demands, 36
    exclusive dealing campaigns of, 37
    justification for involvement of, 37
    organisation of, 36
    physical force and, 37
Chase, Malcolm, 36, 180
Chew, Ada Nield, 104, 105, 109, 110
Chew, George Nield, 104
Childs, Sarah, 191
Chorlton vs Lings, 61
Church League for Women's Suffrage,
    70–1
Churchill, Jennie, 93, 94
Churchill, Sarah, 17, 18, 22
citizenship, 25, 156
Clarion, 91, 102, 108, 110
Clarion Van, 105

Clark, Anna, 36, 37, 175, 177, 180
Clark, David, 104–5, 189
Clements, Samantha, 3, 171
Clere, Mary, 12
Clery, E. J., 23, 177
Clydeside rent strikes, 111
Cobbe, Frances Power, 89, 90, 95
Cobden, Jane, 84
Cockermouth, 108
coffee houses, 23–4
Cohen, Gidon, 140, 193
Cole, Margaret, 118, 190
Cole, Martin, 146, 194
Collette, Christine, 106, 137, 146, 189, 193
Colley, Linda, 24, 27, 178
Colne Valley, 104–5
Coming Day, 71
Common Cause, 65
Communist Party of Great Britain,122, 132, 139–42, 147, 148
    attitude to women members, 140–1
    internationalism of, 139
    women candidates for, 122
    Women's National Committee, 139
    Women's Sections, 140
Conciliation Bill, 65, 67, 86
Conciliation Committee, 67, 87
Connors, Richard, 176
Conservative Party,5, 55, 88, 102
    agents, 134–6
    organisation of women by, 96, 132, 134–7, 145–6
    women MPs and, 122
    women's suffrage and, 61, 96
    women voters and, 136–7
Conservative and Unionist Women's Franchise Association, 76, 97–9, 111, 134
Conservative and Unionist Women's Franchise Association Review, 98
Consultative Committee of Women's Organisations, 125
Contagious Diseases Acts, 44, 134
Cook, Kay, 66, 184
Coombs, Marybeth, 181
Cooper, Selina, 63, 157
Coote, Anna, 128, 147, 191, 195, 197, 198
Corn Laws, 39

Corrupt Practices Act (1883), 30, 77, 78, 91
Courtney, Katharine, 152
covenanting, 9
Cowan, Brian, 23, 177
Cowman, Krista, 184, 186, 189
Craig, Edith, 72
Craig, Maggie, 175, 179
Craigie, Jill, 128
Crawford, Elizabeth, 185
Crawford, Patricia, 9, 11, 20, 172, 173, 175, 176
Crawshay, Rose, 52
Cresswell, Elizabeth, 37
Cross, Máire, 189
Cruikshanks, Eveline, 175
Cullen, Stephen, 143, 194
Curzon, Georgina, 93
Curzon, Lord, 91

Dagenham strike, 128, 164
Dahlerup, Drude, 198
Dalrymple, Alexander, 174
Darlington, 79, 80
Davenport, Constance, 96
Davidoff, Leonore, 27, 178
Davies, Charlotte Aull, 195
Davies, Emily, 41, 42, 43, 52, 59, 60, 89, 90, 99
Davies, Natalie Zemon, 17, 175
Dawson, Julia, 102, 108
Daybel, James, 20, 172, 176
de Larrabeiti, Michelle, 39, 181
debating societies, 1, 11, 24–5
Despard, Charlotte, 69, 75, 118
Devine, T., 173, 177
Devonshire, Georgiana, Duchess of, 22
Dingsdale, Ann, 181
Divorce Act (1867), 44
Doebner, Richard, 174
Drummond, Flora, 142
Duby, Georges, 175
Dundee, 39,
Durham, 164
Durham, Martin, 143, 144, 193, 194
Duval, Victor, 73

Eales, Jaqueline, 172
East London Federation of Suffragettes, 70, 76
Eatwell, Roger, 193

Edinburgh, 47, 52
education, 28, 38, 49
    of girls, 42
    of women, 28, 81, 106
Education Act (1870), 51
Edwards, John, 104
Eger, Elizabeth, 177
Elam, Bertha, 145
electioneering, 21–2, 65, 82, 87, 92–3,
    94–5, 108
elections, 20, 77, 79, 108, 116, 117–9,
    144
Elias, Norbert, 17, 175
Eliot, George, 44
Ellliot, Baroness, 127
Ellis, Markman, 24, 177
Elizabeth 1, 13
Elmy, Elizabeth Wolstenholme, 43, 44,
    45, 47,60, 62
Engels, Frederick, 102
English Civil War, 10, 12, 23
Englishwoman's Journal, 33, 41, 42
Englishwoman's Review, 31, 32, 55, 93
Enlightenment, 11, 24–6, 28, 32
Eoff, Shirley, 153, 195, 196
Equal Franchise Act (1928), 131
Equal Opportunities Commission, 128
equal pay, 127–8, 154
Equal Pay Act (1969), 128
Equal Pay Campaign Committee, 128,
    160, 162
Equal Rights International, 156
Eustance, Claire, 186
Evans, Dorothy, 154
Evans, Neil, 66, 184
Evans, W. G., 42, 181
Ewen, Elizabeth, 172, 175
Ewing, Winnie, 122, 147

Faithful, Emily, 41, 42,
Falkner, James, 175
family allowances, 152
Fawcett, Millicent Garrett, 43, 59, 63,
    74, 79, 83, 131, 181, 185, 186, 192
feminism
    Conservative, 28, 89–90, 102
    equality, 11, 151–3, 162
    first wave, 3, 89
    imperialism and, 35, 136
    liberal, 81–2, 102, 134
    liberalism and, 78, 84

origins of, 11, 30, 41–3
radical, 89, 166;
second wave, 123;
socialist, 89, 102–3, 147, 166
third wave, 3
varieties of: Black, 166
Ferguson, Rona, 175
Fieldhouse, R., 176
Figes, Eva, 163
First World War, 72, 73–5, 87, 88, 90,
    99, 101, 103, 105, 111–12, 115,
    125, 138, 142
Fitzpatrick, Martin, 178
Flatman, Ada, 66
Flinn, Andrew, 140, 193
Flint, Caroline, 169
food riots, 11, 28
Ford, Isabella, 189
Foreman, Amanda, 176
Forrester, Lillian, 155
Forward, 104
Forward Cymric Suffrage Union, 72
Foulton, Margaret, 52
Fox, Adam, 172
Fox, Helen, 69
Fox, Norah Dacre, 118, 145
Frances, Junita, 154–5
Francis, Martin, 187
Fraser, Antonia, 175
Free Church League for Women's Suf-
    frage, 71
Free Church Suffrage Times, 71
French Revolution, 11, 25–6, 54
Friends' League for Women's Suffrage, 71
Frow, Edmund, 180
Frow, Ruth, 180
Fry, Sophia, 79–81, 84
Fyrth, Jim, 195

Garrard, John, 179
Garrett, Elizabeth, 52, 59
Gaskell, Mrs, 44
Gawthorpe, Mary, 108
Geddes, Jenny, 9
Gelbe, Joyce, 198
General Strike (1926), 141, 143
George, Prince of Denmark, 16
Girls' Friendly Society, 34
Girls' Public Day School Company, 42
Girton College, 42
Gladstone, Catherine, 80, 81

Gladstone, William, 1, 79
Glasgow, 34, 36, 37, 69, 74, 104, 105, 111
Glasgow Women's Labour Party, 106
Glasier, John Bruce, 104, 107, 189
Glasier, Katharine Bruce, 102, 104, 105
Glasier, Lizzie Bruce, 106
Gleadle, Kathryn, 28, 35, 49, 50, 178, 180, 181, 182
'Glorious Revolution', 10, 14–15, 28
Glucksman, Miriam, 195
Goodhart, Celia, 146, 194
Goot, Murray, 187
Gorbals, 38
Gordon, Eleanor, 101, 188, 189, 195
Gorham, Deborah, 195
Gottlieb, Julie, 143, 144, 194
Gould, Barbara Ayrton, 75
Gowing, Laura, 11, 172, 173
Graham, Rose, 176
Grant, Charlotte, 177
Graves, Pamela, 138, 193
Green, Barbara, 68, 184
Gregg, Edward, 16, 17, 175
Grey, Sandra, 165, 171, 197
Grieg, Teresa Billington, 63, 68, 108, 161, 162, 164
Griffiths, Paul, 172
Griggs, Annie Brock, 144
Grimmett, Jennifer, 38, 39, 180
Grimshaw, Pat, 179
Guest, Harriet, 28, 178
Gullace, Nicolette, 75, 185

Habermas, Jürgen, 27, 178
Hagan, J., 173
Hall, Catherine, 27, 178, 179
Hall, Robert, 180
Halifax, 37, 38,
Hallinan, Hazel Hunkins, 158, 163, 190, 196
Hamilton, Anne, Duchess of, 19
Hamilton, Cicely, 72
Hamilton, Lord, 92
Hamilton, Mary Agnes, 191
Hamilton-Phillips, Martha, 174
Hannam, June, 50, 102, 105, 110, 182, 188, 189
Hardie, Agnes, 126
Hardie, Keir, 109, 189
Harker, Elsie, 109

Harris, Frances, 176
Harris, Tim, 173
Harrison, Brian, 68, 120, 123, 132, 151, 184, 190, 191, 192, 195, 196
Harvey, Miss, 133
Hays, Mary, 26
Hays, Matilda, 41
Heeney, Brian, 70, 185
Heyrick, Elizabeth, 34
Higgins, Patricia, 13, 173, 174
Hills, Jill, 146, 194
Hindle, Steve, 172
Hinscliffe, Rev. Claude, 70
Hinton, James, 159, 196
Hirsch, Pam, 178, 181
Hirshfield, Claire, 86, 87, 132, 186, 192
Holcombe, Lee, 44, 181
Holledge, Julie, 185
Hollis, Patricia, 48, 53, 54, 83, 85, 182, 183, 185, 186
Holmes, Geoffrey, 18, 175
Holton, Sandra, 47, 60, 65, 74, 78, 79, 181, 182, 183, 184, 185
Holtby, Winifred, 152
Home and Politics, 136
Home Service Corps, 73
Hope, George, 39
Hornsby-Smith, Pat, 122, 125, 190
Houlbrooke, Ralph, 172
House of Commons, 116, 120, 124, 125
House of Lords, 126–7
Houston, R. A., 172, 173
Howard, Rosalind, 84, 85
Hughes, Ann, 12–13, 173
Hume, Leslie Parker, 186
Hume-Rothery, Mary, 44
Hunt, Karen, 102, 104, 105, 106, 110, 142, 188, 189, 193
Hyde, Ann, 13, 17

Independent Labour Party, 55, 63, 64, 73, 81, 99, 101, 102, 103, 105, 109, 138
  women's suffrage and, 107
Independent Suffragette, 74
Independent Suffragettes, 74
Inglis, Marie, 143
Innes, Sue, 172, 195, 196
International Alliance of Women, 160
International Women's News, 160
International Socialists, 148

International Women's Suffrage Alliance, 153, 155
Ivens, Frances, 74

Jacob, Margaret, 24, 177
Jacobite Movement, 10, 14, 15, 19–20, 29
Jarvis, David, 90, 136, 187, 192
Jeffreys, Sheila, 182
Jersey, Lady, 95, 97
Jewish League for Women's Suffrage, 71
Joannou, Maroula, 183
John, Angela, 5, 171, 183
Johnson, Harry, 67
Jones, David, 180
Jones, Clive, 176
Jones, Helen, 128, 157, 158,161, 196, 197
Jones, Peter, 178
Jordan, Constance, 174

Kaplan, Cora, 178
Kanner, Barbara, 176
Kedge, Alice, 66, 68
Keeling, Eleanor, 102, 103, 104
Keighley, 116
Kenney, Annie, 64, 66, 86
Kensington Debating Society, 42, 52, 60, 89
Kent, Susan Kingsley, 151–2, 195
Kerr, Harriet, 67
Kerrigan, Rose, 140
Kinnaird, Joan, 187
Kirk, Neville, 189
Kishlansky, Mark, 173
Klein, Lawrence, 177
Knellwolf, Krista, 178
Knight, Anne, 33, 60
Knightly, Lady Louisa, 96, 98
Knights, Mark, 176
Knott, Sarah, 177
Knox, W. W. J, 172
Koonz, Claudia, 178
Kough, Kathleen, 109
Kushner, Tony, 193

Labour Party, 88, 99
    suffrage and, 107;
    women MPs and, 122
    organisation of women, 137–8

Labour Representation Committee, 106, 109
Ladies' National Association, 45, 47, 48
    class composition of, 45, 46–7;
    links with other movements, 48, 62
    men and, 47
    provincial strength of, 45
    work with prostitutes, 46–7
Ladies' Society for the Relief of Negro Slaves, 33
Lancashire and Cheshire Women Textile and Other Workers' Representation Committee, 63
land clearance protests, 12
Landsbury, Nellie, 139
Lane, Penelope, 177
Lane-Fox, George, 92
Langford, Paul, 176
Langham Place Circle, 41, 89
Lapworth, Mrs, 37
Larkin, Jim, 70
Law, Cheryl, 3, 150, 171, 190, 196
Lawes Resolutions of Women's Rights, 1
Lawrence, Emmeline Pethick, 69, 71, 75
Lawrence, Frederick Pethick, 69, 71
Lawrence, Susan, 169
Lee, Jennie, 126
Leeds, 27, 50
Leicester, 36, 107
Leigh, Mary, 67
Leneman, Leah, 66, 183, 184, 186
Levellers, 9, 12–13
Levine, Philippa, 31, 54, 179, 183, 185
Lewis, Gifford, 183
Lewis, Jane, 151, 195
Lewis, Sarah, 48
Liberal Party, 5, 55, 77, 78, 102
    appeal to women's votes, 133
    organisation of women by, 132–3, 145–6
    Women's Liberal Federation and, 82–3
    women MPs and, 122, 146
    women's suffrage and, 61,78, 86–7
Liberal Women's Suffrage Union 87
liberalism, 78
    feminism and, 78, 84
Liddington, Jill, 63, 64, 103, 109, 183, 184, 185, 189, 196
Liverpool, 24, 65, 71, 74, 81, 82, 83, 94, 105, 152, 157
Lloyd George, David, 117

Lloyd George, Megan, 120, 132
local government, 4, 20, 21, 32, 48,
  51–4, 148, 156–7, 168
Local Government Act (1894), 63
Lovenduski, Joni, 90, 122, 166, 187,
  190, 191, 192, 194, 197
Lovett, William, 36
Lunn, Kenneth, 193
Lytton, Lady Constance, 96
Lytton, Lord, 87

Macarthur, Mary, 110, 116, 118–19
Macaulay, Catherine, 26
Macaulay, Rose, 152
MacCubbin, Robert, 174
MacDonald, Flora, 19
MacDonald, Margaret, 106
MacDonald, Margot, 147
MacDonald, Ramsay, 106
Mackay, Fiona, 165, 172
Mackinosh, Ann ('Colonel Anne'),
  19
Maclachlan, Leigh, 125, 192
MacPherson, Mary Fenton, 106
Maguire, G. E., 89, 90, 187, 192
'male equivalence', 4, 120
Manchester, 39, 40, 53, 60, 63, 83, 105,
  109, 143
Manchester Women's Suffrage Society,
  44, 61, 63
Manea Fen, 32
Mann, Jean, 127
Manning, Brian, 173
Manning, Charlotte, 42, 60
Manning, Roger B, 173
Mansfield, 37
Marcievicz, Constance, 118
Markham, Violet, 119
Marlow, Joyce, 184
Married Women's Association, 151
Married Women's Property Acts, 44
Married Women's Property Committee,
  44
Marshall, Catherine, 75, 87
Martin, Jane, 53, 182
Martin, Mary Clare, 49, 182
Martyn, Caroline, 105
Martyn, Edith How, 116, 119
Marwick, Arthur, 75, 185
Marx, Eleanor, 102
Mary I, 13, 14

Mary II, 10, 13–16
  conception of queenship , 14, 15, 17
  death, 15
  education, 14;
  marriage, 14;
  regnancy, 15;
  relationship with husband, 14, 15
  religious beliefs, 14, 15
Masham, Abigail, 18
Mason, Bertha, 2, 61, 85, 87, 171, 183
Mason, Frances, 185
Masson, Ursula, 66, 79, 184, 185, 186
Matters, Muriel, 69
Maxse, Majorie, 134, 135, 192
Maxton, James, 155
Maxwell, Lily, 61, 62,
Mayhall, Laura Nym, 61, 183
McAllister, Laura, 147, 172, 195
McCalman, Iain, 178
McCrillis, Neal, 135, 192
McDowell, Paula, 176, 177
McIntyre, Stuart, 141, 193
McLaren, Eva, 82, 84, 85, 86
McLaren, Priscilla Bright, 44, 61
McMillan, Margaret, 105
Meehan, Elizabeth, 195
Meikle, Maureen, 175
Melton, James van Horn, 23, 177
Men's League for Opposing Women's
  Suffrage, 97
Mendelson, Sara, 9, 172, 173, 175
Merrington, Martha, 52
Meux, Sir Hedworth, 1, 116
Middleton, Mary, 106
Midgley, Clare, 179, 180
Mill, Harriet Taylor, 60
Mill, John Stuart, 60, 61, 78,
Miller, Millie, 122
Mitchell, David, 185
Mitchell, Hannah, 104, 155, 189
Mitchell, Juliet, 78, 180, 185
Monad, Paul, 19, 175
Montefiore, Dora, 109, 110
Moorhouse, Mary, 139
More, Hannah, 11, 28, 34
Morgan, Kevin, 193
Morgan, Simon, 27, 40, 50, 178, 181,
  182
Morley, Ann, 67, 184
Morrill, John, 176
Morrison, Sybil, 161

Mosley, Oswald, 143, 144, 145
Mothers' Unions, 158
Mott, Yolande, 144
Municipal Corporations (Franchise) Act (1869), 51
Murphy, Mollie, 140
Murray, Eunice, 119
Murrell, Christine, 123

National League for Opposing Women's Suffrage, 116, 169
National Unemployed Workers' Movement, 141
National Union of Societies for Equal Citizenship, 119, 123, 132, 151, 152–3
National Union of Women's Suffrage Societies, 63, 68, 96, 99, 101, 119, 125, 156
  branch network, 64, 65
  election fighting fund, 65, 66, 87, 88, 101, 111
  in First World War, 74, 75
  'mud march' (1907), 65
  political composition, 63, 64, 65, 101
  relationship with other organisations, 65, 71, 72, 87
National Union of Women Teachers, 152, 155
National Union of Women Workers, 156
National Vigilance Association, 47
Nava, Mica, 50, 182
Nelson, 157
Nevill, Meresia, 94, 95
New, Edith, 67
'New Woman', 63, 103
Newcastle, 79
night cleaners, 164
Nithsdale, Lady, 19
Norris, Jill, 63, 64, 103, 109, 183, 185, 189
Norris, Pippa, 90, 122, 187, 190, 191
Nottingham, 46, 50

O'Brien, Karen, 173, 178
Ó'Gallchoir, Clíona, 177
O'Gorman, Frank, 10, 21, 172, 175, 176
Oakley, Ann, 180
Offen, Karen, 177, 179
Oldfield, Sybil, 194

Open Door Council, 151, 155–6, 161, 164
Open Door International, 156
Oppenheim, Sally, 124
Oram, Alison, 159, 197
Origins of the Family, Private Property and the State (Engels), 102
Orme, Eliza, 84, 185
Orr, Clarissa Campbell, 13, 1784, 178
Owen, Robert, 32
Owenism, 32
Oxford, 164, 165

Pankhurst, E. Sylvia, 40, 66, 70, 74, 106, 181, 189
Pankhurst, Christabel, 64, 66, 68, 69, 70, 72, 73, 108, 110, 117
Pankhurst, Emmeline, 32, 62, 64, 67, 69, 72, 73, 105, 117
Pankhurst, Richard, 61, 64
Parkes, Bessie Rayner, 33, 41, 43, 44,
Parkes, Wendy, 68, 184
Parliament (Qualification of Women) Bill (1918), 116, 117
Parmar, Pratibba, 166, 198
party politics, 10, 20, 21, 77–8
  as a career for women, 45, 66, 105, 108, 135, 163
  cultural dimensions of, 10, 20, 72, 92, 93, 94, 101, 104–5
  participatory nature, 31
  women candidates in, 82–3, 116–26, 145, 146, 157, 161, 244
Payne, Helen, 10, 172
peace campaigns, 12, 75–6, 111, 133, 145, 147, 164
Pearce, Isabella Bream, 106
Pease, Elizabeth, 50
Pedersen, Susan, 152, 195
Pelling, Henry, 189
'People's Charter', 35
People's Suffrage Federation, 110
Perot, Michelle, 175
Perrigo, Sarah, 145
Peterson, R, 173
petitioners
  anti-corn laws 40
  anti-slavery, 33
  Chartist, 36, 37
  Leveller, 13
  property rights, 44
  suffrage, 60

Petrie, Charles, 175
philanthropy, 31, 48–50, 80
    women and, 31, 80, 115
Philips, Baroness, 127
Philipson, Mabel, 120
Phillips, Ann, 185
Phillips, John, 21, 176
Phillips, Marion, 137, 138
Phillips, Nora, 82, 84, 85
Pierson, Ruth Roach, 179
Pincus, Steven, 24, 177
Pittock, Murray, 175
Plaid Cymru, 122, 132, 147
    women candidates and, 122
political history, 2, 4
Poor Law Guardians 51, 82
    women's work as, 52–4, 83, 105, 106
Prentice, Archibald, 181
Priestman, Anna Maria, 85
Primrose League,78, 79, 91–5, 96, 99,
        103, 134
    class composition, 92
    Cycling corps, 94
    origins, 91;
    organisation, 91–2
    philosophy, 91;
    political education and, 93–4
    propaganda van, 94
    role of women in, 92–5
    women's suffrage and, 95, 96, 98
Primrose League Gazette, 91, 92, 93, 96
print culture, 10, 22–4, 36,
Prochaska, Frank, 48, 182
Procter, Adelaide, 41
prostitution, 45, 46, 47
protective legislation, 152–3, 155
Pugh, Martin, 54, 68, 86, 91, 92, 97,
        123, 128, 154, 159, 183, 184, 187,
        188, 190, 191, 192, 194, 196, 197
Purvis, June, 182, 183, 184, 190

queens as regnants, 13, 14
    see also individual name entries

'Radical Suffragists', 64
Rae, Janet, 105
Raeburn, Antonia, 63, 183
'Rag Plot' (Oxford), 23
Railway Women's Guild, 106
Randall, Vicky, 164, 166, 191, 194, 197,
        198

Rathbone, Eleanor, 66, 116, 119, 125,
        151, 152, 156, 161, 190, 196
Ravensdale, Baroness, 127
Rawson, Mary Anne, 33
Reading, Lady, 159
Redbridge, 122
Reddish, Sarah, 63
Rees, Teresa, 171, 195
Reform Acts
    (1832), 20, 30, 31, 35, 51, 77
    (1867) 30, 77, 91
    (1868), 30, 77
    (1884) 30, 75, 77, 91
Reid, Elizabeth, 187
Reidi, Eliza, 188
Rendall, Jane, 25, 32, 40, 41, 43, 62, 173,
        177, 178, 179, 181, 183, 186, 195
Representation of the People Act (1918),
        2, 75, 111, 115, 116, 131, 145, 150
reproductive rights, 163, 166
Reynolds, Kim, 4, 171
Reynolds, Sian, 172
Richards, Judith, 174
Richardson, Mary, 69, 145, 184
Richardson, Reginald, 36
Richardson, Sarah, 175, 178, 181
Rigby, Edith, 158
Rights of Women (Richardson), 36
Robb, Janet, 90, 92, 94, 187, 188
Roberts, Krisztina, 73, 185
Robins, Elizabeth, 158
Robinson, Annot, 104, 106
Rochdale, 37
Rogers, Helen, 180
Rogers, Nicholas, 12, 173
Roper, Esther, 63, 64
Rose, Craig, 175
Rosen, Andrew, 68, 184, 190
Routh, Martin, 174
Rover, Constance, 87, 186
Rowan, Caroline, 189
Rowbotham, Sheila, 164, 165, 166, 195,
        197, 198
royal court, politics at, 17
Rubinstein, David, 182
Runciman, Hilda, 132
Rupp, Leila, 2, 171
Russell, Dora, 138
Ryan, Joan, 186
Rye, Maria, 42
Ryley, Kate, 84

St Joan's Social and Political Alliance, 151, 155
Salt, Thomas, 36
Samuel, Herbert, 116
Sarah, Elizabeth, 68, 184
Sawer Marian, 165, 171, 190, 197
Scatcherd, Alice, 50, 62
school boards, 51–2, 83
Schwarzkopf, Jutta, 37, 38–9, 180
Schwoerer, Lois, 10, 13, 21, 172, 174, 175, 176, 177
Scott, Joan, 25, 177
Scott, Rachel, 108
Scottish Nationalist Party, 122, 132
women candidates and, 122
Scottish Parliament, 147
Scottish Women's Hospitals Association, 74–5
Second International, 75, 101, 105, 139
Second World War, 122, 123, 126, 127, 150, 155, 159–61
Selbourne, Countess, 97
separate spheres, 26
Serious Proposal to the Ladies (Astell), 23
Sex Discrimination Act (1975), 128
Sex Disqualification (Removal) Act (1919), 126, 131
sexuality, 26, 32, 42, 45–6, 166
Seymour, Elizabeth, 18
Shackleton, David, 63, 64
Sharpe, James A., 175
Sheffield, 33, 39, 53,
Shield, The, 45
Shilston, Bessie, 83
Shoemaker, Robert, 173
Shrewsbury, 50
Sieff, Rebecca, 159
Silcock, Helen, 110
Siltanen, Janet, 187
Simm, Lisbeth, 106
Simonton, Deborah, 71, 195
single-issue campaigns, 31, 32, 41–3
Sinn Fein, 117, 118
Six Point Group 123, 151, 153–5, 162
'blacklist' of MPs, 154
formation, 153
membership, 153
philosophy, 153, 154
relationship with Women's Liberation Movement 163

Slack, Paul, 176
Smilie, Robert, 108
Smith, Angela, 73, 185
Smith, Harold, 63, 64, 123, 129, 151, 153, 183, 184, 190, 191, 195
Smith, Hilda (historian), 4, 171, 172, 176
Smith, Hilda (labour activist), 146
Smith, Mary, 60
Smout, T. C., 177
Snowden, Ethel, 116
Social Democratic Federation, 101, 105, 106, 109
women's circles, 105, 106
Social Democratic Party, 146
social purity, 45, 47
Socialist Sunday Schools, 104
Society for Promoting the Employment of Women, 41
Society for Promoting the Return of Women as Poor Law Guardians, 53
Spare Rib, 166, 167
Spearman, Ann, 11
Speck, William, 174
Spencer, Lavinia, 21
Spender, Dale, 2–3, 163, 166, 171, 195, 197, 198
Stacy, Enid, 104, 105
Standing Joint Committee, 137
Standing Joint Council of Women's Organisations, 156–7
Stanley, Liz, 67, 184
Stanworth, Michelle, 187
Statham, Arnold, 92
Status of Women Committee, 151, 163–4
Staves, Susan, 21, 176
Steinbach, Susie, 52, 181
Stevenson, Flora, 52
Stewart, L, 172
Stobaugh, Beverley, 120, 123, 190
Stott, Anne, 28, 178
Stott, Mary, 167
Strachey, Lady Jane, 96, 97
Strachey, Ray, 28, 30, 59, 68, 118, 119, 120, 131, 178, 179, 181, 184, 190
Strickland, Agnes, 174
Strictures on Female Education (More), 28
Studlar, Donley T, 190
Styles, John, 173
Suffrage Atelier, 72

suffrage militancy, 64, 67–8, 69
Suffragette, 69
Suffragette Fellowship, 66, 126, 151
Suffragette News Sheet, 74
suffragettes of the WSPU, 74
Summers, Ann, 182
Summerskill, Edith, 128, 161
Swanborough, Baroness, 127
Swanwick, Helena, 75
Sweet, Rosemary, 177

Tague, Ingrid, 20, 176
Taithe, Bertrand, 188
Tanner, Duncan, 76, 185
Tate, Mavis, 122, 162
Taylor, Barbara, 32, 177, 178, 179
Taylor, Clementia, 61
Taylor, Miles, 31, 179
Taylor, Rosemary, 184
Taylor, Stephen, 176
Taylor, Verta, 2, 171
Terrinton, Lady Vera, 129
Thale, Mary, 177
Thane, Pat, 88, 129, 131, 132, 172, 183,
    186, 190, 191, 192, 193
Third International (Comintern), 139
Thomas, Margaret Haig (Lady Rhondda),
    67, 126, 153, 154, 157, 184,
    196
Thomis, Malcolm, 38, 39, 180
Thompson, Dorothy, 180
Thompson, E. P., 173
Thompson, Laurence, 189
Thompson, William, 32
Thornton, Tim, 188
Thorpe, Andrew, 138, 141, 147, 193
Thurlow, Jessica, 3, 154, 161, 171, 196,
    197
Tickner, Lisa, 185
Time and Tide, 123, 153, 154
Topping, Robert, 125, 192
Townswomen's Guilds, 158, 167
transport strike (1911), 107
Tremblay, Manon, 190
Trimble, Linda, 190
Tuke, Mabel, 69
Turner, Beth, 140, 141
Turner, Elizabeth, 105
Twells, Alison, 34, 179
Twining, Louisa, 49
Tyrrell, Alex, 40, 181

Ugolini, Laura, 186
Union of Practical Suffragists, 85
United Suffragists, 70, 74, 76
Urban Space, 68, 77, 94

Vallance, Elizabeth, 117, 120, 122, 124,
    128, 129, 190, 191
Van Wingerden, Sophia, 63, 183
Vellacott, Jo, 63, 74, 183, 185, 186
Vernon, James, 30, 35, 179, 180
Vervaecke, Philippe, 95, 188
Vickery, Amanda, 2, 27, 171, 178
Victoria League, 34, 97
Victory Corps, 142
Villiers, Elizabeth, 18
Vincentelli, Moira, 171, 195
Vindication of the Rights of Woman (Woll-
    stonecraft), 25, 54
Von den Steinen, Karl, 20, 175, 176
Votes for Women, 69
Votes for Women Fellowship, 69
Voyce, Hollie, 146, 194

Walker, Linda, 84, 85, 94, 186, 187, 188
Walkowitz, Judith, 47, 181, 182
Walter, John, 11, 173
Walthall, Dorohy, 142
Warburton, Penny, 177
Ward, Arnold, 116
Ward, Mrs Humphrey, 54
Ward, Irene, 124, 128
Ward, Joseph, 172
Ward, Stephanie, 193
Ware, Vron, 33, 179
'warming-pan scandal', 18
Watson, Janet, 73, 185
'wave' metaphor, 2, 3,
Webster, Nester, 144
Weil, Rachel, 13, 174, 175
Welsh National Assembley, 147
Wentworth, Charlotte, 21
White, I, 173
Widdrington, Percy, 104
Wightman, Mrs, 50
Wilberforce, William, 33
Wilkinson, Ellen, 124, 125
William of Orange, 14–16
Wilson, Elizabeth, 147, 164, 194, 197
Winslow, Barbara, 184
Wintringham, Margaret, 120, 121, 132
Wollstonecraft, Mary, 2, 25–6, 28, 32, 89

'Wollstonecraft School', 26, 28
Woman Power Committee, 160
'Woman Question', 102
'Woman's Mission', 40, 48,
Women Citizens Associations, 132, 153,
   156–7, 162, 164
women MPs, 115–30
   collective work by, 123, 125–6, 159,
      166
   elevation to Lords, 127
   eligibility of women to stand as, 116
   facilities for, 124
   first election of, 119
   independent, 119
   numbers, 121
   party affiliations, 121, 126
   press portrayals, 124, 169
   selection, 118, 121;
Women for Westminster, 123, 151, 160,
   161, 162
Women's Aid, 166
Women's Amalgamated Unionist and Tariff Reform Association, 96–7, 134
Women's Auxiliary Army Corps, 73
Women's Co-Operative Guild, 138, 156
Women's Election Committee, 123
Women's Franchise League, 62
Women's Freedom League, 69, 72, 75,
   116, 117, 119, 123, 151, 162
Women's Guild of Empire, 142
Women's Institutes, 5, 158, 167
Women's International League for Peace
   and Freedom, 75, 110
Women's Labour League, 102, 106–7,
   110, 111, 138, 156
Women's Liberal Federation, 62, 78–88,
   96, 97, 103, 110, 132
   class composition, 80
   formation, 78
   Home Rule and, 84
   organisation, 80
   women's suffrage and, 83, 84–7
   'test question' and, 85
Women's Liberal Federation News, 86
Women's Liberal Unionist Association,
   84, 96
Women's Liberation Movement, 147,
   150
   class composition, 164
   conferences, 165, 166
   demands, 165

   early campaigns, 164
   organisation, 165
   relationship with earlier feminist move-
      ment, 163, 165
   use of history by, 165
Women's Local Government Association,
   157
Women's Local Government Society, 53
'women's movement', 30, 43, 115, 153,
   185
   media coverage, 162
Women's National Anti-Suffrage League,
   97
Women's National Liberal Association, 85
Women's Party, 117, 119, 125, 126
Women's Peace Crusade, 111
women's political writings, 10, 13, 23,
   25, 26, 31, 43, 102–3
women's politics
   in anti-slavery movement, 33–4
   class composition, 3
   critiques, 12, 24, 26, 27, 33
   definitions, 4–5
   domestic content, 134, 136, 137, 149,
      152, 154
   economic dimensions, 33, 34, 37, 39,
      134
   in English civil war, 12, 29
   family dimensions, 4, 19, 20, 29, 31,
      34, 38, 81–2, 90, 99, 104
   in French Revolution, 25, 29
   impetus for, 9
   in Jacobite movement, 19–20, 29;
   in local government, 51–54, 82–3,
      107, 108
   at local level, 4, 11, 20, 21, 22, 31, 33,
      48, 51–4, 99, 102, 108, 111, 148,
      166
   in Owenite Movement, 32–3
   petitioning *see* petitioners
   political parties and, 10, 79–88,
      90–101
   religious dimensions, 23, 33, 39, 48–9,
      50
   Scottish, 6, 12, 19–20, 23, 24, 32, 33,
      34, 51, 61, 65, 80, 91, 101, 120,
      141, 147, 165
   Welsh, 5, 33, 42, 52, 65, 66, 72, 79,
      80, 91, 106, 120, 147, 165
   see also under individual parties, move-
      ments and organisations

Women's Publicity and Planning Association, 151, 159–60
Women's Royal Naval Service, 73
Women's Volunteer Reserve, 73
Women's Social and Political Union, 64, 86, 96, 98, 118, 145, 154
  branch network, 66
  in First World War, 74
  formation, 64
  militancy, 64, 66, 67–8
  move to London, 66
  relationship with other organisations, 65, 71, 72
  socialism and, 64, 69, 73, 109
  splits within, 69
women's suffrage, 35, 36, 42, 54
Women's Suffrage Movement, 31, 32, 59–76
  diversity, 69–73
  in First World War, 73–5
  geographical spread, 59–61
  organisation, 62

  origins, 60–62, 78
  relations with other campaigns 59, 63
women's theatre, 72
Women Under Socialism (Bebel), 102
Women's Voluntary Service, 159
Wood, Andy, 173
Woolf, Daniel, 175
Workers' Birth Control Group, 138
Workers' Socialist Federation, 70
Workers' Suffrage Federation, 70
Worley, Matthew, 142, 193
Wrightson, Keith, 9, 172

Yeo, Eileen, 171, 181, 195
York, 48, 67, 68, 79
Young, J. R., 177
Young Women's Christian Association, 158

Zetkin, Clara, 75, 111, 139
Zweiniger-Bargielowska, Ina, 187, 191